100 GREATEST

BABY BOOMER TOYS

MARK RICH

Published by

krause publications

The World's Largest Hobby & Collectibles Publisher

700 E. State St.
Iola, WI 54990-0001
Telephone 715-445-2214
www.krause.com

Please call or write for our free catalog. Our toll-free number to place an order or obtain a free catalog is 800-258-0929 or please use our regular business telephone 715-445-2214 for editorial comment and further information.

Library of Congress Catalog Number: 99-68134

ISBN: 0-87341-880-8

Printed in the United States of America

Dedication

To Charles and Kikue Rich
For being there at my introduction to the world of toys

and Martha Borchardt
For being there at my re-introduction

Contents

Chapter Four: Locket Dolls and Magic Crayons

Chapter Five: Squeaks to Finks

Chapter Six: More Honorary Boomer Toys

Chapter Seven: Flip Your Wig!

Chapter Eight: The Life-Size Kitchen & Electric Football

Chapter Nine: More Honorary Boomer Toys

Chapter Ten: Bash!

Chapter Eleven: From Pogo to Play-Doh

Chapter Twelve: Last Words

Boomer Toy Value Guide

Acknowledgments

Additional Reading

Index

Introduction

The 1954 Woolworth's *New Christmas Book* had everything a child could want, from coloring books, records, and activity sets to dolls, trucks, blocks, cap guns, and trains. It showed over 150 toys, many of them new to the season. Every one of them was some child's favorite in that 1954 to 1955 season of Eisenhower, the Red Scare, *The Lord of the Rings*, *Lolita*, and the Bikini Atoll hydrogen bomb explosion. Every one of them.

Or open the Sears Toy Book of ten years later. While Woolworth's took the approach of beguiling the child with comic book reading material, having the toy ads slipped between the pages of a comic story featuring Phineas the Pelican and the two children of a circus ringmaster, Sears took the hardcore approach. It just showed the stuff itself, on glossy pages - over 200 of them, with many in color. Toys, toys, toys! Race tracks and life-size kitchen appliances and typewriters and chairs and dolls and cars and trucks and soldiers and puppets and wagons and costumes and scooters, all arrayed in such a way that the children gazing there would lose their souls forever.

Those 200 pages held over 1,500 items. Somewhere in this country, at least one person will stand up for each item in that fabulous catalog, and will tell you how that particular item belongs on anyone's Top 100 list, because It Was The Greatest Ever.

They are right to do so. How could they be wrong, after all? Yet in the list that follows, I have had to make choices. I have given weight to the novelty of the toy, the popularity of the toy, the significance of the toy, and to some degree the amount of current collector interest in the toy. Information about collector values I have relegated to the end of the book because this is a book about Then, not about Now.

Toys are sand grains slipping between the floor boards. In that blind period we call our first maturity, or young adulthood, or adolescence - or what have you - we suddenly forget toys. Toys no longer impinge on our sensory universe. They lose their existence.

It is as though toys are made of a strangely changeable substance that renders them invisible, once ignored. Turn away once, and they vanish forever.

Years later ...

Then, then, yes, we feel the loss.

By the time we feel it, it is too late: the basement is cleared, the upper shelf of the closet holds only sweaters and scarves for the winter, those random shoe boxes in the back have only dried-up pens and battered old rulers, and under the bed the floor is littered only with dust and a single, sad sock.

This book, however, will bring back those long-vanished toys.

Not all, by any means, not all ...

But the best.

Mark Rich

CHAPTER 1

The Triumph of the Style Doll

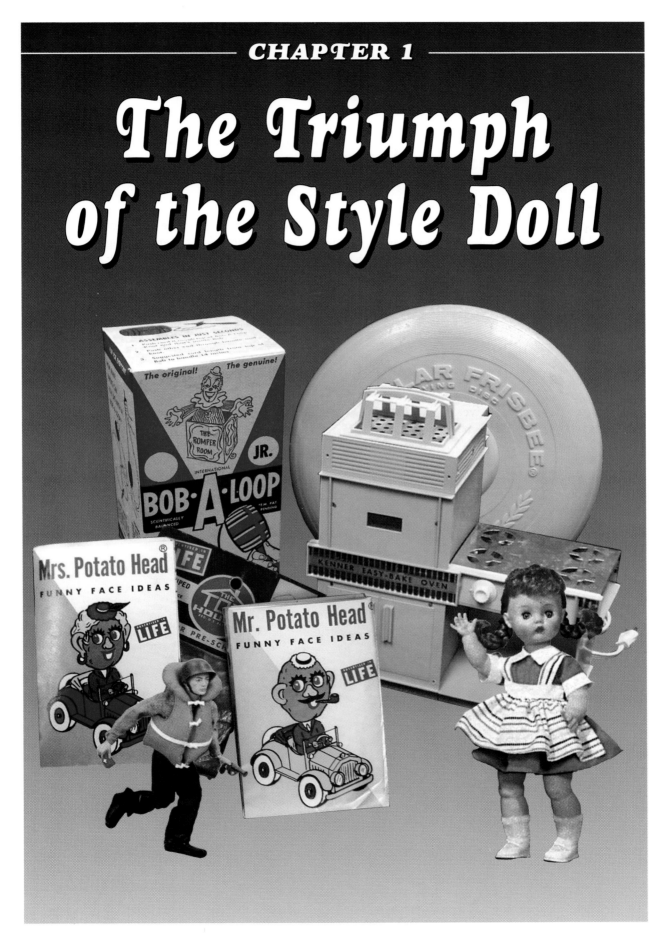

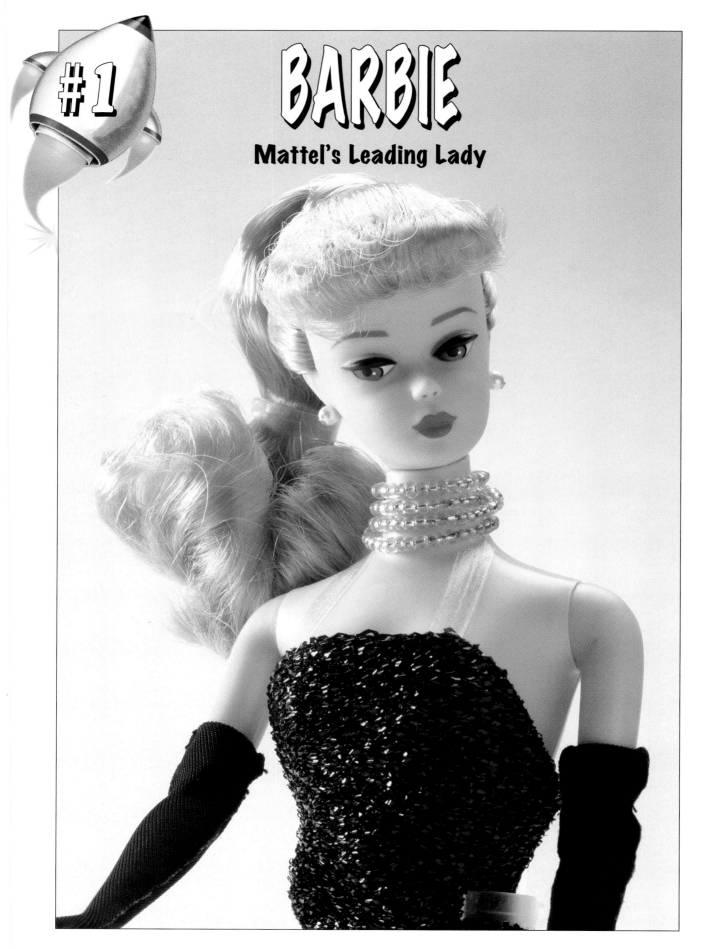

BARBIE

Mattel's Leading Lady

Ruth Handler made an interesting observation while watching daughter Barbara and her friends playing with paper dolls.

The girls had little interest in the paper-doll children. Instead, they spent their time with the paper-doll adults, putting on and taking off their various outfits and then role-playing with these figures.

Conventional wisdom in the toy industry said that girls played with dolls because they liked to pretend to be mothers. This meant they liked to play with baby dolls, or with dolls representing girls close to their own age.

Barbara and her friends may well have been pretending to be mothers. Yet they used dolls of the mothers, not the babies, to do so.

Would girls react positively to dolls that depicted adults and embodied adult ideals, instead of children and child ideals? Ruth Handler thought so. Since she ran a successful toy company, Mattel, with her husband Elliott, she was in a position to test her idea. She ran into resistance first from her husband, then from the industry.

At the 1959 New York Toy Fair, where Barbie made her debut, store representatives thought the doll would never succeed. Yet they had enough faith in Mattel's track record to order some for their stores.

They learned soon enough they had ordered too few.

Ruth Handler had found the physical doll to fit her adult doll idea in Germany. A few years earlier, cartoonist Reinhard Beuthien had created a character named Lilli for a spot cartoon in the daily Bild-Zeitung in mid-1952. The character proved popular, which encouraged Beuthien to draw more cartoons featuring Lilli. Then he designed a doll.

Lilli was a curvaceous, slender-waisted blonde beauty with striking eyes and a taste for tightly fitting clothing. She was both sexy and savvy. She entered the world of toys and dolls with the aid of Max Weissbrodt, who had created the highly prized Elastolin figures manufactured by O. & M. Hausser. The Lilli doll, with sharp-cornered eyes, arched brows, high forehead, thin neck, high breasts, and long, slender legs, made her debut in August 1955. During her brief period of popularity she was shipped around the world.

When sales of the doll declined, Lilli happened to be sold to Mattel, who, in 1959, test-marketed

Fashion Queen. *The Fashion Queen Barbie acknowledged her preeminence in the toy world through her name. Issued without the rooted hair of her earlier incarnations, the Fashion Queen could indulge in the '60s passion for wigs. Mattel, 1963*

and then released a remarkably similar doll with a new name, Barbie, which appropriately enough was the nickname of the Handlers' daughter.

Barbie succeeded for many reasons, not least of which was her sexuality. Never mind her high breasts, which immediately established her maturity to any who saw her, and which the male-dominated toy industry thought would doom her in the marketplace.

The Barbie doll expressed sexuality above all through conspicuous display.

She was a fashion doll.

The age the Barbie doll was born into was an age of accessories. The accessories were not the same as those that came with Sun Rubber's squeezable baby dolls: diapers, water bottles, extra clothes. Useful things. Barbie's were accessories in the sense used by the style industry. They were items serving no intrinsic purpose beyond display. Looking good was enough.

In fact it was more than enough. It was everything.

Barbie was the watershed, turning Baby Boomer toys into something new and distinctive.

Barbie and Ken. General Merchandise Catalog, *Fall-Winter 1962.*

Glittering Gown with stole $2.99

Barbie in Pink. Sears Toys, *1966-67.*

The rest of the Boomer years might be seen as the triumph of the fashion doll, for fashion and style dolls dominated the toy landscape. Even non-doll toys took on the aspect of fashion dolls, or appeared in guises that acknowledged their dominance. Accessories for the sake of accessories ruled.

Just as it had seemed utterly natural earlier in the 1950s that a popular toy robot, Robert the Robot, should have plastic sides that mimicked austere, undecorated sheets of metal, so it seemed utterly natural, not long after Barbie's appearance, that Yakkity Yob, a popular toy robot of the early 1960s, should appear wearing a tie and good-luck ring. Gone was the austerity. Fashion and style-defined personality were in.

By the mid-1960s, children were of the mind that everything needed to be accessorized, even their school books and notebooks, which sported every kind of sticker and decal available. Unlike the colorful rub-on decorations of wild animals and alphabet letters found inside children's books from the late 1800s, these decorations were conspicuous. Far from being designed for the quiet enjoyment of the solitary child, they were bright and loud and meant to be noticed by the crowd. They added not to the book or notebook, but to the person. They were that person's "style."

Accessories mattered to even the youngest, of either sex.

Barbie caused none of this. The trend was building in society to value appearance above all else. Neat, indistinguishable lawns enhanced neat, indistinguishable suburban houses, while housewives wearing the current hairstyle sent husbands driving the latest car off to work. The way to excel and stand out was through conspicuous excellence of display - perhaps over-conspicuous excellence. Barbie coolly achieved that among dolls, and made everyone follow suit.

The fashion dolls of the remainder of the 1960s were legion. Among Barbie look-alikes alone were generic "Fashion Dolls" from Sears, Polly the "Livin' Doll model" from Alden's of Chicago, and Ideal's Mitzi. How many casual rip-off dolls from Hong Kong appeared on dime store shelves will probably remain forever unknown.

Made in the shade. *Barbie relaxes on a covered swing in a 1964 advertisement.* Playthings, *March 1964.*

Barbie's own corner of the toy world gradually expanded through the 1960s, with her innocuous boyfriend Ken appearing in 1961, her friend Midge in 1963, her little sister Skipper and Ken's buddy Allan in 1964, Skipper's friends Skooter and Ricky in 1965, and Barbie's Mod cousin Francie in 1966.

She came full circle as early as 1962, becoming a paper doll from Whitman Publishing Co.

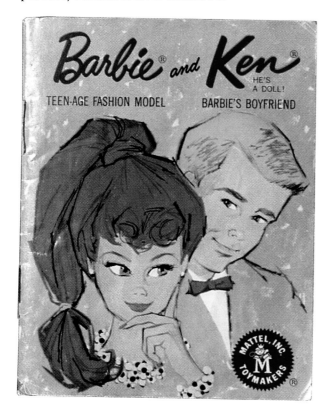

Don't accept imitations! *Booklets such as this one provided dozens of style options for Barbie and Ken. All too aware of copycats flooding the toy marketplace, Mattel included warnings against imitations. "Look for the Mattel identifying wrist tag attached to each genuine Barbie and Ken Doll. For perfect fit and finest quality, always insist on the genuine Barbie and Ken fashions, made only by Mattel." The toy company even trademarked such phrases as "Teen-Age Fashion Model" for Barbie and "He's a Doll!" for Ken. Mattel, 1962.*

#2 MR. POTATO HEAD
Everyone's Favorite Vegetable

The road to the plastic beauty doll was paved, oddly enough, by potatoes.

Potatoes turned their eyes in every direction except toward fashion until seven years after World War II. That year, by introducing potatoes to the toy fashion world, one of the smallest companies in the business, Hasbro, changed the way children looked at their food almost overnight.

Food, in its raw, original form, became a plaything through a box filled with plastic pieces.

It was called the Mr. Potato Head Funny-Face Kit.

Hasbro issued plastic bodies, eyes, hats, pipes, noses, mouths, eyebrows, ears, feet, and hands, all of them expressly meant to decorate food. The spike-like necks of the hard plastic bodies stuck upward into the potato, while the hands and feet went into the bodies. The eyes, nose, mouth, ears, and hat had small pointed spikes that went directly into the raw vegetable. Once this was accomplished, your average potato took on a distinguished, if somewhat ridiculous, appearance. He wore a tie, a respectable hat, had bushy eyebrows of felt held in place by the eye-spikes, perhaps a mustache, perhaps some hair if you chose to be creative and use some scrap felt or garden foliage for that purpose. His nose and ears were large. His eyes were round and the tiniest bit buggy, or else oval and comic-bookish.

Were kids delighted? Fabulously.

Not long before, Hasbro had been Hassenfeld Brothers, a manufacturer of stationery, pencils, and pencil boxes. Merril Hassenfeld, a son of one of the original Hassenfeld brothers, had been inching into the toy business. The company started selling junior doctor and nurse kits before the war, then junior air raid warden kits during the war for coastal cities that were starting to experience black-outs. He followed these with junior sewing, mailman, jewelry, and school kits, and started dipping a toe into licensing, which resulted in Donald Duck doctor kits and Roy Rogers pistol-shaped pencil cases.

In 1951 a man named George Lerner offered Merril the set of noses, eyes, ears, and other plastic features that would become Mr. Potato Head. The toy pieces had been packaged earlier as a cereal premium, which meant Hassenfeld Bros. had to obtain rights. It did so, and gave Lerner an advance against royalties - a small one, since prospects for the success of a toy that everyone else in the business had turned down seemed small.

Yet that toy succeeded far beyond Lerner's or Merril Hassenfeld's imaginings. It succeeded in part because of intrinsic charm. Children saw the toy and saw how it could always be a different toy from playtime to playtime. It seemed to increase

Food for funny thoughts. *Hasbro advertised its Mr. Potato Head pieces as usable on apples, bananas, cucumbers, oranges, pears, and peppers, too. Hasbro Mr. Potato Head pieces from the 1950s and '60s, in apple, potato, and tangerine.*

The Hassenfeld legacy.
In its early days, Hassenfeld Bros. specialized in school supplies, especially pencils and pencil boxes. When the toy division made waves with Mr. Potato Head, the school supplies division cashed in with tie-in pencil boxes. The acceptability of taking toys to the classroom increased during the Boomer years, even becoming routine through "Show and Tell" periods. School Days Potato Head Pencil Case, 11˝ long, Hasbro, 1950s.

the possibilities of make-believe rather than decrease them, as some toys managed to do.

Yet it succeeded even more because of where children first saw this toy.

Parents may have first seen it in the pages of *Life* magazine.

Kids saw it on TV.

Toys in the United States after the war took a few years to become Baby Boomer toys. For a time they remained the same as those issued in the war years - yet those wartime toys were not quite the same as the ones that came before. Toy makers were working under restrictions, cut off from their usual supplies of various metals and rubber. They were forced to become adept at working with wood again, as well as paper and cardboard.

Nearly everything could be made of wood, from puzzles, riding toys, alphabet boards, pull toys, alphabet blocks (which in the late 1940s still lacked the interlocking ridges to which we have become so accustomed) and push-puppets to toy cars, trucks, ships, trains, and airplanes. A few of the more popular construction toys of the prewar years were made of wood anyway and were largely unaffected by the rationing of materials.

The expertise manufacturers developed during the war no doubt helped them hold onto wood as a toy-making material in the Boomer years - probably for longer than would have been the case otherwise.

Cardboard, which had filled in for other toy-making materials during the war, likewise continued to be important afterwards. Play sets with card-

board farms, tractors, implements, people, and animals gave children their imaginary life in the country. Other sets used Masonite, which made sturdy service stations and doll houses.

Toys made of such restricted materials as lead alloy, tin, and pressed steel slowly returned to production after the war: toy trucks and cars, windup spinning toys, wheeled toys, toy sewing machines and typewriters, construction sets, and cap guns. Even toys made of thick, heavy rubber returned, looking unchanged from their prewar, Deco-inspired predecessors.

Yet change was in the air. Some children were playing with toys their parents never had, and never could have had. The plastics industry had moved decisively beyond celluloid and Bakelite into newly formulated acetates and other plastics. Plastics manufacturers began courting toy makers, who, they thought, should be perfect consumers of synthetic materials.

They were right. A few companies had already experimented with new plastics before the war. They resumed production afterwards, and found themselves joined by other forward-looking manufacturers.

By the second Christmas after World War II, plastic seemed to be headed for a permanent place in the toy industry. The new plastics made ideal material for doll house furniture, for one. It was advertised as "well proportioned, beautifully made. Copied from fine adult furniture in color, finish. Details are expertly reproduced." No toy maker could have made such claims for its toy furniture before the advent of hard plastic - not, at least, for

$.98, which bought a dining room set, including some pieces with moving parts, or for $1.98, which bought the living room set, including grand piano.

The new plastic also worked extremely well for small vehicle toys, which could be sold for less than $1.50 a dozen, and for tea sets. A tea service for two might cost $.95, while a 40-piece set for six cost only $2.25. Manufacturers also saw the potential for hard plastic for the very young, such as pull toys made of "washable plastic in bright harmless colors."

Most of us will look back at these toys of the later 1940s and wonder what was missing. Plastic was part of the picture, certainly. Yet some color or vital spark is absent. Some element of excitement we associate with the toys of our lost Boomer childhoods is missing.

What was that spark?

It was akin to the one given off by the Yellow Kid and other early cartoon characters at the end of the 19th century. By the early 20th, cartoon personalities were becoming as well known as real ones - often better known. Things really started taking off in 1906 to 1907, when *Mr. Mutt*, the first daily comic strip, was making a name for itself, and again in 1933, the year that saw *Funnies On Parade* and its immediate successors, the first true comic books in the modern sense of the word.

In the meantime, Winsor McCay's 1911 animated film *Little Nemo* set in motion a series of events that would result in Walt Disney's 1928 film *Steamboat Willie*. It was the first to combine animation with synchronized sound, and the beginning of an animation empire.

The "funnies" gave the toy industry the push it needed to change playthings into something we now recognize as Modern. Where would the childhoods of the 1920s, '30s, and '40s have been without Popeye and Olive Oyl, Dick Tracy, Buck Rogers, Flash Gordon, Blondie, Superman, Happy Hooligan, Barney Google, Little Orphan Annie, Krazy Kat, Felix the Cat, and, of course, Mickey Mouse and the rest of that rubbery and ebullient Disney cast?

The new media of radio and the movies also provided characters for toys in the Modern period, including Tarzan, who appeared in film as early as 1918, and Hopalong Cassidy, who was first portrayed in film by William Boyd in 1935.

The groundwork for the media influence that would make the most difference in the Boomer years was laid at the same time. A far-sighted farmer's boy, Philo Farnsworth, dreamed up a practical way to deliver images electronically. The first scheduled television broadcast was made in 1928 by WGY in Schenectady, New York. Within a year, Bell Labs was experimenting with color television. It was an explosion waiting to happen.

As the 1950s got underway, toy manufacturers were showing signs of a new sophistication. Toys appeared in catalogs and advertisements with the following statement, presented as a worthy and notable credential: "As advertised in *Life*."

Toy makers including Auburn Rubber, Banner Plastics, Doepke Manufacturing, Electric Game Co., Milton Bradley, Nosco Plastics, Parker Brothers, and Structo Manufacturing Co. adver-

Nationally known funny faces. *While Mr. Potato Head is now famous for being the first toy advertised on TV, in the early 1950s far more prestige accrued from another claim: "Advertised in LIFE." Mr. and Mrs. Potato Head* Funny Face Ideas *instruction pamphlets, Hasbro, 1950s. Behind the pamphlets, a package of metal jacks with the same claim.*

tised in America's leading popular magazine. From the start, *Life* magazine captivated readers with its pictures of both the everyday and the unusual, its focus on the rich and famous, and its large format. Most importantly, the magazine fed the huge public appetite for fine photography, at mid-century an art form still seen as exciting.

At the same time, the new medium of television was making huge strides. Broadcasting stations, only two in number in 1941, television's first year as a viable medium, numbered over 100 by 1948. After briefly dropping back, they surpassed that number permanently in 1950. By mid-decade, over 400 stations were broadcasting across the country. For the biggest pool of Boomers in the late 1960s, over 600 stations telecast commercial programs.

Alongside growth in the number of cities with broadcasting stations and the number of stations per city, viewer growth kept pace. Many people saw their first TV broadcasts in circumstances related to the New York World's Fair of 1939, where the medium had its public debut. My father remembers being taken by my grandfather, a young pastor at the time, to the DuMont dealership in New Jersey to see a student choir perform at the Fair's opening ceremonies on the dealership's TV screens. As stations developed, people congregated at bars to watch wrestling or *Author Meets the Critics*, a popular program of verbal-sparring that began as a local New York show. As TV programming increased, TV ownership spread, with the TVs themselves becoming conspicuous symbols of social status.

Eight thousand households owned TVs in 1946, a number that nearly doubled in a year. Then the explosion set in. In 1948, nearly 200,000 house-

holds had TVs; in 1949, over 900,000. In 1950, the number zoomed upward to nearly four million, and to ten million in 1951. The increasing numbers meant advertisers took greater and greater interest, to the tune of $58 million in 1949, nearly $200 million in 1950, and over $300 million in 1951.

In 1952, over 15 million households owned television sets, and advertisers were spending an amount on TV sponsorships closing in on $600 million. The year marked a watershed, for those advertisers were close to spending as much on upstart TV as they were on radio.

In that year CBS also delivered one of many blows the pioneering network DuMont would suffer by luring Jackie Gleason away from DuMont's two-year-old hit program, the *The Cavalcade of Stars*. Art Carney, the June Taylor Dancers, and the Ray Bloch Orchestra followed him from DuMont to CBS, where increased resources, monetary and otherwise, helped make their new show an even bigger hit.

In that year, too, Hasbro's Mr. Potato Head appeared on the burgeoning media scene. In a time full of firsts, Mr. Potato Head became the first toy to be advertised on TV.

It appeared on *The Jackie Gleason Show*.

Television ads invited kids to "Meet Mr. Potato Head - the most wonderful friend a boy or girl could have." "The most novel toy in years," said the Hasbro catalog. "The ideal item for gift, party favor, or the young invalid." While the promotion was unsophisticated by later standards, the ads did the job. A million Hasbro sets, each containing several dozen accessories, went out to a million buyers. At a time when the Arthur Godfrey Flamingo Ukulele

Advertised on TV. Telling kids that a toy was advertised on television remained important through the late Boomer years. Hasbro Mr. Potato Head logo, 1968.

#2050 MR. POTATO HEAD ON THE MOON

Space Age! By the mid-1960s, many accessory-based toys established some connection with America's push for the moon. Hasbro's decorated potato beat Neil Armstrong by only one year. Mr. Potato Head On the Moon, 1968.

cost $5, an Auburn Rubber farm set cost $3, and American Logs or a Wolverine tin pull train cost $2, the Mr. Potato Head Funny-Face Kit ("Any Fruit or Vegetable Makes a Funny Face Man") sold for $1. The pieces, while small, promised unlimited fun, for they were endlessly reusable and could be employed in a multitude of ways. The new Hasbro catalog showed the face pieces inserted into all the standard products from the grocer's produce aisle: not only potato, but apple, banana, cucumber, orange, pear, and pepper. To keep him from being lonely in his popularity, Hasbro introduced Mrs. Potato Head, son Spud, and daughter Yam the next year.

The toy remained a steady seller for the growing toy company through the Boomer years. It went through several changes, most notably in 1964 when the first kits appeared with the potato provided, in hollow plastic form. Once Hasbro crossed that threshold, Mr. Potato Head's universe started expanding to include other roots, fruits, and vegetables. Dubbed his Tooty Frooty Friends, they included Katie the Carrot, Cooky the Cucumber, Oscar the Orange, and Pete the Pepper. Later in the decade the Picnic Pals appeared, including Mr. Soda Pop Head and Franky Frank. The end of the decade saw the appearance of the most complex Mr. Potato Head toys, including the whimsical Mr. Potato Head On the Moon play set.

Although Hasbro continued issuing kits to be used on actual fruits and vegetables through the middle 1960s, by the end of the decade new child safety laws blunted the piercing ends until they were useful only for poking through pre-poked polyethylene potatoes.

Mr. Potato Head is perhaps the single most characteristic toy of the Boomer years. It appeared early enough, and with enough fanfare, to be a factor in the childhoods of even the first Boomer children. It established for the first time the connection between everyday toys - as opposed to "premiums" - and the then-blossoming medium that would end up largely defining the times: television. It consisted entirely of the material that would come to dominate toy making by the 1960s: plastic, in both hard and soft forms.

In almost pure form it encapsulated one of the greatest trends to be seen in toys of the Boomer years, the ascendance of the accessory toy. For its first decade and more, Hasbro was not selling the toy itself, the potato, but simply accessories for the toy. A generation starved for accessories embraced Mr. Potato Head as their own, recognizing kinship.

At the same time, Mr. Potato Head stood for the ever-growing American postwar wealth, which the industry perceived as "disposable income." The country was enjoying such economic success that

In the Parade. In the late 1960s, many kits still promoted the use of real fruit and vegetables. This Mr. Potato Head In the Parade kit suggested kids make a lemon majorette, onion clown, and cucumber calliope. Hasbro, 1968. Courtesy Becky Stubbe.

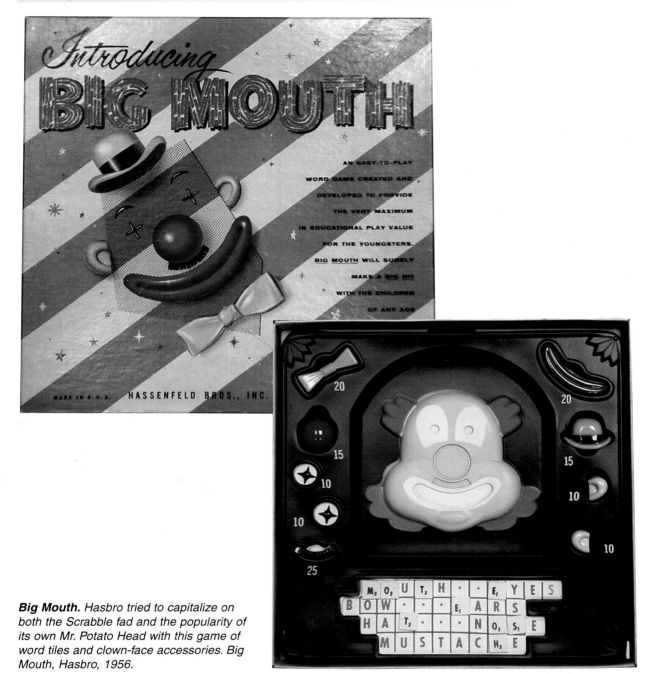

Big Mouth. *Hasbro tried to capitalize on both the Scrabble fad and the popularity of its own Mr. Potato Head with this game of word tiles and clown-face accessories. Big Mouth, Hasbro, 1956.*

America's children could play with their food, with adult sanction.

In the change from the emphasis on real fruits and vegetables to artificial ones, Mr. Potato Head moreover represented changes in the toy world that increasingly took children farther and farther from home-made toy experiences to industry-made ones. In that and other changes, Mr. Potato Head's development also reflected the changes forced on childhood by government safety standards.

For all these reasons, Mr. Potato Head ranks as the top toy for many Boomers, especially those millions who never played with - who may never have even *seen* - Barbie.

The toy as it was known to Boomers then would give joy and hours of quiet fun to no other generation - at least not in quite the same form, not in quite the same way. The toy's name would remain the same, while the rest would change.

Much as happened with all of us.

G.I. JOE

According to conventional wisdom at mid-century, girls played with baby dolls, not adult-looking dolls. Conventional wisdom also said boys never played with dolls at all, however cute the babies might have been.

Unless, that is, someone looked away and the boy-kid nabbed a baby doll and started playing with it - which happened all the time, because boys, like girls, grew up in Boomer America knowing what a toy was: anything in reach.

The postwar stiffness of gender roles would hit the boy-kid soon enough, but not until he stretched his fingers and made that reach. Then came the slap. "That's for girls, kid," said the gentle guardians of social behavior.

Conventional wisdom followed this postulate to its necessary corollary: boys would never play with adult-looking dolls either.

Child play by its nature is weighted towards make-believe. Make-believe embraces the worlds outside the child's reach. In the times before the war, those out-of-reach worlds were presented to children through storybooks, comic strips, radio serials, and the adult lives around them. The adult lives were always the most important. The adults lived in a world so full of complexly organized noises, smells, textures, appearances, and words that it endlessly fascinated kids. They play-acted being those adults.

Characteristic of the postwar years was the increasing intrusion of the toy industry into those make-believe moments. Before the war and immediately afterwards, boys would move directly from having no wood-working tools at all to having actual, working tools. The tools might be designed for children and made in accommodating sizes, yet the tools would be real. Even if they started off with a building set from Erector, Meccano, or Structo, the tools in the sets were real, working tools, made expressly for the job.

For much of the Boomer period, children could emulate mother's or father's use of tools at an earlier age, with realistic but not actual tools. For some companies this was a vital niche in the toy world. Handy Andy made tin boxes with toy tools, and Auburn Rubber manufactured rubber saws and hammers. Adults instinctively approved of these toys and bought them in great numbers.

Toy manufacturers devoted increasing inventory to toys that helped kids project themselves into ever more varieties of adult experience. Kids could spend less time imagining and more time being "just like Mom" and "just like Dad." Not the same as, but just like.

Even so, the toy industry stopped short of giving boys a fashion-doll figure whose clothes could be changed to reflect different careers and different aspirations. Many boys undoubtedly played with Ken dolls or the figures of Dad and Ted from Ideal's Tammy line, or Dr. John from Remco's Littlechap Family in the early 1960s. As they did, they probably glanced over their shoulders to see who was looking. These male figural toys came from the doll aisles at department stores and from the doll pages of toy catalogs. This was enough to make boys nervous.

E ven though the Boomer generation was America's largest, what was more significant was that it was being raised by the largest pool of war veterans in the country's history. That was what mattered. Long before the war, Americans had coined the word "Siss" for sister or young woman. Its diminutive, "Sissy," took on such derogatory power for Boomer boys that the word by itself could stop almost any behavior, even if it

was the normal behavior of a boy imagining being older than he was. Girls casually played being men, and frequently had to because of the nature of playing house. Even as girls grew older, engaging in male-stereotype activities led to relatively few social repercussions. Boys hewed closer to the line. The pressure to do so started early.

The 1960s saw rising social unrest and change, in part as a reaction to the stiff social conventions people pulled up around them like blankets as comfort against the triple threats of war memories, the Bomb, and the Communist scare. Since toys often reflected society instantly, by that decade toy manufacturers were veering farther from the dictates of traditional wisdom than ever before. The fashion doll marketed specifically for boys was bound to arise.

It did so in 1964 from Hasbro, a company still struggling to recover from the debacle of its Son of Flubber tie-in toy, a putty that had caused allergic reactions first and lawsuits second. Not surprisingly, since war toys were in ascendance while Western-style toys declined, Hasbro's fashion doll was a military figure. All his style changes and accessories were military. He was America's Movable Fighting Man, marketed under a severe policy that steered clear of the sissy word "doll." He was the G.I. Joe Action Soldier, G.I. Joe Action Marine, G.I. Joe Action Sailor, and G.I. Joe Action Pilot.

Action Pilot, from G.I. Joe America's Movable Fighting Man, Hasbro catalog, 1965. Photo courtesy Krause Publications.

"He's over 11˝ tall, has 21 movable parts, stands, sits, kneels! Takes combat-action poses. Has equipment authentically scaled from actual G.I. issue. Even has dog tag and training manual." Joe, Hasbro said, "is ready to carry out your orders!"

At the same time, the Louis Marx Co. released its Stony, a paratrooper who had molded-in fatigues but still plenty of accessories in the form of hats, helmets, packs, and weaponry. Even the veterans of battles in Europe and Asia could only approve the purchase of such dolls for their boys, who would all grow up, they knew, to be men.

The timing turned out to be right. G.I. Joe enjoyed phenomenal sales in his first two years, bringing Hasbro's toy division well out of its losses in 1964 and bringing in a profit of $6 million in 1965.

The time was also wrong. The true nature of America's involvement in Vietnam was settling in. The fact of the draft loomed over the older brothers of the boys who received G.I. Joes. Even those younger boys felt the knowledge dawning that the draft calmly awaited them too. Part of maturing in the 1960s meant coming to realize what a body count was. The romance of war was wearing thin.

In an effort to prop up G.I. Joe's declining popularity, Hasbro introduced outfits that made him more a civilian. He was a boater, a scuba diver, a hunter. Yet he never lived down his initial image, trapped in the amber of his name. He was G.I. Joe. He was a grunt. A scuttlebutt for others, he fell short of mastering his own fate. What was happening to his ilk overseas, after all? They were being shipped and flown into a slaughterhouse and sent home in body bags.

G.I. Joe as Green Beret. Sears Toys, *1967-68.*

Hasbro learned one lesson from Mattel without absorbing another. Barbie started without a specific career or calling. Instead, she simply depicted success. She had a great sense of style and an obviously ample purse. She could be only one thing in the theaters of imagination: a celebrity. Being a celebrity meant being a television star or member of high society - close to the same thing since high society tended to appear on television. Above all, being a celebrity meant having glamour, which, in the TV Age, mattered immensely. Even boys wanted glamour. They wanted TV's glamour. They happily played at being Roy Rogers or a *Bonanza* star, pretending to fight rustlers or run a ranch, because doing so meant having glamour. They played *Rat Patrol* because being on the *Rat Patrol* jeep had glamour. They played *Captain Video* or *Star Trek* because of the glamour of television science-fiction. They played *Ben Casey* because of the glamour of television hospital work.

Was Barbie a hard worker? Her self-assured, side-glancing eyes made the question superfluous. She had glamour. What more did she need? Did she ever follow anyone's orders?

"What kind of question is that?" the girls would have wondered.

Boys never had to wonder about G.I. Joe.

They were told.

Action Sailor, from G.I. Joe America's Movable Fighting Man, Hasbro, 1965.

Accessories of war. *The G.I. Joe line gave boys a chance to participate in the fashion revolution, but within a narrow range. G.I. Joe accessories, Hasbro, 1960s.*

Johnny West, Louis Marx Co., 1960s.

Best fashion dolls of the Old West. *While the Louis Marx Co. went head-to-head with Hasbro with its Stony soldier figure, it enjoyed more success with its Western line called Best of the West. Unlike the Mattel and Hasbro plastic fashion dolls, the slightly larger Johnny and Jane West came with molded-on clothing. Also unlike the Mattel or Hasbro lines, the Best of the West line of cowboys and cowgirls, Indians, cavalry, horses, buffalo, dogs, buckboards, and Fort Apache stockade appealed to both boys and girls of the later 1960s. Accessories came in the form of vinyl guns, canteens, hats, vests, and chaps for the people, and bridles and saddles for the horses. Jane West, the "fully jointed cowgirl," with Thunderbolt and Thundercolt, Sears Toys, 1966-67.*

Meet the boldest, bravest hero!
CAPTAIN ACTION with Batman Costume and Quick-change Chamber

Fully jointed 12-inch figure in uniform, fully armed, ready for adventure. Then *presto* . . transform him into another popular hero in the quick-change-chamber

Only Sears offers this complete Captain Action Set

$8.29

Uniformed plastic figure with lightning sword, scabbard, action gun, belt, hat . . even removable boots. Batman costume includes plastic cape, helmet-mask, belt, weapons. Colorful, detailed cardboard transformation chamber with swinging door. Sets up quickly. About 18 inches high and 13 inches wide.
79 N 6018C—Shipping weight 3 pounds.....................Set $8.29

Total makeovers. *While never as widely popular as G.I. Joe or Best of the West, Ideal's Captain Action was perhaps the ultimate fashion doll. Kids could transform the versatile Captain into their favorite superheroes by changing clothes, weapons, and even faces, which were tight-fitting, rubbery full-head masks that could be pulled over Captain Action's craggy features. By 1967, Action Girl and Action Boy joined the line. Sears Toys, 1966-67.*

MATCHBOX CARS #4

The first revolution that would forever change American sandbox motoring happened quietly in, of all places, England, where a young man back from the war had the sensible idea that children would enjoy having toy cars that could be slipped into English-size matchboxes, which could then be slipped into the pocket and carried to school.

Jack Odell did more than dream about the idea. He made a small brass road roller for his daughter, which she did immediately slip into a pocket and carry to school, where the novelty of its scale and design created an instant demand for more.

Odell worked in die-casting with Leslie and Rodney Smith, unrelated friends who had joined forces after leaving the Royal Navy to found

Sixties favorites. *The flow of Matchbox cars to America from England reached flood levels by the late 1960s. Lesney Matchbox cars on a Kenner Bridge & Turnpike road.*

Lesney Products, basing the name on their own first names. Among other products, they made miscellaneous die-cast toys, including a large Coronation Coach.

The toy road roller that fit in a matchbox started Lesney Products down an entirely new road, however. Lesney started its line of Matchbox cars in 1953. Roughly the same scale, all were nicely detailed, and all were good fun. Odell and his co-workers based the designs on existing vehicles and provided the toys with base plates. The master strokes were two: they packaged them in those

Fifties favorites. *Matchbox toys from England showed a realism and attention to detail that put Chicago-manufactured Tootsietoys to shame. These three vehicles, the No. 25 Bedford "Dunlop" Van, No. 43 Millman Minx, and the No. 44 Rolls Royce Silver Cloud, were originally issued with metal wheels. These examples have the second wheel type, made of gray plastic. In the 1960s, the wheels were made of black plastic. Lesney Products, late 1950s.*

Ford G.T., No. 41, 1965.

Ford tractor, No. 39, 1967.

GMC Tipper Truck, No. 26, 1968.

"matchboxes," and, through the years, adopted a 1 to 75 numbering system, which proved to have great appeal to young collectors.

Many companies followed in the wake of Matchbox. Fellow British company Budgie released charming vehicles almost indistinguishable from early Lesney products. Japanese company Tomy later produced Tomicas, which enjoyed some success in this country.

American companies never quite seemed to get the hang of it. Hubley, a venerable presence in the toy world, turned out a few slightly larger vehicles for its Real Cars line. The likewise venerable Tootsietoy launched a short-lived HO series of toy cars, which had much of the appeal of Matchbox toys, but which were few in number.

Since the boxes of these toys proved almost as popular as the cars themselves, for a while even extremely cheap soft-plastic cars made in Hong Kong were issued in Matchbox-style boxes. Through the 1950s and most of the '60s, nothing else quite caught on, however. Children were perfectly content to play with the toy cars made by other makers, but showed their true allegiance by calling them all by the same name: Matchbox cars.

The floor-level highways, congested as they became with the dozens of attractive models always available, prepared much of the generation for the car-dominated world they were entering.

Eight Wheel Crane Truck, No. 30, 1965.

CHATTY CATHY
& Friends

**Just Pull the
Chatty Ring**

Mattel put a defiant flag of ownership in Noisy Toyland when the '60s started. This flag was not your ordinary flag. It was a small box, which fit inside a toy, which was set into motion by something called the Chatty Ring. You pulled the Chatty Ring and the toy talked.

Mattel suddenly found itself with a new spokesperson, in the form of a 20″ vinyl doll with sleep-eyes and freckles who could speak Toylandese: "Please change my dress." "I'm so tired." "I love you." "Please brush my hair."

Her name?

"Hi! I'm Chatty Cathy!"

Once the company had a firm grasp on its new toy technology, Mattel started putting it everywhere. "Just pull the Chatty Ring and they each say many different things," Mattel promised. "You never know what they'll say next!"

"How about some haaay," said Mattel's talking-galloping horse, whose Chatty Ring was located in the neck, within easy reach of any young cowboy or cowgirl rider. "Whee-ee-ee! My name is Blaze!" Blaze, Mattel promised parents, "gallops, bucks, AND talks! Provides lots of thrills for active youngsters - his legs actually move when they ride him. When they lean in the saddle, he rears or kicks up his heels! Hours of fun!"

Chatty Baby was born in 1961, becoming available in 1962. Like Chatty Cathy, she came with various outfits. Mattel also gave her a cradle, and Cathy a new bed, so kids could have the pleasure of trying to put to sleep little ones who wouldn't hush up.

By 1962 everyone in the Mattel toy cart seemed to talk: Bugs Bunny ("What's Up, Doc?"), Casper the Friendly Ghost ("Let's play ghost!"), Donald Duck ("I live in Disneyland!"), Mickey Mouse ("Pluto is my dog!"), Popeye ("Blow me down!"), and Beany ("Help! Save me!") and Cecil ("You called?"). Colonel Claxton and Calvin Burnside appeared, as did Pinocchio and even Matty Mattel, who had to say, "I am Matty Mattel," since kids had no idea who this kid was, with his striped shirt, red hair, and crown. I suspect Matty also told his young owners, "Buy Chatty Cathy!" "Buy Chatty Baby!" "Buy me!" (Remember what Mattel said? "You never know what they'll say next!") I have yet to confirm this suspicion, however.

So clever for so young. Changeable Charmin' Chatty, "The Educated Doll," had 120 sayings, thanks to interchangeable records that were inserted in her left side. Playthings, *March 1964.*

By 1963 and '64 Mattel was using the Chatty Ring in more animals, including the new Animal Yackers series figures Crackers and Larry, the talking plush parrot and lion, and a talking Woody Woodpecker Hand Puppet.

Mattel once again chose dolls to represent the cutting edge of Chatty technology, especially with "changeable Charmin' Chatty, the educated doll," who was everyone's precocious little talker. Dressed in a sailing outfit and wearing dark-rimmed glasses over her side-glancing sleep eyes, Charmin' had 120 sayings at her beck and call,

Ha-ha-ha-ha-ha! Woody Woodpecker, with vinyl head and soft cloth body, joined the Mattel pull-string crowd in 1964.

Monstrous for the laughs. *Mattel's line of talking toys included several stars of TV and the movies, including this talking doll of Herman Munster, leading man of the popular 1964 to 1966 TV comedy* The Munsters. *Mattel, 1964. Photo courtesy Robert G. Johnson, Comet Toys.*

Minis are smashing! *In 1968, Barbie seemed to have everything: bending legs, eyelashes, and voices. "I have a date tonight!" "Would you like to go shopping?" "I think minis are smashing!" The Livin' Barbie Dolls were Talking Barbie, Talking Stacey, and Talking Christie, costing less than $5 each that Christmas.* Alden's Christmas *catalog, 1968.*

thanks to the five extra records she came with, to be inserted in her left side.

Shrinkin' Violet made her debut in 1964 - a cloth doll with fluttering eyebrows and a mouth that moved while she talked. The talker even moved into games: the Animal Talk Game of '64 featured an "Oink-oink! Whinee! Baa-aah! Moo-oo-oo" Chatty Ring barn.

Traditional "boy toys" were not entirely forgotten. Mattel invested heavily in its V-RROOM! campaign of 1964, which featured the V-RROOM! Real Motor Roar Guide-Whip Racer, Dump Truck, and Skiploader. The racer could be guided through obstacle courses or simply raced. The faster it went, to the delight of boys, the louder it got. The Dump Truck idled, roared, and revved; the Skiploader, in addition to being capable of scooping and dumping loads, featured actions that were guided by control handles, and was "big, powerful, loud, and sensational!"

The talking barn of '64 may have pointed the way to one of Mattel's most significant new toys, introduced the next year: the See 'n Say Educational Toys.

At last even Barbie, long given to lengthy, demure, and yet self-assured silences, gave in. She became yet another chatterbox.

She was nine years old by 1968. Perhaps it was time.

Chatty Cathy. *Mattel's new doll greets the world in the company of two Ruthie Dolls by Horsman.* Toys, *1960-61.*

KENNER EASY-BAKE OVEN

Light-Bulb Inspirations

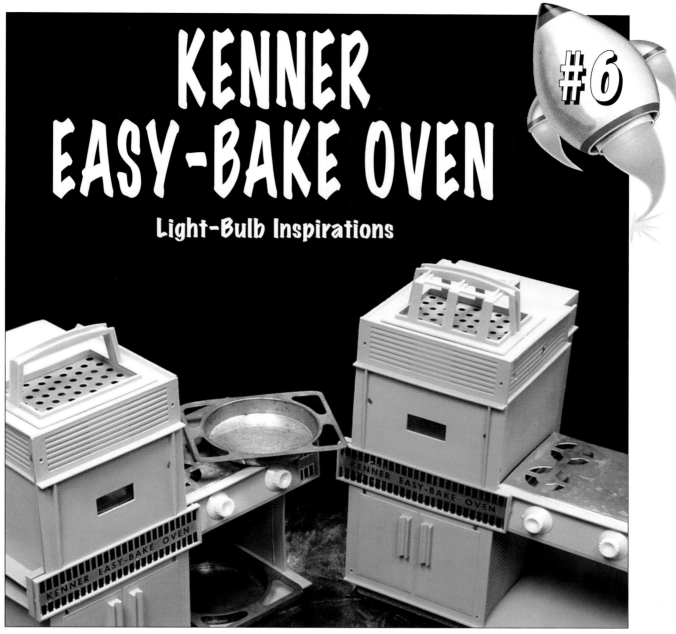

Girls had access to play ovens from well before the war, ranging from cast-iron toys made by such companies as Hubley and Arcade, to working electric appliances from companies including electric-train giant Lionel.

Electric appliances came into their own in the 1950s. Early in the decade, Metal Ware offered the Little Lady Electric Range, capable of operating on either A.C. or D.C., with separate elements for burners and oven. The oven even had the feel of the real thing: baked enamel finish and a clear glass oven window. The set came with utensils and a cookbook.

Meanwhile, another company offered its Alumode Kiddykook cookware, which could be safely used on actual stoves. The percolator was touted as capable of percolating. The teapot, it was promised, would whistle.

The smartest companies capitalized on brand names mothers already recognized. Model-Craft issued Kay Stanley's Cake Mix Set featuring boxes of kid-size Pillsbury cake mixes, as well as the Heinz Kitchen with utensils, chef's hat, and six cans of "genuine Heinz products." Within a few years, Ideal came out with the competing Betty Crocker Junior Baking Kit. Amsco, in the mid-'50s, promoted its Campbell Kids' Chuck Wagon Set, complete with pots, pans, utensils, cans of soup for heating over the campfire, Chuck Wagon Cook Book, two Western-style neckerchiefs, and a phonograph record that played a Western tune, just to set the proper campfire mood.

Everything Mom has, for $15.95.
The early Easy-Bakes came in a distinctive turquoise color. Many earlier toy ovens, working and non-working, had more standard appearances and came in standard department store colors. The early version had an exposed metal ventilation plate beneath the handle and cautioned users only to use 100-watt bulbs. The subsequent version added a protective cage at the top, a caution on back about possible burns from hot surfaces, and a warning against immersion. Kenner, 1964 and later 1960s.

These enjoyed tremendous success, with catalogs listing kid's baking sets with 35, 60, and over 100 pieces by the mid-1960s.

Food-related toys were flooding the market by then. Kids popped popcorn in the Empire Electric See 'Em Pop, hosted cookouts with their Electric Hot Dogger Jr., served refreshments from their Pepsi-Cola or Coca-Cola Dispensers or Kool-Aid Kooler, and spun cotton candy desserts in electric-powered plastic spinners.

In the midst of all this child cookery, a quiet, light bulb driven revolution had happened. In 1964, Kenner introduced a toy oven made of turquoise-colored plastic. Designed to be utterly safe and care-free, kids could use it to bake a cake with little or no parental supervision. Using no more heat than could be supplied by two 100-watt light bulbs, it turned specially formulated Betty Crocker cake and cookie mixes into not-quite-steaming-hot goods - and they were, Kenner promised, "just like Mom's."

The toy it announced to the industry was the Safety-Bake Oven. It came with 12 mixes (Devil's Food Cake, White Cake, Chocolate Icing, Brownies, Vanilla Cookies, Biscuits, Pie Crust, Pie Filling, Pretzels, Pizza Dough, Pizza Cheese, and Candy) in aluminum foil packages. Although replacement packets were available, Kenner was large-minded enough to include a recipe book for making Safety Oven baked goods using ingredients available at home - in other words, by a little sneaking-away of mother's supplies.

For accessories, it had a mixing spoon, measuring spoon, spatula, rolling pin, and three metal slide-through baking pans.

The name was intended to appeal to the safety-conscious parents of the '60s. Broadcasters, however, expressed their concern about Kenner's ability to fully back up the claim implicit in the name. They urged a change. When it appeared on store shelves, the Safety-Bake Oven carried the name that was to remain familiar for many Christmases to come: The Kenner Easy-Bake Oven.

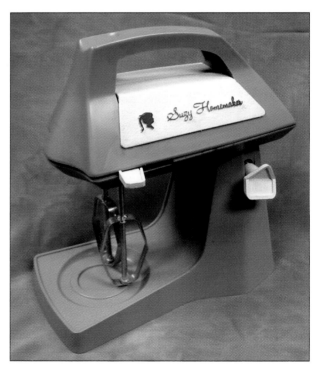

Mix batter just like Mom! *As did all successful toy innovations, the Easy-Bake inspired imitation, most notably Topper Toy's Suzy Homemaker Super Oven of 1966, which made even bigger cakes. Topper issued a full line of kitchen devices, including this battery-operated mixer. De Luxe Reading, 1960s.*

FROSTY SNO-MAN SNO-CONE MACHINE

Hassenfeld Brothers of Pawtucket, Rhode Island, enjoyed considerable success in the late Boomer years with its Frosty Sno-Man Sno-Cone Machine.

"Your cleverly designed Sno-Cone Machine will shave ordinary ice cubes into snow," said the instructions that came with the red and white plastic machine in 1967. "Remove snow with shovel and place into cups, top with fruit flavor to make a delicious frozen treat."

It may have been a toy that frustrated children as much as it pleased them. You could only work one ice cube at a time into shavings. And while Frosty came with ten flavor packets, which were mixtures of sugar and both artificial and natural flavors, the machine had only two flavor bottles for dispensing them. Children running their pint-sized soda fountains found themselves embarked on a particularly labor-intensive playtime, with the reward of only two flavors to try at a time, unless they were creative and began freezing juices into ice cubes for grinding.

The sheer pleasure of creating palatable treats won over all difficulties. For those with friends who could be suckered out of nickels for sno-cones, it was the best of all possible toys.

#7

FRISBEE

From Flyin' Saucers to Flyin' Pie Pans

The one we all threw. *Wham-O's Regular Frisbee Flying Disc, "for toy flying saucers, for flying games," dates from 1966. The instructions on the underside assume ignorance: "Play catch - invent games - To fly, flip away backhand-ed. Flat flip flies straight. Tilted flip curves - Experiment!"*

For some, the greatest phenomenon of the late '40s was the flying saucer scare, arising from an Air Force pilot's sightings of disc-shaped objects over the Cascade Mountains in the Northwest.

Newspapers leapt on the story, making the words "flying saucer" the nation's hottest phrase. The Roswell incident in 1947 fanned the fires, with witnesses swearing they saw dead alien beings in the wreckage of an unfamiliar flying craft. Soon editors such as Ray Palmer of *Amazing Stories* and *Fate* magazines were working hard to put a sensational spin on the saucer scare.

Other people worked on the toy spin. Of those, none developed that spin to greater effect than Warren Franscioni, an Air Force Major who saw service in the Near and Far East in World War II, and Fred Morrison, another Air Force pilot who flew missions over Italy before being shot down and being imprisoned in Germany's notorious Stalag 13.

In 1947, Morrison came looking for work at the Franscioni and Davis Butane Co. in San Luis Obispo, California. While Franscioni took Morrison on, the business proved too slow to support all three families involved. This prompted Franscioni and Morrison to undertake a side business.

The flying disc has a history much like the yo-yo. Discs were used for sport in ancient Greece and disc-like shields were flung by Roman soldiers as weapons. The throwing of lighter flying discs as casual recreation probably occurred any number of times and places in history. Certainly it had a firm place in New England culture by the time the second World War arrived. The most famed occurrence of this centered around Yale University and the nearby bakery of the Frisbie Pie Co., founded in 1871 in New Haven and famed for not only its pies but also its cookies. The pie pans flew nicely, and also hummed, since they sometimes had holes around the center. The cookie tin lids flew nicely too. Just as college students anywhere rarely show reticence when it comes to the opportunity to throw things around, Yale students flung around various pieces of round tin, yelling "Frisbie!" for the safety of oblivious bystanders, much as golfers yell "Fore!"

Everywhere in the country the materials were at hand for flying-disc sport: paint can lids, hubcaps, tin plates, and pan lids.

When World War II arrived, soldiers stationed around the country and abroad sought their diver-

Before the UFOs. *The Frisbie pie tins started such a popular Ivy League recreation that the word "Frisbie" was in widespread use long before Wham-O came along, according to flying disc historian Victor Malafronte. The famous pie company closed its doors just before Wham-O's Frisbee became a widespread success. Frisbie pie tin, 1940s. Photo courtesy Victor Malafronte.*

sions wherever they could find them. Since lids and coffee can tops could be found anywhere there was a mess hall, the simple recreation probably went around the globe. It grew in this country for logical reasons: kids from the East, with their back-and-forth games with cookie can lids and pie pans, mingled in Army, Navy, and Air Force units with California kids, who were used to vying against each other to see who could hurl paint can lids farthest across the ocean.

Wartime developments in plastic opened the doors to innovative production after the war. All a manufacturer needed to do was think of something old that could be redone in the new material. Plastic and flying discs were natural mates in the minds of Franscioni and Morrison, who apparently conceived of the notion together. Franscioni created the first plastic disc, designing aerodynamic features to make the plastic variety better than any previous metal version. As designer, mold-maker, and original partner in the company that probably provided equipment and resources, Franscioni might reasonably be thought originator of the plastic flying disc if any one person needed to be identified.

Franscioni and Morrison, working out of Franscioni's basement, made a prototype out of Tenite, a plastic made by the Tennessee Eastman Co. Tenite, an advanced variety of cellulose ace-

The Mystery "Y." *Other companies manufactured flying plastic discs, including Empire Plastics of Pelham Manor, New York. This Mystery "Y" shows a disc thrower wearing a "Y" on his t-shirt, presumably for Yale. Empire Plastics, late 1950s. Photo courtesy of Victor Malafronte.*

Identified flying objects. *An important early form of the plastic flying disc made its Outer Space allegiance plain, with "Flying Saucer" in the center and the planets depicted around the rim. Pluto Platter, Wham-O, 1957-63. Photo courtesy Victor Malafronte.*

tate, was already a popular plastic for manufacturing, having been used for such items as football helmets, army whistles, tool and utensil handles, and radio housings. It was tough, lustrous, and took colors well. Even Tennessee Eastman itself hinted at a problem, however: "Like most materials, natural and synthetic," the company said, "Tenite is tougher at high than at low temperatures."

In flying disc terms, this meant that as day cooled toward night, the toy might start chipping. It might even shatter if the other person failed to catch it.

Franscioni and Morrison's company, Partners in Plastic, or Pipco, contracted with Southern California Plastic Co. of Eagle Rock, California, to produce the new disc in a softer plastic, at a cost of $.25 per disc.

Pipco sold its new Flyn' Saucer for a dollar, the same price Wham-O would get for Frisbees 20 years later. The Flyin' Saucer took more salesmanship than the company could muster, with Franscioni usually tending the business end of things in San Luis Obispo and Morrison going on the road to demonstrate and actively sell the toy. At a point when the company was still struggling to cover the costs of the original dies, a marketing agreement with Al Capp, creator of *L'il Abner*, must have seemed a godsend.

Capp thought Pipco went beyond the agreement, however, and sued for damages. Franscioni borrowed $2,500 from his mother and another

$2,500 from his mother-in-law to pay off Capp. Pipco and Franscioni and Davis Butane Co. failed at about the same time, and Franscioni rejoined the Air Force out of necessity.

Southern California Plastic somehow continued making the Flyin' Saucer, however. Morrison continued to sell them, while developing a new disc of his own on the side. When Wham-O took an interest in 1955, Morrison signed a deal that would eventually earn him millions.

The first Wham-O Pluto Platters, which looked more like flying saucers than ever, hit the market at the beginning of 1957. Sales were slow at first. When Wham-O's Richard Knerr belatedly discovered the New Haven "Frisbie" tradition, the company renamed the flying disc. It seemed to add the magic touch. Wham-O registered the Frisbee trademark in 1959.

In what seemed no more than a blink of an eye, America's youth and Frisbees were inseparable.

By coincidence, the year Morrison was awarded the flying disc patent, 1958, was also the year the Frisbie Pie Factory in New Haven closed its doors.

Warren Franscioni was left out of the Wham-O deal. He was never mentioned in the patent claim, which he hoped to challenge at the time of his death.

The toy brought joy to millions of children. I know, for I was one of them.

Franscioni never received a cent for his role in having made that joy possible.

HULA-HOOP #8

Hooping. Even in Europe and the States, "hooping" was familiar before 1958 through juggling acts. Bob Bramson, who came from a juggling family, achieved fame during the Boomer years for his superlative and unequaled performances with hoops. Bob Bramson, publicity still, 1950s-60s.

Even if hoop toys, hoop-rolling, and hoop exercise apparently go back to the ancient Greeks and Egyptians...

Even if missionaries may have first drawn the connection between hip-whirling Hula dancers in Hawaii and the sport of hoop-twirling in far-away England...

Even if Australian health-nuts were thinning their waists by whirling wooden hoops just the year before...

Even if these things were so, the advent of the Hula Hoop in 1958 remains very much a Boomer phenomenon.

The reason is plastic. When Wham-O's Richard Knerr and Arthur Melin decided to adapt the Australian fad for the American market, they made prototypes of colorful plastic, tested it with local children, and discovered they had a toy on their hands with far greater potential than any other they had produced thus far.

Be Bop a Hula! *Teresa Brewer, a singing prodigy who began her singing career well before kindergarten, recorded a popular version of Donna Kohler and Carl Maduri's "The Hula Hoop Song." The song also worked its way up the Hit Parade in a version by Georgia Gibbs.*

Knerr and Melin had started their toy business in 1948 in a garage, making inexpensive slingshots. Ten years later they unleashed the Hula Hoop, starting a one-season fad that at its crest would see them producing 20,000 hoops per day, all of them flying from stores at a price of $1.98 each. Since Wham-O was unable to patent the toy, competing toy companies jumped in with Spin-A-Hoops, Hoop-D-Doos, and probably many others. Plastics manufacturers had trouble keeping up with the demands of the toy manufacturers, while toy manufacturers found it impossible to keep up with demand. For one dizzying summer, all of America had a thinner waistline.

Since the hoops were a summertime recreation, as the weather grew colder sales started slumping. Wham-O responded by marketing the plastic creation overseas and made the sensation a world-spanning, even if brief, phenomenon.

Romper Room "sensation." *The same year the Hula Hoop took the nation by storm, a small toy company was billing its Bob-A-Loop as "the game sensation of the nation!" Consisting of two pieces of thick wood connected by string, the toy probably knocked the most heads and broke the most windows of any toy before Klackers came along. Romco Enterprises, 1958.*

HOT WHEELS
Greased-Wheel Revolution

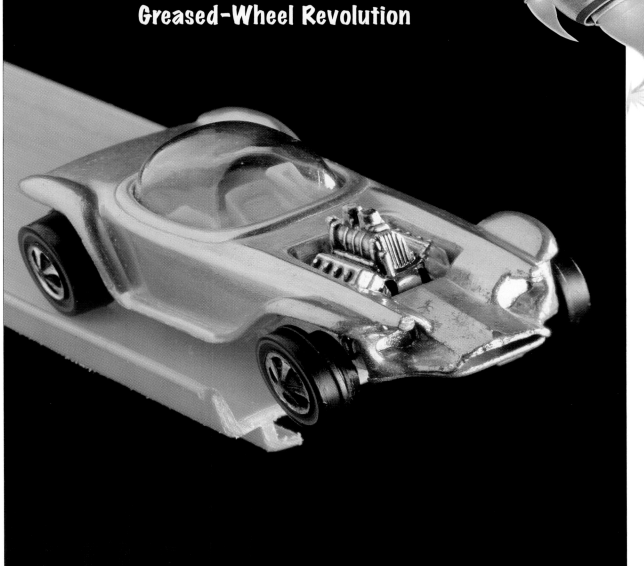

In the 1960s, the English company Lesney ruled the sidewalk highways. Suburbs were growing at a fantastic pace around every major city, all following the basic suburban model: wide streets, pleasant houses, lawns, trees, and sidewalks.

Millions of toy cars poured into this country from England, proving such a phenomenon that Mattel executives decided they needed something like Matchbox cars in their line. Their designers set to work in this direction, but ended up being slightly more influenced by the

Big Daddy's bubble-top. *Daring designs helped place Mattel's Hot Wheels at the top of the die-cast heap in 1968. Such custom show cars as this Beatnik Bandit, based on a car designed by Ed "Big Daddy" Roth, and the Silhouette, based on a Bill Cushenberry design, stood in startling contrast to the staid Matchbox cars of the time. Mattel, 1968-71. Photo courtesy Krause Publications.*

California ethic: beaches and surfing, crazy cars, and Ed Roth.

When the first Hot Wheels appeared on toy stands in 1968, Mattel had a revolution on its

Performance car accessory. *The metal tab-buttons packaged with early Hot Wheels toy cars became as much a part of the play scene as the cars themselves. Mattel showed its usual good sense regarding the fashion needs of children with the innovation. Ed Roth Beatnik Bandit and Maserati Mistral buttons, Mattel, 1968 and '69.*

hands. For the first time, a manufacturer was selling die-cast car toys based not on model accuracy or roll-on-the-floor fun, but on speedway performance. To be fully appreciated, Hot Wheels cars needed tracks. Why? Because the low-friction wheels made the cars run so fast they could do stunts, including leaping from one ramp to the next, or doing loop-the-loops on special sections of track.

Although they arrived relatively late in the Boomer period, Hot Wheels had enormous influence, changing the toy scene much the way Barbie had a decade before. The new dominance of the performance car, as opposed to the model car, was made startlingly clear by the waves of imitations that attempted to compete with the head of the pack. Topper introduced its sleek Johnny Lightning cars, which some said were faster than the original Hot Wheels. Although well liked by children, the line had a short life due to the bankruptcy of the company for reasons unrelated to the toy car.

The Louis Marx Co., ever eager to follow any toy trail scent, came out with its relatively tame

Custom cool. *Hot Wheels capitalized on the "custom" craze sweeping an already car-obsessed nation, and issued hot rod versions of popular cars. Custom Volkswagen, Mattel, 1968.*

and clunky Mini-Marx Blazers. Being low-budget imitations of Hot Wheels, these toys made little inroads into the toy market and ended up having only a few models in its line.

Even Matchbox faced the music. By 1971 most of the Matchbox line had Superfast wheels, which were not quite the fast-spinning Mattel wheels but still satisfying to kids.

I remember having a collection of "regular wheel" Matchbox cars, as they are now called, then becoming the proud owner of one of the new Superfast cars. To me, it was better than the Hot Wheels: it still looked like a real car and had doors that opened and a detailed interior. It fascinated me.

Yet so did Hot Wheels. I ended up with only one, a Volkswagen bug. I had one Johnny Lightning, the Custom Turbine, with its bubble top that hearkened back to old science fiction pulp covers of spaceships and space cars, or even to Ed Roth's Beatnik Bandit issued by Hot Wheels in 1968.

Instead of a Hot Wheels set with tracks, I received a then lower-end Marx set. It suited me fine, after the initial qualms I must have felt at not having gotten the TV-endorsed brand name. The set included a couple primitive-looking die-cast cars, a Chaparral racer and a Jeep, and a track with a device for making a loop.

That loop made the toy. We tried the Matchbox (not bad) and Marx cars (pretty good) and Hot Wheels Volkswagen (it tended to get halfway and not make it all around the loop) and Custom Turbine (oooh). Then we tried marbles and had loads of fun shooting marbles down the track and through the loop-the-loop. Marbles outraced Hot Wheels or Johnny Lightnings any day. Then, of course, we had to try the huge steel ball-bearing from the Hit the Spot game, and made the whole thing collapse.

Best evidence of the fact that Hot Wheels redefined toy cars at the end of the '60s came from Barclay, a toy-making outfit operating since the mid-1920s that produced what is known as "slush-

Hot on Mattel's wheels. *Companies including Topper and Marx jumped on the idea of the high-performance toy die-cast car after Mattel's massive success with Hot Wheels. Chaparral, Marx, late 1960s.*

mold" or "white-metal" cars. The operative word is this: cheap. Cheap, but not unappealing, as toys. Many kids appreciated them, just as many collectors highly appreciate them now. They had a simplicity and no-frill approach that left lots of room for the imagination.

The marketing department at Barclay must have had lots of imagination too, since they started a small set of Barclay racers with normal axles and plastic wheels and a length of track. This was meant to draw the low-penny crowd who couldn't afford the high-penny, fast-wheeled competition. It might have drawn them - but how long would it have held them? Barclay cars could barely roll when pushed along by hand, let alone on gravity power down a track.

Barclay swiftly passed away. Mattel's Hot Wheels thrived and became such a fixture that many Boomers find it hard to realize that it was, among toys, one of the latecomers, touching only the tail end of the generation.

10

SLINKY

Early boxes for Slinky, made by James Industries, Inc. of Philadelphia, spelled out the facts of the new toy. "Place Slinky on the top step of your stairs, then lift one end and let go, so that the end falls on the middle of the next lower step. Slinky will then walk down the stairs step by step, or down an inclined surface. ... See how Slinky moves as if he were alive."

This soon became common knowledge.

Richard James, inventor of the walking spring, had trouble convincing people his toy would sell. When they looked at it, they saw no more than an unpainted pile of coiled metal wire. Why would people buy it? After considerable effort, James convinced Gimbels Department Store of Philadelphia to let him introduce Slinky to the public. It was nearing the end of 1946. James had already arranged with a local machine shop to manufacture 400 of the metal coils. They measured 2-1/2″ tall and each included 98 coils of a high-grade, blue-black Swedish steel.

In addition to the toys, James took with him a small set of stairs for the demonstration. His wife Betty and a friend came along, each bringing a dollar so he would have at least two sales.

Customers shopping at Gimbels that day saw something much different than the skeptical store management had seen earlier. On one level, true enough, they did see that it was no more than a bare metal spring. Yet the spring was more than a spring. It conjured up for them all the amusing animated films they had seen where cars broke down and the inner springs spewed forth, bouncing across the landscape with lives of their own - or the accordions that flipped, end over the other, wheezing discordantly.

Springs already had a comic history. When folks saw a live-action comical spring in person at one of their favorite downtown stores, they reacted accordingly. This Slinky acted strangely lifelike. It walked down stairs. It could be shuffled back and forth between your hands like a supernaturally controlled pile of cards. It made such a pleasing sound, too. How could anyone see it as no more than bare metal wire?

The 400 sold within hours.

The year before, Richard James had become intimate with metal springs of every variety. An engineer, he had been struggling with the challenge of isolating a sensitive marine torsion meter

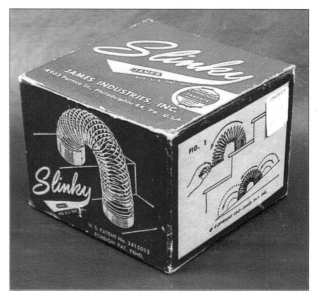

The Gimbels Slinky. *The 1947 box for the James Slinky, in brown and white, is almost as simple as the toy within. The price on the side, from Gimbels: $1.*

from outside motions caused by heavy weather around the boat or the firing of a shipboard gun. He experimented with spring after spring. At one point when he had springs piled on a table, he happened to knock one over and watched in surprise

Rover or roller? *The Slinky Dog was one of the most charming of Boomer toys, and, with its wagging, springy tail, probably the friendliest. Pairs of wheels attached to the feet allowed the dog to roll forward. The short Slinky between the front and back halves helped the latter catch up with the former. James Industries, 1950s-60s.*

The '60s Slinky. While the earliest Slinkys were coppery in color, the dull silver look became the one most Boomers knew. James Industries, 1960s.

Soldiers, Seal, and Handcar. *James Industries knew it would take more than just Slinky itself to compete in the 1950s. Offerings included a Slinky Train, Slinky Worm, and Slinky Eyes.* Life *magazine, Nov. 11, 1957.*

as it acted in a manner unlike any he had seen before. He soon discovered it could "walk" down piles of books. The spring's action was no mere fluke, for it performed the same trick over and over again.

Amused, he took it home to his children, who promptly shared it with their friends and made it a neighborhood phenomenon. Its immediate popularity started him down the road to Gimbels.

Near Philadelphia, in Holidaysburg, the new James Industries built a half-dozen machines that could make a Slinky out of 80 feet of wire in less than 12 seconds. The machines would last through

hundreds of millions of Slinkys, and would serve the company through its entire life as a family-owned venture.

Although the original dark steel was replaced with a more silvery steel, the toy likewise remained much the same through the Boomer years. Only the addition of crimped ends made the toy different for the last Boomers. Even the price remained roughly the same. It started at $1 in Philadelphia and never went too much higher.

What was true for the toy was not true for the family, where things changed drastically. Betty James, who named her inventor husband's toy, took over control of the company in 1960 after Richard apparently fled the toy-making life, abandoning wife, six children, and Slinky to pursue their own fortunes.

Slinking along. *The Slinky connections between body parts gave charming realism to this multi-wheeled larva. James Industries, 1950s-60s.*

CHAPTER 2

...And the Triumph of Television

"A recent survey shows that, today, more people watch shows on television than on any other appliance. Toasters are second." - Pat Paulsen on The Smothers Brothers

By the mid-1960s, when over 50 million households in the country had TVs, the connection between television advertising and toy success had become a matter of common-sense. Rather than boast of the play potential of their toys and games, toy manufacturers convinced retailers to carry their toys by proudly proclaiming how much they were spending on TV ads.

The example of De Luxe Reading's Topper Toys in 1964 is typical. In support of its Johnny Seven military toys and Penny Brite doll line, Topper had a vigorous program for Saturday mornings, with 48 minutes of fall commercials for the *Alvin Show* at 9:00 a.m., 99 minutes for *Tennessee Tuxedo* at 9:30 a.m., 57 minutes for *Quick Draw McGraw* at 10:00 a.m., 30 minutes for *The Jetsons* at 10:30 a.m., 46 minutes for *Roy Rogers* at 11:30 a.m., over an hour for *Bugs Bunny* at noon, and 30 minutes for *The Magic Land of Allakazam* at 1:00 p.m.

Even the Louis Marx Co., which initially viewed television advertising with wise-owl disdain, claimed that same year that "Marx starts with the premise that the Toy Business begins with 'toys' (not TV promises)," but then trumpeted, "We're starting off with the greatest line of TV merchandise in toy history ... All supported by the most powerful wave of network and local spot TV ever rolled out by Marx - the toy maker who 'pays off' on TV promises!"

Did a toy work in a TV spot? The question was suddenly more pressing than whether it worked on the playroom floor.

Fortunately, some toys ended up being pretty good, despite the hoopla.

#11 TV's HOWDY DOODY
and the Home Puppet Theater

AND CLARABE

TV's Happiest Face. *Howdy Doody introduced many children to puppet theater, with which they could then experiment themselves with the aid of such toys as this hand puppet from the 1950s. While Howdy Doody marionettes were widely available, most kids in the '50s played with less expensive toys or simply collected books, comics, or premiums off bread packages. Howdy Doody hand puppet, marked "Bob Smith," 1950s.*

Howdy Doody, famous marionette star of his own TV show, was born on radio, on WEAF's *Triple B Ranch* out of Buffalo, New York. The show featured Big Brother Bob Smith, who created at least a few parts of Howdy on air. The first part was the voice. Since it seemed to fill a void in Smith's children's show, the popular broadcaster created a dunce-hatted hick with a "hyuck-hyuck" laugh, forever fond of saying "Howdy Doody!"

While this character was at first named Elmer, that name proved slippery. Kids, after all, had already started asking who this "Howdy Doody" was. Entertainment figures change their natures at will. Even imaginary entertainers.

The name change presaged other changes. The radio star turned into a TV star in 1948, becoming a marionette with an ungainly, doltish appear-

ance. Then the sudden need for a wholly new marionette, brought about by a disagreement of the sort that arises in show biz (let me just say it involved questions of money and who owned what), forced the situation. Howdy Doody had to change again. This time he became the affable, freckle-faced figure that came to be known to millions as Howdy Doody.

Puppet maker Velma Dawson, who had worked for Walt Disney, created the new marionette

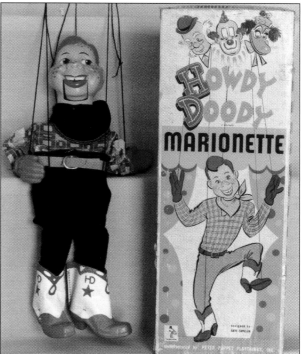

It's Howdy Doody time! Howdy Doody on-air promotions encouraged enthusiastic buying of everything from loaves of bread and breakfast cereal to items of apparel. Sales counter display, Howdy Doody Wrist Watch, Ingraham, 1954. Photo courtesy Krause Publications.

Strung along. Television may have been perfectly suited for puppet and marionette shows, since the square screen mimicked the small stages used by traditional puppeteers. Marionettes naturally became desirable playthings in the early TV years, with the Doodyville cast taking a preeminent place. Howdy Doody marionette, Peter Puppet Playthings, 1950s. Photo courtesy Krause Publications.

Toy TV. Toy makers evoked the new center of the Boomer child's universe wherever possible. Toy "TV" sets were frequently no more than cardboard or plastic boxes with a "screen" through which simple film strips could be rolled. Dime store toy manufacturer Lido produced a great many such viewers. Others included American Plastic, who made this Howdy Doody and Friends Color Television Set, with five film strips. Kagran/American Plastic, 1950s. Photo courtesy Krause Publications.

based on drawings submitted to Smith by Disney artists. The new Howdy was a ten-year-old boy dressed in cowboy hat, boots, flannel shirt, blue jeans, and a Western neckerchief. Bob Smith changed Howdy's voice slightly to match the new look - less doltish - while talented puppeteer Rhoda Mann brought the figure to life.

Many elements besides Howdy himself contributed to the success of *The Howdy Doody Show.* Tantrum-throwing Clarabell the Clown, played by Bob Keeshan, certainly helped. Fellow puppet characters including Flubadub and Phineas T. Bluster added more than just wooden dimensions. Human characters helped too, including Bill Lecornec's Chief Thunderthud, who gave the Boomers, not to mention a later generation, the nonsense cry, "Kowabonga!" When Judy Tyler took over the role of Princess Summerfall Wintersummer from a puppet predecessor, she added an energy of an entirely different kind. Now even fathers watched.

The main responsibility for the show's success,

Dream destination. *Most children in the early TV years could only dream of visiting the set of the Howdy Doody show, where a few extremely lucky souls could sit in the Peanut Gallery during filming. The Howdy Doody TV Game capitalized on this dream. "A Visit to Howdy's Own T.V. Studio," it promised buyers. Milton Bradley, 1950s. Photo courtesy Krause Publications.*

however, rested with Bob Smith, a musician with not only a talent for voices but for selling, too. He could sell kids on the existence of a marionette named Howdy. He could sell them on a whole cast of Doodyville regulars, half wooden, half flesh. He could sell them on anything, in fact, as he learned when the hodgepodge, dragon-like creation named Flubadub made its first appearance and declared its diet to be flowers. It ate nothing else. Upset mothers quickly wrote in: now their kids ate flowers. Immediately thereafter, Flubadub ate spaghetti and meatballs.

Endorsements from Howdy Doody and Buffalo Bob, as Smith came to be known, could sell anything from toothpaste to shoes to bread. They also sold toys, marionettes, a popular series of Little Golden Books, and comic books. Doodyville was a productive little town.

The show enjoyed enormous success across the country in the early to mid-1950s, then suffered a slow slide from its place at the top of the television pile. Something of the spirit of the show lived on, however, since Howdy Doody puppets, marionettes, and painting sets kept appearing through the next decade. They even enjoyed a resurgence of popularity in the early 1970s, just in time to catch the last of the Boomers.

Zippy, by Rushton. *The most enduring toy to emerge from Doodyville was based on neither puppet nor human actor, but upon Zippy the Chimp. Zip, a trained chimp originally used in a "blue" act in Louisiana, tended to cause chaos on the Howdy Doody set, thereby becoming greatly beloved by children. Zip toys were popular from the 1950s well into the 1970s. Rushton specialized in stuffed, plush toys with soft vinyl faces.*

Mr. Bluster and the Princess. *Miniature marionettes in hard plastic, these toys had one moving part each: the lower jaw, which could be moved by a lever behind the head. The Princess appears here in the puppet form she had before she transformed into a living, breathing person. Tee Vee Toys, Inc., early to mid-1950s.*

ROBERT the ROBOT #12

Something surprisingly different appeared on department store shelves and in store catalog pages in time for Christmas 1954.

His name was Robert.

Robert was 14″ of gray plastic, with two arms that moved back and forth, flashing eyes, and a flashing light at the top of his head. The head was a cube set on squared shoulders, while the body was shaped like an angular bell. Wheels hidden beneath the "skirt" of Robert's body allowed the figure to move when the controls, which looked like a space gun, were used.

He was, of course, a robot. Robert knew this about himself, for when the crank turned on his back, his high-pitched voice would say, "I am Robert the Robot, the mechanical man."

Robot toys had been circulating since the late '40s, with the first ones arriving in this country

***Mechanical man of tomorrow.** "This mechanical man of tomorrow moves forward, reverse, left or right, swinging his arms, carrying objects in his hands - all by battery-operated remote control," enthuses one toy catalog over the first toy robot to reach widespread acceptance through department and catalog stores. Ideal, Robert the Robot, 1955 version.*

from overseas, especially Japan. Japan was rebuilding its economy in part through the production of inexpensive but attractive tin toys of every variety, much of which sold through American dime stores.

Robert the Robot, however, was made by Ideal, a long-established toy and novelty company with a well-deserved reputation for its dolls. Being made by a major American toy manufacturer meant that Robert benefited from merchandising and sales efforts that foreign-made robot toys never received.

Robert was also made of hard plastic, not metal, even though the surface of his body had bumps, square edges, and seams as though actually made of riveted metal. In the eyes of many, metal, especially tin, was the "old" toy-making material. Plastic was the new one. Not for nothing did Dillon Beck Manufacturing Co. choose plastic for its popular futuristic Coupe in the late '40s, or Mattel for its Modern Dream Car in 1953, or Ideal itself for its own line of smaller futuristic vehicles.

Plastic was the future.

Roving robot. *Early metal robots had simple faces, features, and functions - and often no fixed identity. This Japanese-made robot was known as Flashy Jim in its battery-operated form. As a wind-up, it appeared under such names as Robbie the Roving Robot and Sparking Mike the Robot. The name of this particular version is unknown. Roughly 7″ tall, Sankei, 1950s.*

Danger, Danger, Will Robinson!

One of the most memorable TV stars of the 1960s was the *Lost in Space* Robot. Even though Gene Roddenberry's 1966 to 1969 science-fiction TV series *Star Trek*, with its cast of Kirk, Spock, Bones, Scotty, Sulu, Chekov, and Uhura, was to prove far more enduring in its appeal, *Lost in Space* had two things *Star Trek* never had: an on-ship villain named Dr. Smith, played by Jonathan Harris, and his mechanical accomplice, played by Bob May within the ultimate science-fiction accessory any Boomer kid would have swooned to step into: a full-body robot suit. The robot had no other name than what it was - Robot.

Even if many of the story lines left much to be desired, the cast kept audiences interested for most of the show's 1965 to 1968 run. Billy Mumy played the adventurous and appealing Will Robinson, Guy Williams, already popular for his role as Walt Disney's TV series *Zorro*, played Professor John Robinson, and June Lockhart, who played Timmy's mother on *Lassie*, was Maureen Robinson. The family and crew also included Marta Kristen as Judy, Angela Cartwright as Penny, and Mark Goddard as Major Don West.

Appearing a little more than ten years after Ideal's Robert the Robot, Remco's plastic *Lost in Space* Robot was the most popular robot toy of its time. It appeared in 1966 in blue-and-red and black-and-red versions.

Photo courtesy Robert G. Johnson, Comet Toys.

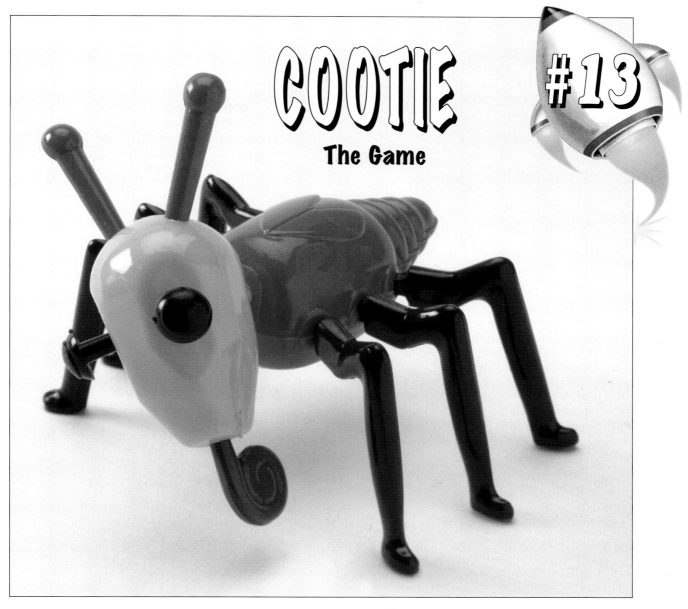

COOTIE
The Game

#13

Many who rattle off a personal Top Ten Toys list start with games. For perfectly good reasons, too. Especially in the TV age, kids tended to spend more time fussing over how they wanted a toy, how they "needed" it, how they "had" to have it because, look, it's so much fun there in the TV ad on my favorite show that I really really "got" to have it please, please, please Mom.

Then they had it in their hands, found it not much fun, and went back to another game of Monopoly.

Children may have loved their non-game toys more than their game toys and may have invested more imagination time in them. Even so, they usually spent more hours of play time at games, with friends or family, and sometimes even alone.

Cootie has become an icon representing a generation. It appeared at the same time as the

Boomers, having its first commercial appearance in 1949, and lasted through the Boomer years in essentially unchanged form.

As a game, Cootie was simplicity itself: you tossed the die, hoping to be the first to piece together your Cootie bug. The bug itself was a thing of beauty to many kids. Probably to many adults too. Made of shiny hard plastic, it consisted of a beehive-like body, six bent legs, antennae, eyes, and, best of all, a coiled proboscis.

Herb Schaper, Cootie's inventor, ran a shop selling wood toys he carved himself. He also fished, as to be expected of an Upper Midwesterner. One day in 1948 he realized that a fishing lure he was carving had turned into an attractive bug. Within a year his Minnesota company, named after him, became a contender in the national toy stakes.

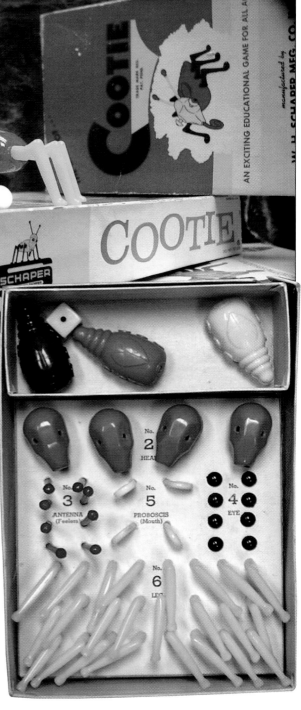

The best of all possible bugs. *The early box, with its remarkably homely example of 1940s-50s graphics, was used for more years than it probably should have been. The Cootie itself remained much the same for most of the Boomer years: buggy, in the extreme. In the late '60s, Sears offered an exclusive Cootie House, featuring a vinyl mat and enough parts for eight Cooties. Schaper, 1950s.*

I have friends who contend that Cootie was one of those games you never played. You simply put together the pieces and played with the toy. Yet I find foggy memories emerging of worrying over the results of the die. I have no memories of triumphantly completing my Cootie bug first. I remember that dire frustration of watching brother, sister, or parent finishing theirs first.

And *I* was the one into bugs.

The Cootie assembly plant. *Interior of a box, with the Cootie parts in their early arrangement. Schaper, 1950s.*

Oddball game empire. *Schaper's many game creations through the Boomer years included Ants in the Pants, Don't Spill the Beans, Don't Break the Ice, and the popular Ticklebee. Skunk, Schaper, 1950s-60s.*

DAVY CROCKETT'S COONSKIN CAP

Coonskin icon. *This vinyl figure, with flintlock rifle, fringed buckskin clothing, and coonskin cap, was issued as a generic pioneer figure but was instantly a Davy Crockett figure for millions of children. Auburn Rubber, 1950s.*

Walt Disney's new weekly television series *Disneyland* was barely underway when it started the nation singing about a frontier hero.

The original format of *Disneyland*, which started in October 1954, called for a rotation of programs under the banners of Frontierland, Fantasyland, Tomorrowland, and Adventureland. On Dec. 15, in the Frontierland slot, Disney aired *Davy Crockett, Indian Fighter*, in which the resourceful scout tracks down and confronts Chief Red Stick. It featured a low-key young actor, Fess Parker, whose prior claim to fame was a bit part in the science fiction feature Them.

Disneyland was already ABC's first hit program. Even against that background, *Davy Crockett, Indian Fighter* was one of the biggest overnight successes in TV history, giving rise to an instant coonskin craze and a chart-hogging hit single, "The Ballad of Davy Crockett."

The sudden success of the show caught Disney by surprise. By the time the first show aired, the studio was busily killing off the frontier hero in the last

Pioneer glory. *The author in 1964. Photo and costume (and kid) by Kikue Rich.*

of the three segments it was filming. In the second segment, *Davy Crockett Goes to Congress*, which first aired on January 26 the next year, the hero successfully runs for office only to be hoodwinked by his former General, President Andrew Jackson. In the last segment, *Davy Crockett at the Alamo*, first aired on Feb. 23, Crockett leads a heroic and hopeless defense of an old fort against the Mexicans and is last seen swinging his rifle as a club.

Even having killed off their hero, Disney was not without resources. Disney cannily had been producing his black-and-white ABC programs in color, which allowed the studio to patch together a feature film for summer release. The notion of live-action features from Walt Disney was not entirely new. In July 1950, Disney released its first entirely live-action feature film, *Treasure Island*, followed by the popular *The Story of Robin Hood* in 1952. The release in 1955 of *Davy Crockett, King of the Wild Frontier*, far from being taken as a rehash of TV material, was greeted with all the enthusiasm of an entirely new production.

The enthusiastic endorsement of *Boy's Life* magazine that summer was typical: "Fess Parker, who plays Davy, is six feet, five inches tall, and a good likeness of the historical hero. 'Fess' is his real name; it means 'proud' in old English, and Parker's proud of it. The movie shows the legendary Crockett as hunter, fighter, frontier statesman, and hero of the Alamo. Best of this month's motion picture releases," the magazine told its more than one million readers.

While some portion of the American populace wanted nothing more than to wear Mouse ears later in 1955 due to Disney's next TV hit, *The Mickey Mouse Club*, a far greater percentage yearned toward wearing coonskin.

A list of available gifts available through Montgomery Ward's that Christmas gives a good indication of the scope of the fad. They included a Davy Crockett Outfit, Girl's Outfit, Hunting Jacket, Canteen Outfit, Holster and Knife Set, sparks-shooting "Old Betsy" Shootin' Iron, Pistol, Camera Outfit, Scouting Set, Flashlight, Play Tents in two sizes, Lamp with plastic figure of a horse-riding Davy, Dish Set, a Guitar as well as a "Ge-Tar" with a crank handle that played the hit song, Dancing Doll ("Tall as a child, ideal dancing partner when elastic on his feet and hands are slipped over child's shoes and hands"), album of three Tru-Vue Davy Crockett Film Card Stories, Walt Disney's Davy Crockett on Record, Phonograph with recording of "The Ballad of Davy Crockett," School Bag, Lunch Kit, Binocular Set, Wallet, Barlow Knife with genuine rabbit's foot key ring charm attached, and Watch.

Which was not all. Ward's also offered a twill shirt-and-pants set, pajamas, three-piece shirt set, knit shirt, girl's jackets, suede vest, beanie, girl's challis square ("The girls want their hero with them wherever they go!"), Miss Davy's Blouse and Skirt, mittens, steer hide gauntlet gloves, combed cotton blazer, stretch nylon blazer, dude tie, steer hide belt, plastic wallet, moccasins, slippers, slipper socks, towel set, quilt, and a pinpoint-chenille, buckskin-tan spread, available for four bed sizes. It

Gumball charms. *Plastic charms became commonplace in the Boomer years. These two celebrated one of America's biggest pop heroes. Davy Crockett charms, 1950s-60s.*

also offered Walt Disney's Official Davy Crockett at the Alamo Model Set by Marx, with a small figure of Crockett modeled on Fess Parker.

Strangest of all was the Davy Crockett Bear's Head Trophy, a shield-shaped birch plaque bearing the head of the animal Davy shot when he was only three. "Realistic enough for recreation rooms," Ward's promised.

And, best of all, coonskin caps.

Why the proliferation? Despite the phenomenal drawing power of Fess Parker's character and the Walt Disney name, almost every toy, clothing, and novelty company in the business capitalized on the fact that Davy Crockett's name and story were historic in nature.

Only Walt Disney could issue licenses for "Walt Disney's Official Davy Crockett" items, but anyone could issue a plain old Davy Crockett item. So everyone did, with the result that the quickly created market was equally quickly flooded.

Davy Crockett as a pop-culture figure was kept alive by Walt Disney during subsequent years. It received a further boost in 1964 when NBC launched the long-lived *Daniel Boone*, also starring Fess Parker. While the TV show focused on another character altogether, the closeness of the two figures' outfits and outlooks, not to mention the identical nature of their screen appearance, made the two melt into one in the minds of children growing up in the 1960s. *Boy's Life* even devoted a cover to Boone when Davy Crockett came out, which may mean kids were confused from the start.

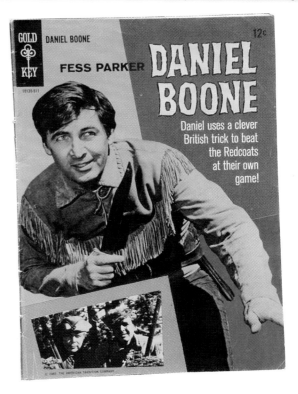

Still wearing coonskin. *The* Daniel Boone *TV show inadvertently helped keep the memory of Davy Crockett alive. Daniel Boone, No. 3, K.K. Publications, 1965.*

I remember having discussions with friends about who we liked better: Davy Crockett or Daniel Boone. The former usually won, probably because of the song.

Not that it mattered. All that mattered was having that coonskin cap.

Riding the crest of the West. *The prewar fascination with the Old West continued through much of the Boomer period, with Crockett mania bringing it to a high spike of popularity. Western toys gave many children their first hands-on experience with altering their own identities through accessories. Western costumes, Ward's Christmas Book, 1947.*

Before the war it would have been unimaginable that the Louis Marx Co. not have its toys ranked among the Top Ten of the time.

After the war, while not quite resting on its laurels, Marx took the stance of the time-tested and firm-footed Old Man of the industry. The toy-making giant went about its business of making toys, eschewing the new ways of massive promotional budgets and kids-oriented television advertising. It had risen to the top of the pile on the strength of its excellent toy making and it thought it would stay there.

To a degree, Marx was right. It could succeed without advertising - partly because of the excellence of the play sets it issued in the Boomer years, many of which were offered through catalog stores that gave them all the advertising necessary.

Among its play sets, the Farm Set proved a reliable seller for the company as well as a solid source of entertainment for children through the 1950s, '60s, and early '70s. Sears and other catalog outfits regularly gave full pages to showing off these tiny farms.

For good reason. These were among the most attractive toys of the time, incorporating enough different elements to keep almost any child happy, with enough detail to kick off hours of serious daydreaming.

The barns usually had two stories, with the roof cut away to allow play on that second level. The tin walls were lithographed inside and out. Sometimes even the undersides of floors were lithographed, as was the case with the later raised-foundation barns. These, the largest of Marx's barns, first appeared at the tail end of the 1950s and were offered as part of the Giant Happi-Time Farm Set, among others, through the '60s. The "stone" lower level gave room to house the dairy herd, while the uppermost hayloft could be filled by means of the block-and-tackle extended from one end of the roof. The silos and chicken coops were also tin.

The true fun came from the multitude of little parts, some of hard plastic, some of soft. The minuscule implements included shovels, hay forks, saws, lanterns, and fire extinguishers. Buckets, milk cans, milking stools, feed sacks, troughs, and fences added to the sense of realism. Various vehicles came with the sets - sometimes trucks and cars, sometimes grain elevators, but always the farm tractor, with a selection of heavy equipment to haul behind. Farm hands were seen tossing hay, carrying feed sacks, or hoeing the garden. One molded-in farmer sat on the tractor, while others could be placed on the trailers to ride along.

Most important of all, the sets had marvelously modeled, solid-plastic farm animals. There were roosters, chickens, and chicks. Pigs and piglets. Goats, sheep, and a Lassie-type dog. Then there were the cattle, calves, horses, and colts. For those lucky miniature farmers who had parents willing to shell out the extra $.98, there was the Prize Livestock assortment. The prized set included ten solid plastic, carefully detailed animals based on favored farming breeds, measuring from 1-3/4″ to 3″ high.

The country charm of the farm. *No doubt far more Boomer kids visited the tiny world of Marx farm play sets than ever set foot in real, working farms. The play sets included plastic farm hands, tractors, feed sacks, milk cans, tools, and animals of every domestic variety. Louis Marx Co., 1960s.*

A hay wagon pulled by horses, a combine, a milk truck, a crop-duster airplane, even a working irrigation system ...

At least one set played with by late Boomers, issued in 1973, had not only irrigation but dried pellets that burst into green and growing crops with watering.

Different sets through the years offered different accessories. All, however, offered a breath of the calm, quiet countryside that seemed increasingly distant as Boomer toys moved deeper into the Space Age.

Top breeds only need apply. *Marx issued a special set of Prized Livestock as farm play set accessories. Solid plastic and carefully detailed, they rank among the best plastic figures of the 1960s. Clydesdale, 3-1/2″ long, Louis Marx Co., 1960s.*

THINGMAKERS

Toy makers have probably always realized who their biggest competitors are: kids themselves. Kids, after all, take pride and pleasure in making their own toys from whatever materials are at hand. Some clever company realized, probably as early as the 1920s or '30s, a way to capitalize on even this tendency. They marketed the tools for toy making. Soon, kids were buying molds for pouring their own lead soldiers. On kitchen ranges they melted small ingots of lead, or "slush" metal, for their miniature armies. When they ran out of those, they melted whatever they could get their mitts on: toothpaste tubes, Brill Cream tubes, maybe even dispatched soldiers from the enemy army.

In 1964, however, Mattel put a twist into the old home-casting idea, introducing a low-temperature hot plate that heated the molds themselves instead of the raw material, and a plastic that hardened, instead of softening, with heating. The plastic was called Plastigoop. The kits were called Thingmakers.

Or maybe the children were the Thingmakers. With their hot plates, molds, and goop, they found themselves fantastically empowered. With some kits they could make superhero figures. They could

make toy soldiers with two-piece molds. They could make flowers with Fun Flowers. They could make Picadoos, which were odds and ends designed for use in arts and crafts projects. The Mini-Dragons kit promised "a whole silly world of crazy mixed-up wigglin' jigglin' creatures."

Or kids could stick to basics and make the original and most popular Things of all: the Creepy Crawlers, which were everything from snakes, lizards, and frogs to centipedes, spiders, cockroaches, and trilobites.

The Creeple Peeple of 1965 proved especially delightful to kids. The Creeple People molds made various parts - heads, arms, feet - that transformed the contents of the school desk pencil box full of Eberhard Faber #2s into a mysterious population of oddities. As a nod to the troll fad sweeping the country, garish plumes of hair topped the Creeples. Since the feet were the part stuck onto the sharpened tip of the pencil, they were the part always lost. They simply fell off. The loss was not a great one, however. If you yourself had no kit for making new feet, by the end of the school day (you always took your Creeple Person to school) you could

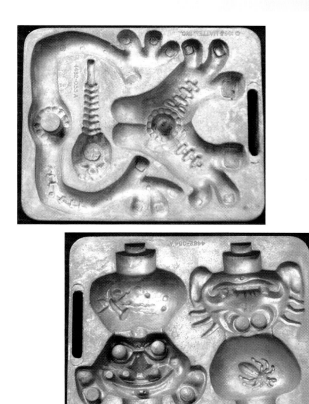

Grotesqueries. *Mattel marketed the Creeple Peeple Thingmaker as an accessory toy: "Make lovable Creeple Peeple! Creeple Peeple pencils you make and take everywhere! Wear 'em! Clip 'em on pockets, notebooks! Write & erase with 'em! Stand them up! Give 'em! Wear 'em! Trade 'em!" Creeple Peeple molds and figure, Mattel, mid-1960s.*

walk home, eyes to the sidewalk, and find the feet someone else had dropped. Almost everyone came into a pair of Creeple feet this way.

Children could even make toys they could eat, which was a definite step up from eating crayons or white paste.

My particular Thingmaker was a Creepy Crawler set intended for children already equipped with the basic hot plate. My mother let me use the electric range on the kitchen stove. I put the trays in an aluminum pie pan, then tried to bake that yellow or green Plastigoop in the molds. I heavily favored the trilobite mold, since it provided accessories to go with my MPC dinosaurs, even though I knew with boyish erudition that the trilobites and dinosaurs never coexisted. But then, too, I knew most of the dinosaurs never coexisted, either. Except in Toy Time.

Invariably I undercooked my goop, and produced a good many toys with soft, sticky centers, which fortunately (or unfortunately, for the surfaces involved) were on the undersides of the toys.

Undercooked toys ... another '60s innovation from Mattel.

Mattel led the pack with its Thingmakers, yet was not quite alone at the top. Topper Toys was

breathing down its neck with a popular kit using "Super Plastic." Rings'n Things, introduced in 1968, enjoyed considerable vogue among the young earring-and-necklace set, who were delighted to be making all the gaudy personal accouterments they always knew they deserved.

Other toy-making kits enjoyed considerable success as well. Mattel issued the Electric Vac-U-Form, with plastic sheets and molds that shaped those sheets into numerous toys and novelty items. Similarly, Topper issued the Johnny Toymaker as a partner to its successful Suzy Homemaker toys.

Surprisingly, the innovations of the Thingmakers line still left room for old-fashioned home casting. Kits, now marketed under such names as the Electric Metal Casting Set and sold through Sears in the mid-'60s, allowed kids to melt ingots of metal and pour them into matched molds.

Emenee released several 1965 kits using the same idea with plastic. Its Formex Casting Sets allowed kids to cast soldiers or monsters using a reusable plastic. It also made a Munsters Casting Set, using "Castex 5" for one-time use in producing Herman and his family.

Kenner came up with the most up-to-date version of home casting, however, with its Electric

Mold Master. The kit made soldiers, tanks, jeeps, cannons, and even a pistol that could shoot bullets. The kit put plastic injection molding into the hands of children with a machine called the Mold Master. At low heat it melted the plastic compounds, which came in four colors. A plunger then forced the material into the molds, making a variety of three-dimensional toys.

They were good toys. They just weren't crazy and weird. Mattel almost took out a patent on crazy and weird with its Thingmakers.

I remember no one in my various classes in elementary school voicing the desire to grow up to be a toy maker. They all already knew better. They knew you didn't have to grow up to be one.

COOK UP SOME FUN! FRIGHTFULLY DELICIOUS! SUGARLESS!

Make 'em Fast & Easy with Gobble-Degoop! *The trend started by Mr. Potato Head of making toys of food found its ultimate expression in Incredible Edibles from Mattel. "Cook up some fun," the box instructed kids. Parents took heart from the sugarless nature of the Gobble-Degoop, and from the Good Housekeeping Seal of Approval. The set featured the Sooper-Gooper, a covered hot plate in the shape of a buck-toothed, orange-wigged head, with round aluminum molds featuring two or three shapes each. They made Bug Bites, Luscious Lizards, Fancy Flowers, Fabulous Frogs, Gourmet Goldfish, Funny Fruit, Sweet Snakes, and Ginger-Men, as well as butterflies, octopi, skull-and-crossbones, cats, and a haunted mansion. The flavors? Cinnamon, licorice, cherry, raspberry, root beer, butterscotch, mint, and tutti fruit. Replacement Gobble-Degoop packets cost $1.25 per pair of flavors. Mattel, 1966.*

TV's MICKEY MOUSE CLUB EARS #17

The four-fingered hand. Mickey Mouse hand puppet, 1960s.

The Walt Disney film crews must have welcomed the end of the war. Finally they could stop producing such wonderful titles as *Weather at War* for the U.S. Navy, or *Ward Care of Psychotic Patients* and *Operation and Maintenance of the Electronic Turbo Supercharger* for the U.S. Army.

To be sure, Disney had kept up production of animated shorts through the war, and immediately afterwards released major films including *Bambi* in 1946, *Cinderella* and Disney's first live-action feature *Treasure Island* in 1950, *Alice in Wonderland* in 1951, the live-action *The Story of Robin Hood* in 1952, and *Peter Pan* in 1953.

Disney also moved into the new medium of TV. In December 1950, the Coca-Cola Co. sponsored *One Hour in Wonderland* on NBC. The next year, *The Walt Disney Christmas Show* aired on CBS,

sponsored by Johnson and Johnson Co. That year Walt Disney also established Disneyland, Inc., followed in 1952 by Walt Disney Inc., which was to develop ideas for a family entertainment park. Things moved quickly enough that ground was broken two years later for the Magic Kingdom of Disneyland.

Even the ground-breaking had its TV connections. The ABC TV network had invested a considerable sum, and had guaranteed an even larger loan to help build Disneyland. In return, ABC TV received a share of Disneyland and a commitment for a weekly Walt Disney TV show. The first one-hour weekly, *Disneyland*, made its debut on ABC only months after the ground-breaking, in October 1954. The show, under various names, went on to become the longest-lived prime-time series in network history.

On the verge of TV stardom. *The Disney cast of animated characters, enormously popular before the war, reached ever more audiences in the postwar years through TV. The medium introduced a new generation to prewar Disney animated films. Well into the early Boomer years, new Disney toys closely resembled their prewar predecessors. Walt Disney tray, J. Chein & Co., 1950s.*

Disneyland itself opened in July of 1955, with more than 28,000 people attending. The next month, in Fantasyland, the Mickey Mouse Club Theater opened, followed in October by Disney's second ABC TV show, *The Mickey Mouse Club.*

In addition to bringing children the cartoons of their parents' childhoods, the daily show featured such live-action serials as The Adventures of Spin and Marty and Annette, and, best of all, the talents of the Mouseketeers, a group of ebullient, always-cheerful, always-on-the-go adolescents who made all of us look bad and feel good about it.

The show, as it happened, permanently changed the world of toys. Mattel, only ten years old in 1955, made the unprecedented move of committing itself to a full year's worth of advertising on the new *Mickey Mouse Club* TV show. Never before had toys been advertised on a year-round basis.

Mattel had made its name with various noise-making and musical toys, including the Uke-A-Doodle, which was a child-size ukulele, and hand-cranked music boxes. In 1955 the company had a major hit with its Burp Gun, a kind of automatic cap gun. With its new sponsorship of the Disney daily show, it introduced a new musical toy which was in no way revolutionary in its underlying nature, but which still became a hit for the company: the Official Mousegetar, bright red and featuring Mickey's smiling face.

"Just like Jimmy Dodd's," Mattel promised the young members of America's largest kid's club. "Plays real music - Big Mouse size... Jimmy Dodd's musical instructions enable youngsters to actually learn to play!"

Learn to play what? Mickey Mouse Club songs, naturally.

The Mousegetar Jr. followed soon thereafter. Mattel and other companies released a variety of Mickey Mouse Club toys in the following years, the most notable of them film-related, including the Mickey Mouse Club Projector and Theater with 12 films, and the Mickey Mouse Club Newsreel, which added sound.

Other toys in the last few years of the 1950s included Mouseketeer hand puppets, Jacmar's Mickey Mouse Club Magic Arithmetic Series, which were electronic quiz games, and the Hasbro

Never say "Grow Up." *Many toys played off the popularity of postwar Disney movies, including the Walt Disney's Peter Pan game. Transogram, 1952.*

Pencil Craft Set, a colored pencil set with six cards with "pre-sketched pictures of Mickey Mouse Club Walt Disney characters."

After the cancellation of the show in 1959, Disney toys were more likely to promote the Disneyland name over the Mickey Mouse Club name, or to promote the characters who were stars of the current Disney shorts - Pluto, Goofy, and especially Donald Duck.

Even so, later Boomers saw in syndication the endless reruns, so the early 1960s Boomers grew up feeling they knew, in a somehow intimate way, the Club members: Jimmy Dodd, Roy Williams, and the Mouseketeers Annette Funicello, Darlene Gillespie, Cubby O'Brien, Karen Pendleton, Bobby Burgess, Doreen Tracy, Sharon Baird, and Cheryl Holdridge.

And what of Mickey himself? Mickey Mouse had made his last new film appearance of the Boomer years in 1953 in *The Simple Things*. Reruns of older films on TV and perhaps the re-release of *Fantasia* in 1956 and 1963 made it seem the Mouse had not so thoroughly changed from Disney Studios film star to Disneyland Spokesmouse.

Yet he had. If he was a force in the lives of Boomers, it was not in the same way he was in the lives of their parents. He left the center stage for others: Donald, Alice, Robin Hood, Annette, Peter Pan, Davy Crockett, Old Yeller, Mary Poppins...

It took a great many to fill his place. But they did.

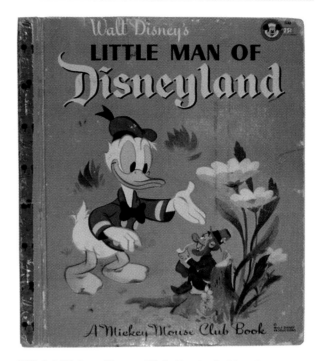

Official Mickey Mouse Club Book. *Golden Books and their imitators provided much of the earliest reading for the Boomer generation. Walt Disney's* Little Man of Disneyland *showed the Disney animated gang hard at work building the theme park. "Who are we?" cries Donald Duck, in the book, to the last Leprechaun in California, on whose land the park was rising, who did not recognize the gang. "Don't you go to the movies? Don't you watch TV?" Simon and Schuster, 1955.*

Mouseketeers. *Mickey Mouse's constant presence on TV made it seem the famous animated character had not retired from films. Mickey Mouse Club costume, nylon, 1950s.*

#18 TAMMY

The girl next door. *Tammy gave children the option of playing with a fashion doll who was first and foremost a hometown sweetheart, unlike a certain other citified, European-inspired fashion doll. Ideal, 1960s.*

It surely reflects on the American public, or at least on our Boomer generation, that the first doll to come to mind from the Boomer years is Barbie, not Tammy.

A late friend of mine, who was possessed of a homespun Kansas wisdom her entire life, had a piece of advice she dispensed to those trembling on the edge of tumbling into romance, especially romance that might have some tinge of the dubious: "Always choose wholesome," she said.

Although Barbie herself would ultimately transmute into an all-too-wholesome model of teenage perky cheer, in the '60s her leggy seductiveness and predatory glances found their antithesis in Tammy, who represented America's apple-pie Girl Next Door.

Like Barbie, Tammy was a fashion doll, but a more teenage one. Introduced by Ideal Toy Corp. in 1962, she found easy acceptance among children and parents. They liked her. How could they not?

She built an unassuming childhood empire through the mid-decade, helped in part by her parent company's willingness to grant Tammy licenses to other toy companies. Tammy dishes, housewares, paper dolls, and nurse kits appeared from various manufacturers to bolster the Tammy car, house, tea set, and outfits from Ideal - not to mention Tammy's fellow fashion dolls: Pepper, Pos'n Pete, Pos'n Salty, Dodi, Ted ...

And Mom and Dad. When Mom and Dad became fashion dolls, you knew you were in America.

Leading the cheers. *Tammy, depicted as an everyday, midde-class girl, could let loose and be herself. Barbie, in the 1960s, was still too superbly poised for such antics. Tin plate, Ideal, 1960s.*

Wholesome fun. *The cards for the board game reflected Tammy's orientation: happy at home, and happy at school. The Tammy Game, Ideal, 1963.*

#19 TONKA TRUCKS
Sandbox Workhorses

Rugged style. Dump trucks became the signature vehicle for Tonka after their introduction in 1949. Service dump truck, 13˝, Mound Metalcraft, late 1950s.

In the years immediately after the war, countless companies must have sprung into existence in various odd spaces. Pipco started in a house basement, Mattel started in a house garage, and Tonka started in the basement of a schoolhouse in a suburb of Minneapolis with the humblest of names, Mound.

Lynn Baker, Avery Crounse, and Alvin Tesch founded Mound Metalcraft Co. to make store display racks and garden furniture. They may have enjoyed some success at this, although the evidence suggests otherwise. They happened into toy making by accident, in their first year. Among the materials purchased from a competitor, the L.E. Streeter Co., they found tooling to make a toy metal steam shovel, apparently one with minimal moving parts.

The tooling planted the notion that tough, true-to-life but reasonably priced truck and construction toys might have a place in their company plans. To their surprise, the results of that notion, the Steam Shovel, modified and improved over the original, was a sudden success. So was the other toy also released in 1947, a working model of a

Crane and Clam, which measured about 3˝ longer than the 20˝ Shovel. The toys were extremely sturdy and offered a good deal of play value because they worked more or less as the real things did.

As it happened, the toys sold faster than Mound's other offerings.

Mound Metalcraft named its toys Tonkas in honor of nearby Lake Minnetonka. In the next year, 1948, it expanded its toy offerings to include a Lift Truck and Cart. In 1949, Tonkas became a full-fledged line of toys. New entries included the 22˝ Steam Shovel Deluxe, several versions of a machinery hauler with steam shovel or crane loads, the Tonka Toy Transport tractor-trailer, a Loading Tractor, a Wrecker Truck, and finally, and perhaps most importantly, a Dump Truck. Thereafter, a year of Tonkas without a Dump Truck was no year at all.

Tonka remained a relatively low-profile player in the toy world during its early years, dwarfed by the pressed-metal powerhouses of Marx, Structo, Wyandotte, and Buddy L. It even saw competition from another postwar company, Nylint, which, like Structo and Buddy L, was based in nearby Illinois.

By the 1960s, however, most major toy catalogs reflected the fact that Tonka was the company to watch. Unlike the Tonkas of the '50s, which were modeled on Ford trucks, the Tonkas of the '60s were more generic, and perhaps more broadly appealing for that fact - or perhaps because they were so recognizably Tonkas.

Several innovations early that decade had other pressed-steel companies scrambling to keep up. One, introduced in 1963, was a new line of trucks about 9″ long, made of the same durable

Bulldog toughness. *Tonka built its reputation on straightforward, well-designed, and sturdy vehicle toys, which helped it compete against such prewar giants as Buddy L and Structo. Cabover, Mound Metalcraft, 1949 to early '50s.*

materials as the larger trucks, down to the double layers of real truck paint. Tonka dubbed them Mini-Tonkas in a playful return to the original inspiration for the line's name. The fleet of trucks may have been small, but it sold well: Pickup, Stake Truck, Dump Truck, Wrecker, and Camper. The next year Tonka added a Grader, Cement Mixer, and three semi-trailers featuring a new futuristic cab, in the same scale.

In 1964 Structo followed suit, issuing its Kom-Pak trucks - seven trucks based on a generic cab much like the original Mini-Tonkas. Structo's toys might actually have had more immediate play value, since they included a Vista Dome Kennel Truck with plastic dogs, a Vista Dome Livestock Truck, and a Fire Rescue Truck with ladders.

Tonka's other challenge to the toy-making world took the form, as it happened, of a dump truck. It was the Mighty Tonka Dump Truck of 1964, with its small, square cab, huge tires, and oversize load capacity. Tonka advertised it as super-sized, therefore ride-able. It hauled, dumped, and carried kids down driveways through the rest of the Boomer years, and far beyond.

Construction leaders. *In the early Boomer years, before Tonka rose to the top of the pile, such companies as Doepke Model Toys and Structo had greater fame as manufacturers of sturdy construction toys. Doepke Heiliner, 1951 Toy Fair; Structo Dump Truck, Billy and Ruth, 1952.*

TV's BATMAN COWL

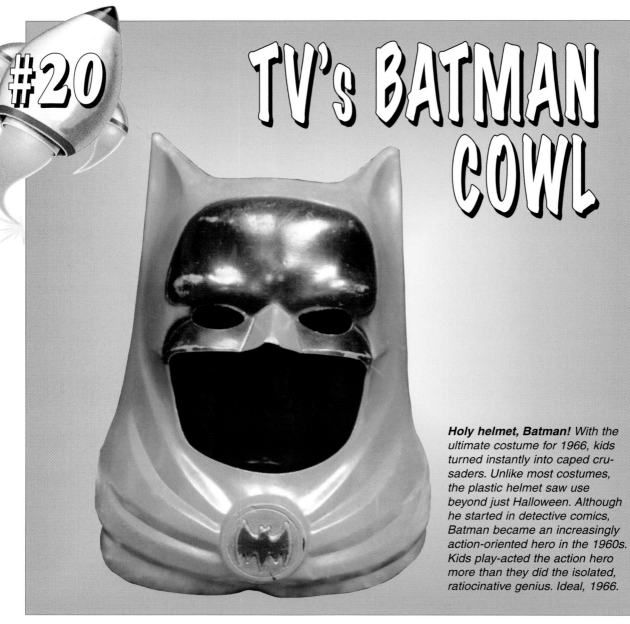

Holy helmet, Batman! *With the ultimate costume for 1966, kids turned instantly into caped crusaders. Unlike most costumes, the plastic helmet saw use beyond just Halloween. Although he started in detective comics, Batman became an increasingly action-oriented hero in the 1960s. Kids play-acted the action hero more than they did the isolated, ratiocinative genius. Ideal, 1966.*

Batman had lingered around the edges of America's popular consciousness since his introduction in *Detective Comics* a few years before the war. He started appearing in a comic book series of his own, on the Superman radio series, and even in 1940s movie serials. Then something happened to bring him front and center in 1966.

In other words: "Holy hit TV show, Batman!" Suddenly kids - probably mostly boys, although I have no hard and fast data to this effect - were whipping around in bed sheet capes and dreaming about having on their heads that Batman hood with those perky bat-ears.

From its first airing on Jan. 12, 1966, *Batman* created a sensation. It starred Adam West as Bruce Wayne, aka The Caped Crusader, and

Burt Ward as Wayne's ward Dick Grayson, aka The Wonder Boy. The two were tended by loyal family butler Alfred Pennyworth, played by Alan Napier, and Aunt Harriet Cooper, played by Madge Blake. For comic foils, Batman had Police Commissioner Gordon and Chief O'Hara, played by Neil Hamilton and Stafford Repp. In its second and last year, the Dynamic Duo were joined by a third, Batgirl, played by Yvonne Craig.

The show's success was short-lived but intense. The campy action, plots, and dialogue were neatly balanced by straight-faced portrayals by the actors. At the same time, in direct reference to Batman's comic book origins, vibrant graphics of BIFF!, BAM!, and POW! filled the full frame of the television screen, giving the show visual novelty.

The villains added another magic touch. Extravagant and well over the top, Gotham City's foes enthralled even the youngest set, who had no idea what acting talents hid behind the masks and face paint. Burgess Meredith played the deviously dapper Penguin, Cesar Romero the singularly sinister Joker, and Frank Gorshin and later John Astin, the twisted Riddler. Vincent Price was the memorably egg-xactly right Egghead, and Victor Buono the majesterial King Tut.

Best of all, the trio of Julie Newmar, Lee Ann Meriwether, and Eartha Kitt played the ultimate femme fatale for a million breathless boys, the Catwoman.

Finger-controlled crime fighter. *Hand puppet heads were easily and cheaply made with one of the favorite materials of postwar toy manufacturers, rubber-like vinyl. Ideal, 1966.*

Masked heroes. *Masked crime-fighters were popular choices for boys at Halloween throughout the Boomer period. Batman and Zorro, Sears Toys, 1967-68.*

Dropping from the Batplane. *Parachuters were popular dime store and convenience store toys in the Boomer years. In the 1960s, Army parachuters made of green plastic, equipped with thin plastic parachutes, were not only cheap but great fun, requiring only the patience to rewind the 'chute and a throwing arm to get the toy aloft again. Batman parachuter toy, 4-1/2˝, manufacturer unknown, 1960s-70s.*

CHAPTER 3

Honorary Boomer Toys

Although World War II cut the century in two, and despite all the 1930s crystal-ball gazing at the future, American culture stayed characteristically Modern afterwards. Toys after the war continued to have largely the same character as prewar toys.

Some of those prewar toys enjoyed such tremendous success after the Bomb, in fact, that most Boomers looking back on their childhoods regard these toys as belonging to them. They take a proprietary interest: these were *theirs*.

It comes as a surprise to these people that, no, these toys were not theirs - at least not first. They were their parents' first. Even their grandparents played with many of these toys. How many Boomers think the Red Ryder air rifles are distinctively a part of the Boomer years? Red Ryders were undoubtedly important to many Boomer kids and teenagers - but no more so than they were to prewar kids, whose enthusiasm made them a hit by the end of the 1930s.

Even though not original to the Boomers, many of the toys became important in countless Boomer childhoods - so much so that I can hardly ignore them. Thus I offer a list of Top Ten Honorary Boomer Toys to run alongside the Top 100 Baby Boomer Toys.

Does it come as a surprise that the #1 slot is taken by yet another toy hearkening back to the Old West?

Honorary Boomer Toy

LINCOLN LOGS

Pioneering the Wright Way

#1

Did any of us examine why we so enjoyed fitting logs together, making earth-brown buildings of the simplest sort, and then setting in place the roof supports, followed by those wonderful green planks?

Did we just like building? Or was there something special about the log cabin itself?

John Lloyd Wright, son of Frank Lloyd Wright and then a budding architect in his own right, thought so. He came up with the idea for this toy in the Woodrow Wilson years, reputedly while watching the construction of the Imperial Hotel in Tokyo.

Is it a coincidence? The elder Wright devised an innovative system of interlocking beams for that hotel in Japan. The younger Wright then devised an innovative toy using interlocking wood "logs" to make toy log cabins for American kids.

Western housing. *The huge interest in all things Western among kids, inspired by movies and TV, helped keep Lincoln Logs among the best-selling construction toys in the Boomer years. Box detail, Lincoln Logs, 1950s-60s.*

Whether the connection is real or apocryphal, the younger Wright introduced a construction toy that was successful from its introduction. He gave it a name meant to conjure the most positive associations possible. The name Lincoln Logs evoked the brightest image of pioneer life, even if it referred to a time when the West was only as far as Illinois.

Lincoln Logs stood poised to greet the new crops of children in the late '40s. Unlike many manufacturers who suspended toy production or significantly altered the nature of their toys because of government-imposed shortages of materials, Lincoln Logs made toys of plentiful wood, with only its production of metal figures to go with its log cabin sets affected. These metal figures appeared after the war: slush-metal frontier people, Indians, horses, and livestock.

The pioneer and Western spirit had already hit Boomer kids hard. They happily embraced Lincoln Logs, imagining themselves so many Davy Crocketts, Daniel Boones, and Rebecca Boones, raising timbers and families in the wilderness. Since most later Boomers never owned the metal figures, the toy company became associated almost exclusively with the "Logs" part of its name. Later log cabin builders had to provide their own frontier populations, usually mined from Marx or MPC play sets.

Lincoln Logs saw spirited competition in the '50s and '60s from Halsam, which had likewise specialized in wooden construction toys since 1917. "American Logs reproduce the natural effect of the rough cut logs," Halsam claimed, "hewn with the adz and ax of the early American pioneer."

Halsam proved itself the more forward-looking and dynamic of the two companies. It ventured quickly into the world of plastic and created some of the most characteristically Boomer-style construction toys of the 1950s and '60s.

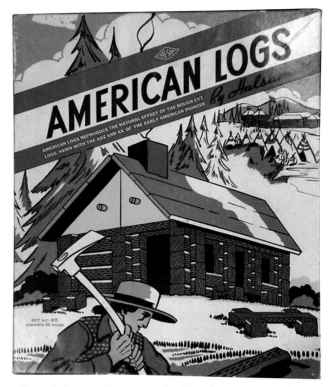

Rough hewn, pioneer style. *Lincoln Logs, manufactured in Chicago, saw competition from American Logs, which used squared interlocking logs, instead of rounded ones. American Logs, Halsam, 1950s.*

Honorary Boomer Toy
MONOPOLY
Everyone's Rich Uncle

#2

Lonely at the top. *The famous Scotty dog stands atop a board now globally famous. Most Boomers can hardly imagine childhood without Monopoly. The game had also been enjoyed by the generation before them. Parker Brothers, 1950s-60s.*

To any American emerging from the trying years of the Great Depression, the opportunity to make money - great, heaping piles of it - must have seemed irresistible. A Germantown, Pennsylvania, man named Charles Darrow apparently entertained himself during the Depression years with a homemade game that involved traveling in a circle without reaching any discernible goal. It also involved real estate, and those great, heaping piles of money. The game arose from a long tradition of finance games, popular in America since the last century when games such as McLoughlin's Bulls and Bears offered players a Wall Street experience, and The Monopolist, also by McLoughlin, put players into "the great struggle between Capital and Labor (which) can be fought out to the satisfaction of all parties." If the players were successful, they could "break the Monopolist and become Monopolists themselves."

After initially rejecting his game and then watching Darrow successfully sell it through Wannamaker's in Philadelphia, Parker Brothers acquired Monopoly and released it in 1935, with four waxed-wood, chess-style pawns for playing pieces. In its first year it rose to be the best-selling game in the country.

Parker Brothers attempted a monopoly over finance games by releasing Monopoly Jr., Finance, and Finance and Fortune in the next few years. They could have saved themselves the effort, since Monopoly did it all by itself.

In 1937 the company made the decision that helped Monopoly become an American institution. Parker Brothers turned to the Dowst company of Chicago to produce a set of die-cast playing pieces, which were of a character now familiar around the globe. Dowst, a name well known among die-cast manufacturing circles in this country from the 1890s, had combined with its fellow

Chicago die-casting company Cosmo in making various trinkets, food premiums including Cracker Jack prizes, and game pieces. For many years Dowst, under its far more famous Tootsietoy brand name, issued the familiar pieces independent of Parker Brothers in bubble-pack assortments through dime stores.

Wartime restrictions forced Parker Brothers to use wooden pawns again. By 1947, however, the company returned to the metal pieces. Offered alongside its $2 Monopoly with wood pawns was the restored $3.50 Monopoly with the full complement of die-cast playing pieces, some of which did not survive through the entire Boomer period: cannon, thimble, iron, top hat, wheelbarrow, Scotty dog, battleship, racing car, airplane, and man atop a rearing horse.

For the first postwar game players, Parker brothers also issued the well-established Finance game, and the game of gold-mine shares, Dig, which had its debut just before the war. Parker also introduced a new finance game, featuring a familiar figure called Rich Uncle. "Fast action, big business! Watch the market quotations shift luck fast!" The new game had, of course, lots of play money.

Baby Boomers played Monopoly games by the millions. Parker Brothers would eventually become famous for variant versions of the game. Perhaps the most notable of Boomer years was the 1964 underwater set built for New England Divers, Inc., with its cellophane-laminated steel board. It weighed 95 pounds.

Probably a good measure of the game's popularity can be measured by events of the 1970s, years when most Baby Boomers were maturing and defining their adult interests. In 1973, the World Championships began for dedicated Monopolists, and in 1978 Monopoly had its sweetest moment when Nieman Marcus offered a $600 solid chocolate full-size version of the game.

Probably the most telling moment had already occurred, however, in 1972. That year the City Commissioner of Public Works promoted a facelift for Atlantic City that would change the names of some streets - including Baltic and Mediterranean Avenues, to Fairmont and Melrose. You can imagine the public's reaction. Edward P. Parker, then president of Parker Brothers, wrote to the commissioner. "Go directly to Jail," he said.

Honorary Boomer Toy
TINKERTOYS
Sticks and Spools

#3

Boy tinker. *A young construction enthusiast, decked out in classic shirt and bolo, enjoys the same stick-and-spool toy his parents probably enjoyed. To his other side are American Plastic Bricks by Halsam.* Toys, 1959-60.

Many toys are given this accolade at some time or another: "Universal appeal!" How many live up to it is another matter.

Probably the closest in our century is the construction toy set made by an outfit based in Evanston, Illinois, since early in this century, named the Toy Tinkers.

Now, nearly everyone in this country knows who Barbie is. I will grant you that. But I would be willing to wager that nearly everyone in this country has a hands-on personal "familiarity" with Tinkertoys.

In fact, if you talk to many Boomers, you will find it is one of the toys that keeps coming up in conversation. It meant something to them. It occupied long hours during their youngest playing years. It usually gave them their first complex construction experience, after graduating from such playthings as the Playskool peg-bench sets and Fisher-Price plastic beads. They fondly remember fitting the sticks into the wheel-shaped connectors. They remember the sound of the sticks rattling and tumbling out of the cardboard tubes.

They even remember the taste of the toys. I was unaware how important this must have been until a friend of mine, who is younger than the Boomers, mentioned the flavor of the red-colored Tinkertoy connectors. Before that moment I had forgotten. Not about red connectors, since I don't remember red connectors myself. But about Tinkertoys in general.

How they tasted. In fact, I immediately went and chewed on an old Tinkertoy stick, and found myself being subjected to a sweet, Proustian welling of deeply buried memory that became this book ...

Just kidding.

A tombstone manufacturer named Charles H. Pajeau started the Toy Tinkers after meditating upon the pleasure children find in playing with sticks and spools. The year was 1914. He soon brought in a friend, Robert Pettit, member of the Chicago Board of Trade. The two of them settled on the tube-shaped container for their toy set. Their Thousand Wonder Builder sold well locally, thanks to creative window displays in Chicago, and then nationally, thanks to a traffic-stopping display at the Grand Central Station pharmacy in New York.

In the first year, 900,000 Tinkertoys were manufactured and sold. Baby Boomers started off with essentially the same kits kids had played with for 30 years. In 1952, the still-growing company was acquired by A.G. Spalding & Bros., Inc. Changes then became the name of the game. In 1953, red sticks started to be mixed with the unpainted ones.

In 1955, other colors followed: green, blue, and yellow.

The Tinkertoy line also expanded with the Tinker Zoo, the Circus Tinker Zoo, and the Toy Maker. Unchanged through the Boomer period, however, was one of the original principals behind the book of designs included with each tube. Earlier, the booklets might have had designs for such things as a Cream Separator or Bi-Plane. In the Boomer era, these changed to reflect the times. Children could now make Tinkertoy versions of the Television Camera or Jet Plane.

But the Tinkers stuck to their guns - so to speak - and never used weapon designs in their instruction books. The set I grew up with must have been a few years older than I was, for, to me, the "classic" set has smooth, fairly shiny red sticks mixed among the plain-wood regular ones.

Yet I only remember how the plain ones tasted.

Merry-Go-Rounds, Giant Tops, Windmills, Airships! *Tinkertoys, its maker promised, could make everything a child could desire. The tube of these prewar Tinkertoys, played with by the parents of the Boomers, included instructions for a Turbine Draw Bridge, Walking Beam, Conveyor, and Monoplane. Early Tinkertoy builders constructed their wonders from uncolored "Spools and Rods," in contrast to Boomer builders, who found increasing numbers of colors tumbling from their Tinkertoy tubes.*

CHAPTER 4

Locket Dolls and Magic Crayons

#21 LITTLE KIDDLES

Locket Dolls

Dangling dolls. *Many Kiddles were small enough to be sold in plastic lockets. Unlike earlier dolls, the Kiddles were themselves fashion accessories. Mattel, 1960s.*

Barbie, Tammy, and Tressy were all very fine for older girls. Younger girls, however, needed something a little more imaginative and perhaps even ridiculous. In 1966, Mattel hit on a winning combination of elements - costumes, storybook associations, and doll-making sense - and came up with the Little Kiddles.

Measuring from 4″ tall down to less than 1″, these miniatures had oversized, rouge-cheeked faces, long, rooted hair (often in attractively unrealistic colors), *I Dream of Jeannie* eyes, and vanishingly small bodies.

The names, though... It must have been the names as much as anything that created the magic aura around these dolls: Bunson Burnie, a Little Kiddle fireman; Anabelle Autodiddle; Howard Biff Boodle; Florence Niddle; Suki Skediddler; Sleeping Biddle; Sheila Skediddle.

Some were quite small, and were sold imprisoned within plastic heart necklaces and brooches, lockets, and perfume bottles. They were dolls that were accessories.

Many children found their favorites among the Storybook Kiddles, based on figures already familiar through nighttime fairy tales and children's books. The sprite-like Peter Paniddle, who had red hair to offset his green outfit and cap, came with Tinkerbell, who was incarnated as no less than a minuscule Barbie doll, and a soft-plastic green reptile, the Crocodiddle. Sleeping Biddle drowsed through the ages on a purple claw-foot bed. Cinderiddle was dressed in rags and toted a broom, but also had a fancy gown and glass slippers - which girls immediately lost, of course, since it was part of the story. Liddle Middle Muffet sat on her tuffett with bowl and spoon, with an octopus-looking spider beside her. Liddle Biddle Peep had sheep and staff, while Alice in Wonderliddle was accompanied by the White Rabbit, with his constantly consulted watch. These all mildly encouraged literacy, coming as they did with their own storybooks.

Except perhaps one Kiddle, who was utterly true to the times: Telly Viddle.

Small fires only, please. *The intrepid firefighter of Kiddlesville measures almost 3-1/2˝ tall - if wearing his hat. Small as he was, he towered over the Kiddles sold in lockets. Bunson Bernie, with fire engine, Mattel, 1960s.*

Walking Goofy. *In the later 1960s Mattel issued Disney toys akin to the Kiddles in spirit. This Goofy measures 4-1/2˝ tall, with a body disproportionately small. They also showed kinship in their name: the Skediddlers. A rod in the back of the small doll moved its arms and legs, making it seem to walk. Mattel, 1967-68.*

Too Cute to Be Trolls

New York's Uneeda Doll Co., enjoying considerable success with its Wishnik Trolls, took the logical next step. Knowing the childlike proportions of Trolls struck a chord with children, Uneeda used a similar body for a new doll line called Pee Wees.

Having some of the tininess of Mattel's Little Kiddles and some of the chunky charm of Trolls, the Pee Wees brightened those three or four inches immediately above the floor for many girls of the mid-1960s.

Pee Wees are marked on one foot with their name and on the other with the year 1965. The Pee Wee Tote, combination tote and dollhouse, were made by Ideal for Uneeda.

LEFT FOOT

RIGHT HAND

Twister

MB

LEFT HAND

RIGHT FOOT

The sedate and serene Milton Bradley Co., which had started in the 1800s with lithographed building blocks and such card games as Curious Bible Questions, found itself with a Mod phenomenon on its hands in 1966.

The year before, a man named Reyn Guyer came up with a new party game. Guyer's business was sales promotions, including the development of packaging and store displays. His game had to do with the placement of hands and feet on a large floor mat spotted with different colors. He called it Pretzel.

When Milton Bradley bought the game, they renamed it, against Guyer's wishes. Yet the new name, Twister, seemed perfect for the times. Milton Bradley advertised it as "the game that ties you up in knots," and "a stockin' feet game." Instead of the usual picture of kids playing, the box featured laughing adults racing to place hands and feet on the colored circles indicated by the spinner, handled by the Referee.

It appeared to be another ill-fated novelty item until Johnny Carson introduced the game on the

Tonight Show, using it as a prop to go with the appearance of Eva Gabor on that evening's program. It then sold - more than three million copies in its first year.

Milton Bradley tried to capitalize on the popularity of the game immediately, releasing in 1967 more zany party games including Feeley Meeley, in which the players, portrayed on the box as young adults, feel inside the box for winning objects, and Slap Stick, "the Wild and Wacky game that makes everyone slap happy." Again, the aim was the young adult: "Indoor and outdoor fun for everyone - a great party 'warmerupper,'" the company promised.

Another new game, Animal Twister, on the other hand, Milton Bradley billed as "just for kids."

"Note," say the instructions of the original Twister. "If a player feels that a new position is impossible or it would cause him to fall, he may concede the game."

Concede? Did anyone concede? Overreaching, tangling, stretching to get that blue spot. Then collapsing !

That was half the fun.

Twister. *The instructions give the "Strategy for Winning at Twister: Good strategy is to advance toward an opponent in an attempt to keep him in his end of the vinyl sheet. This will give him a smaller area of circles on which to gain each position, without going under or over the advancing player." Remarkably, chess held its own against this colorful game of strategy. Milton Bradley, 1966.*

#23

TV's WINKY DINK and YOU

Magic Television Kit

Game Kit. More elaborate than the mail-in kit, the Winky Dink Television Game Kit contained not only the usual items - screen, crayons, and erasing mitt - but also a die-cut puzzle, 40 plastic "doodles" in assorted colors, and game book... not to mention some of the most charming graphics of the 1950s. Standard Toykraft Products, 1955.

One of the earliest attempts at interactive television, *Winky Dink and You*, effected the transformation that was bound to come: It turned the television set itself into a toy.

Winky Dink and You aired on CBS TV from Oct. 10, 1953, through April 27, 1957, hosted by Jack Barry, who had already hosted early game shows including *Juvenile Jury*.

Winky Dink was an animated character with a star-like head and slender, pixy-like body. His voice was provided by Mae Questal, also the voice of Olive Oyl. The cast was completed by Dayton

Interactive TV play set. *The paper envelope of the original Winky Dink Magic Television Kit contained Winky Dink Magic Crayons, erasing cloth, and the Magic Window, which was tinted green. "You may find that you will want to leave the Magic Window up at all times while you are watching your other programs," its makers assured parents. "You will find that the tint is restful to your eyes." Standard Toykraft Products, 1950s.*

Allen, who played the incompetent Mr. Bungle and also provided the voice of Winky Dink's dog Woofer. The show, concept, and Winky Dink animated character were created by Harry W. Pritchett, Sr., and Edwin Brit Wyckoff.

In the fall of 1953, ads invited kids to write in for their *"Winky Dink and You! Super Magic TV Kit,"* which included Magic Screen, Winky Dink crayons, and Magic Erasing Cloth. The kits then arrived at homes around the country: "Here it is! Your own Winky Dink Magic Television Kit! ...a Barry, Enright & Friendly Production."

The thrill must have been unbearable. Here was a magic kit, sanctioned by none other than CBS TV itself, and presumably the parent who surrendered the $.50 needed.

What was the magic? The child was allowed to draw directly on the TV. During the show, Winky Dink would get into an intolerable difficulty. What to do but turn to the audience for a solution? Barry entreated the watching kids to get out their plastic Magic Screen, which could be pressed onto the TV

screen. Then Barry instructed the kids in drawing Winky Dink out of his predicament, using one of the five crayons in the kit.

Tellingly, Crockett Johnson's ever-popular *Harold and the Purple Crayon*, in which the title

Detail of the Winky Dink puzzle from the 1955 Game Kit.

83

Magic Crayons. *Winky Dink's Magic Crayons and their box. The green background is the plastic screen sent in every advertisement.* Modern Plastics Encyclopedia, *1946.*

character draws himself out of predicaments by means of a crayon, came out at the midpoint of the Winky Dink years, in 1955.

Winky Dink and You also involved kids through the tried and true method of secret messages. On the screen, parts of the letters making up the messages appeared, which the children had to trace onto their Magic Screen. Those parts would disappear, so that when the rest of the parts of the letters then appeared on the screen, only kids with Magic Screens were able to read the secret.

The Magic Screen served much as the Radio Orphan Annie and Captain Midnight decoder rings had for the previous generation, updated for the new medium of television.

Standard Toykraft attempted a revival of *Winky Dink and You* in 1969, only to be stymied by the concern that was then quashing other toys and children's activity games: safety. In this case Boomer parents were concerned about the radiation emitted by television sets, and the fact that Winky Dink required that children stand right up against the screen, drawing parts of letters and escape hatches for the beleaguered hero.

Television sets did become radiation-free at the beginning of the '70s - another sign of the ending of an era. By then, however, Winky Dink was gone.

Tiddly Winky Dinks. *Tying in with the Tiddly Winks fad of the 1950s, Barry & Enright Productions produced Tiddly Winky Dinks. The game "board" is a cardboard cube 9˝ to a side. Tryne, 1950s.*

MR. MACHINE

Many toys existed in the minds of children even when they were not lucky enough to own them. Parents couldn't afford everything, after all. Not all girls had Barbies. Certainly not all boys had G.I. Joes. In fact, in my circle of childhood friends, I remember only one who had a Joe. Perhaps because of the kind of children we were, Joe was not an object of envy, unlike other, simpler, and often cheaper toys.

Yet we all knew about Barbie and G.I. Joe. They were part of the mental landscape of childhood, put there by the relentless forces of the Mattel and Hasbro marketing departments.

In the same way, but to a lesser degree, many of us knew about Mr. Machine. Even if we never had one or even saw one in person, Mr. Machine had a strong television presence, was distinctive enough to catch both the attention and imagination of

The Smiling Robot. *Mr. Machine had enough personality to become the spokesrobot for Ideal Toy Corp. in its television ads. The large 1970s version, shown here, could not be taken apart, as could the original. Ideal, 1977.*

children, and had less a feeling of being a "boy's toy" than previous robots. His bolt-nosed head had a friendly expression that seemed a world away from Robert the Robot's mechanically austere face.

Mr. Machine heralded the opening of the third great period of Boomer toys, even if kids were probably unaware of the fact. The toy industry itself may have been unaware of the fact. When this toy was put into the hands of children in 1961, they had no idea it arrived from the inventor's shop of Marvin Glass, via the manufacturing facilities of Ideal Toys. Almost single-handedly, this toy inventor would make the world of toys in the years 1962-69 radically different from the world of toys before.

Suddenly toys became larger, brighter, more complex, and decidedly more zany. Tin started fading away in favor of big constructions of hard plastic, many of which shouted their presence in the playroom with sharp sounds and violent motions.

Marvin Glass was responsible for many of the most prominent toys of the 1960s. His goofy and frog-like Odd Ogg and the aggressive dragon-robot King Zor were big hits. By themselves they would have been enough to put Glass among the notables of 1960s toy innovators. Yet he produced others: Robot Commando, Smarty Bird, Gaylord, and the huge hit of 1963, Mousetrap, for Ideal; Dandy the Lion, for Irwin Corp.; Yakkity Yob for Eldon; Golferino for Hubley; and the Rock'em Sock'em Robots for Marx.

The original 18″ Mr. Machine came with a wrench. Glass fully intended that children use that tool, for the grinning plastic robot could be dismantled and reassembled endlessly.

ROCK'EM SOCK'EM ROBOTS #25

Red Rocker and Blue Bomber

It was inevitable. Since TV thrived on extrava-ganza, action, and conflict, the sports that involved the most physical contest thrived, especially wrestling and boxing. Famed conductor Arturo Toscanini was reportedly a great fan of televised wrestling, which he would watch after dinner on his early, small-screen TV.

And since Boomer toy makers responded to the prompting of television, and since they also vied with one another in making the most outrageous games and toys possible, toy versions of violent sports only seemed natural.

One attempt in the late '50s to capture the excitement of boxing came in the form of Knockout, an electronic game that featured a square boxing ring, bell, buzzer, light, and timer. Two plastic boxers stood on the ends of paddles. Controlled by triggers on the sides of the paddle

Rocker vs. Bomber. *The "rollicking Red Rocker," prize-fighting robot from Soltarus II, fights in the Championship of the Universe against the "beautiful Blue Bomber, pride of Umgluck." The star-traveling robots, according to the box, weighed in at 375 and 382 pounds, respectively. Marx, mid to late 1960s.*

handles, the boxers delivered hard-plastic blows - right! - left! - trying to put each other down for the count. It may have been based on a more elaborate table game designed by Swiss inventor P. Kramer.

The perfect boxing toy for young Boomers arrived in the mid-1960s from the Marx toy company, which had finally overcome its nose-in-the-air attitude concerning advertising budgets and TV. If any toy ever was, the Rock'em Sock'em Robots game was made for the medium.

I must have watched less TV than most kids of my generation - in fact, I am fairly certain of the fact - so I don't have the Mr. Machine song running through my mind at odd moments, or any other toy advertising jingle. Yet I can clearly remember the jousting robots on TV ads, powered by two young "managers." The expected denouement occurs, and the voice-over announces: "He knocked his block off!"

It may not have happened exactly that way. Those may not be the exact words. Whatever they were, the Rock'em Sock'ems packed a heady punch on black-and-white and color sets everywhere.

Were they as fun to play with as to imagine playing with? I sup-pose it depended on the kid. The controls gave limited control over the robots, who could move back and forth over only a small area. The battling fists were great fun, however. And the left punch that made the opponent's head spring up, with a nice ratchety sound, was strangely satisfying.

When Marx introduced the toy in 1964, it expected the "world's only boxing robots" to be one of the most talked-about toys of the year. Since it was busily trying to catch up with toy companies who already had a well-established TV presence, Marx spent heavily that year, making it something of a self-fulfilled prophecy.

TROLLS

From Under the Bridge

Graduation party. *Although wannabe trolls flooded the market in the 1960s, Uneeda obtained a license from Dam to produce vinyl trolls for the American market. Uneeda Wishniks, 1960s.*

"Homely. Look at those ears."

"And those eyes."

"Ugly!"

"Look - naked! Ecch!"

"So cute," said the little one, taking the trolls in arm and walking away.

Trolls hit with such force that comparisons with another overnight sensation, the Hula Hoop, prompted Uneeda to crow in a 1964 ad, "They call it a 'Hula Hoop' ... Its correct name is Wishnik."

Making troll dolls was a departure for Uneeda. It was known for its dolls with names of sugar-spoon sweetness: Weepsy Wiggles, Dew Drop, Blabby, Yummy Kiss, Needa Toddles, Bundle of Love, and Sweetums.

Sugar-spoon sweet? Wishniks were not quite that. They were squat, round-bellied, pointed-eared, grinning, skin-toned, sexless vinyl creatures. The little ones wore no clothes for a few years, although in 1967 even the 3″ trolls learned modesty, or else style. They started appearing that year in costumes and outfits that did their best to remain on the far side of the ridiculous. Even then, the very smallest, the size of charms and bubble-gum prizes, that being what they were, came naked into the world, and stayed that way.

I forgot to mention the hair. Trolls were all vinyl except glassine eyes and plentiful pelage. The stuff erupted from above their heavy brow-ridges with an exuberance thought to be gone from this world since the passing of the wooly mammoth. It swept up with a shape like that of an onion, or of the flame on a match. At least it did so at first. In the hands of a child, the hair was apt to spread every which way or to come out altogether. Soon the various troll manufacturers of the 1960s grew dissatisfied with traditional hair colors and began the great color explosion. Many Wishniks appeared with red, yellow, orange, and blue hair - great flowing waves of the stuff.

The hair was everything. While they did have bellies much like the Japanese god Hotei, whose

Saving for a rainy day. Larger troll banks such as this slicker-clad example came with clothing permanently attached to the vinyl body. Troll bank, 7˝ tall, Dam, 1960s.

belly is rubbed for good luck, Wishniks came with a contrary injunction: "Rub my hair for good luck."

Vinyl troll dolls were the innovation of a Danish baker, Thomas Dam, who started carving wooden troll figures for his children. He put them up for sale to troll-minded sorts when the baking business was going through hard times after the war. The trolls sold so well he set up a factory in Gjol in 1959, getting a fad rolling that would encourage countless imitators.

In 1964 Dam issued a license to make trolls to Uneeda Doll Co., in the business since 1917. The license was such news that Uneeda gave it bigger press than its other licensing agreement that year: through an agreement with *McCall's* magazine, Uneeda was launching a new Betsy McCall doll. Betsy previously had been made by American Character Doll Co. from 1957 to 1963.

In 1966 Dam entered into another agreement with Skandia House, a subsidiary of Royalty House in Florida. Countless other manufacturers turned out troll-like creatures, with some of the most appealing made as curios out of the material Thomas Dam first used: wood.

Trolls appeared everywhere. On family trips out West when I was a child, I remember it being a highlight to stop at Little America, a tourist trap set up in the middle of nowhere that sold every tourist curio imaginable, including a huge vinyl troll that must have stood taller than at least some of us kids.

By the late '60s the boom was over. Although trolls still rode high on a crest of popularity in Europe, the wave had died down in this country.

But not for lack of stroking the hair.

Hula Hoop. Uneeda's announcement of its license from Dam used a term everyone in the toy industry knew. Playthings, *March 1964.*

SPIROGRAPH #27

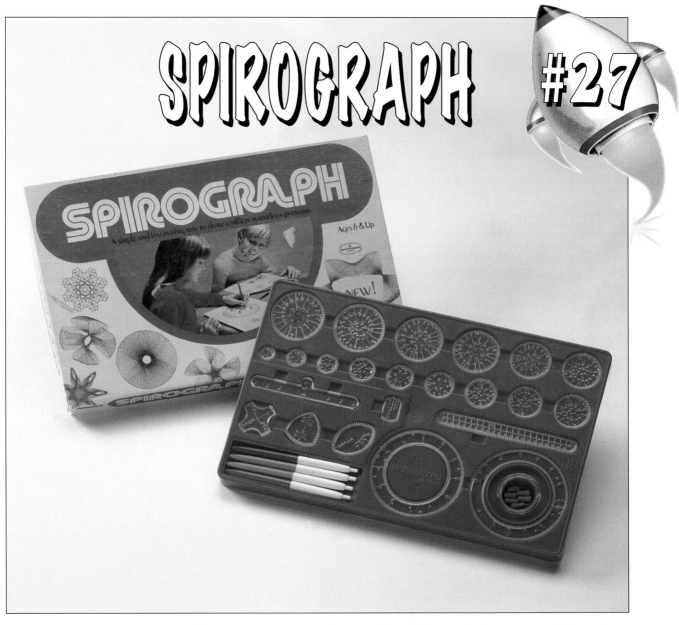

Some toys looked keen as all get-out on TV, then turned out to be duds on the playroom floor. Other toys, however, had a way of staying interesting long after the plastic wrap, or gift wrap, was thrown away.

One of the characteristic toys of the late Boomer years was Spirograph, a radically new art toy. Unlike painting kits or even coloring books, Spirograph required little in the way of intrinsic artistic talent. Instead, it required physical coordination, a slight bit of mechanical talent, and patience.

Invented by British mechanical engineer Dennis Fischer, the toy involved a system of clear plastic pieces with toothed edges, like gears. Some pieces the child had to fix firmly to the page, usually by tacks that went through holes into the drawing board beneath the paper. Other pieces remained free. These had off-center holes in them large enough for the tip of a pen.

The child had to learn to keep an even drawing pressure, not only downward through the moving gear onto the paper but also sideways, toward the center of the fixed gear, which was also the center of the geometric drawing being formed. I remember many a masterpiece flawed by a slip of the pen.

Spirograph was a surprise best seller in its introductory years of 1966 and '67. It sat firmly at the top of toy sales charts both years. I imagine those must have been quieter years than any before.

Five and a half million souls bent over kitchen and den tables, trying to execute the perfect geometric designs made possible by this exasperating and inspiring toy.

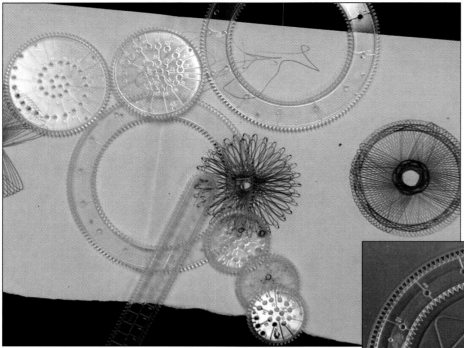

Vintage loops and swirls. *Spirograph made possible elaborate designs such as these, drawn by an unknown child in the 1960s.*

Perfect for a rainy afternoon. *As a drawing toy, Spirograph had democratic appeal: "Anyone can draw beautiful patterns immediately!" The kits contained 22 clear plastic wheels, clear plastic gears, rings, and "racks," as well as ball point pens in four colors. Kenner, 1967.*

Magic Designer. *In contrast to Spirograph, the Magic Designer, originally called Hoot-Nanny, provided a metal platform with gears and drawing area for a round piece of paper. When cranked, the toy produced the drawing mechanically. Northern Signal Co., 1960s.*

GUMBY
TV's Bendy

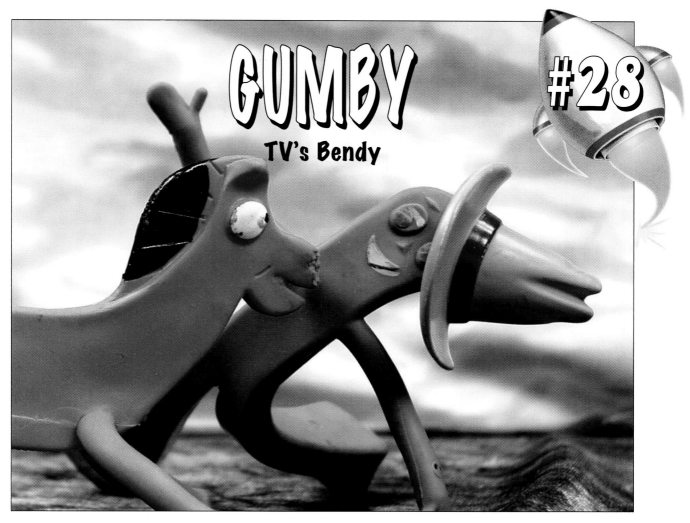

Who or what is Gumby? Gumby is a green clay boy who has a loyal, earth-toned clay horse pal named Pokey, a lemon-colored clay dinosaur friend named Prickle, and a blue clay mermaid friend named Goo. In the *Gumby* television series, Gumby is the son of clay people Gumbo and Gumba.

Gumby might be said, just as truthfully, to be the child of the 1953 art film *Gumbasia*, by Art Clokey. For this film, Clokey animated clay forms as an experiment in movement. A showing for movie producer Sam Engel led to the development of a modeling-clay character for television.

The claymation animator created a flat, easily produced figure with a "bump of wisdom," which recalled for Clokey a picture of his father as a young man, which showed him with a huge cowlick rising like a bump from his head.

The figure's name came from Michigan farm slang - "gumbo," his father's word for the sticky and slippery mud in the roads after a summer rain.

NBC liked Clokey's pilot show and signed him for a series of *The Adventures of Gumby*. Roger Muir, the producer of *Howdy Doody*, agreed to introduce Gumby on that already popular program.

The clay boy first hit television in 1955, with Pokey making his debut the following year. These television appearances gave Gumby the springboard he needed to leap into his own NBC program, *The Gumby Show*, in 1957, with Pinky Lee as emcee. Scotty McKee, portraying Clarabelle the Clown, gave some sense of continuity from *Howdy Doody*.

New shows were produced in 1966, which enjoyed enough success to stimulate a new Gumby series for 1967, which introduced Prickle, Goo, and Nopey, the dog who only said, "No." Dr. Zveegee, the fun-ruining mad scientist, also made his first appearance.

Whether young watchers perceived the fact, Gumby was always a philosophic figure, unfailingly smiling, resilient, and flexible. Even his friends had philosophic natures. According to Clokey, Alan Watts once told him there were two kinds of people in the world: the prickly and the gooey. Prickle and Goo appeared soon thereafter.

Lakeside Industries, having the first license to produce Gumby toys, made available to kids small figures of Gumby and his friends, and accessories to turn Gumby into such grownup characters as Fire Man, Astronaut, and Cowboy. Fortunately for his watchers, that growing-up business on Gumby's part was all make-believe.

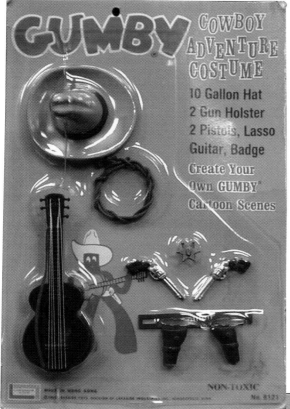

The rubbery Old West. Gumby and Pokey, sold with numerous accessories, were the top bendy toys of the 1960s. Others followed, including Mattel's Major Matt Mason of the last few years of the '60s, and the Colorform Aliens of around 1969. Gumby and Pokey, Lakeside Industries, 1960s, with American Logs.

Sheriff Gumby. Sets such as this gave children the chance to change Gumby's identity the way it changed on TV. This western set included ten-gallon hat, guns, coiled lasso, and badge. The guns and badge had small spikes in the back, to be pressed directly into Gumby's plastic. Lakeside Industries, 1965.

Rocky and Boris. The combination of rubber or soft vinyl with internal wires led to countless effective playthings through the end of the Boomer era. The arrangement worked especially well for cartoon characters, such as Rocky, the flying squirrel, and Boris Badenov, from Jay Ward's *Rocky and His Friends,* which first aired in 1959. Wham-O Co.,1972.

THE BUBBLE-TOPPED COUPE #29

Postwar Christmas best seller. *This futuristic coupe stirred millions of young imaginations, and helped kick-start postwar production of plastic toys. Dillon Beck, 1946-52.*

Steel, lead, and rubber were not the only toy-making materials being rationed and restricted during the war. Plastic was too. As a result, despite the plastic industry's attempts to promote new formulas to the toy industry before and during the war, few manufacturers were poised at war's end to introduce bright new plastic playthings for Christmas.

One of the few was Dillon Beck Manufacturing of New Jersey, which, under its Wannatoys banner, introduced its $.25 coupe.

The Wannatoy Coupe was not your ordinary coupe. It had a bubble top of transparent acetate, through which a simplified steering wheel and seats were visible. The bubble sat squarely on a streamlined body, vaguely reminiscent of a rowboat set keel-side-up.

Children, or at least their buying parents, reacted with enthusiasm to its Art Deco-inspired futuristic design. In the new Atomic Age, it expressed the hope people felt about times to come. A million units moved off shelves in the 1946 Christmas season. The Coupe sold well into the next decade, at the lower price of a dime per car. With plastic

toys being promoted as safe, tough to break, free of sharp edges, and hygienically washable, even toddlers must have had their first lessons in Deco styling from this wheeled, bubbled bauble, a dime-store best seller at the dawn of the Baby Boomer years.

WANNATOY
Plastic Streamlined Toys

CARS · TRAINS
BOATS, ETC.

Send for Catalog Sheets

We also offer highly specialized skills in custom molded plastic toys

DILLON-BECK MFG. CO.
IRVINGTON, N. J.

Dillon-Beck advertisement. Modern Plastics Encyclopedia, *1946.*

#30 PREHISTORIC TIMES PLAY SETS

Shadows of the past. *Marx's Prehistoric Times play sets combined all ancient eras into one. Cave people, prehistoric mammals, dinosaurs, and even earlier reptiles walked and crawled side by side. Marx, 1950s.*

I readily admit my biases. One is for dinosaurs. In this bias, I was far from alone in the Boomer years.

Trips to the Denver Museum of Natural History were a source of great excitement. There I could see massive skeletons from the Age of Mammals and the Age of Reptiles, and ponder the plaster casts of Protoceratops eggs from the Roy Chapman Andrews expeditions, and ogle, through the counter glass in the museum shop, the cast-metal dinosaurs for sale there.

I was a kid. How could I buy things like that? They cost something like $8 each. I could afford plastic dinosaurs, however. Occasionally I would have enough for a bag of brightly colored plastic dinosaurs made by MPC, which the convenience store nearby carried. These I would put in my dino-

saur box, which had other MPC dinos, a few Tim-Mee dinos, a few Frito-Lay premiums, and two or three dinosaurs by the true rulers of Prehistoric Times, the Louis Marx Co.

I had no idea where my treasured, large, gray Tyrannosaurus Rex came from. He was well-worn and obviously heavily played with, for his left toes were smoothed-down to the point he tended to fall over if not judiciously placed so his left foot rested on higher ground.

I do remember where another Marx I had came from. I literally dug it up. At one house where we lived, in an older suburb around Denver, I was engaging in a favorite activity, which was digging in a dirt pile in the backyard. I imagined I was digging for dinosaurs and was thoroughly startled to actually find one. At the time I deeply pondered

March of the ancients. *Instead of elaborate Marx play sets, most Boomer kids grew up with dinosaurs bought by the bag at dime stores, made by Marx or other toy companies. Plastic dinosaurs, MPC, 1960s.*

the differences between these toys and the slightly less elaborate ones made by MPC. I had no way of digging into toy prehistory and finding out about Marx's fabulous Prehistoric Times play sets. Although Marx was still making them at the time, it would be decades before I would see one.

In 1958, Marx gave this description to entice children - as if they needed any enticements other than the plastic dinosaurs and cave people themselves: "You take off in your Time Machine, headed for prehistoric times. There's a dizzying sensation as it hovers over your home - and suddenly the buildings are gone. Instead, you see forest landscape below. Palms and ferns are everywhere. There's a waterfall, and that splash of color is a clear blue pool. Drinking from it are a group of strange, monstrous animals. Dinosaurs! You gasp as you see a big Allosaurus move off in leaping bounds. And there's the Dimetrodon, its spine adorned by a giant 'sail' - the Stegosaurus, with its double row of bony plates - the Brontosaurus, hugest of all saurians! There's the Pteranodon, a flying reptile, with dagger-like beak and 27-foot wingspread.

"And now you gasp again, for you recognize other primitive figures. They're cavemen, attired

in shaggy furs and battling a duck-billed Hadrosaurus with stones, spears, and primitive clubs. And they're winning, too - until another battler enters the fray. It's the huge Tyrannosaurus - 50 feet long, 20 feet high and eight tons of fighting fury! The cavemen flee, but the big monster is gaining. Gunning the Time Machine to top speed, you catch up, then hover just above the Tyrannosaur's head, distracting the awful beast until the cavemen can reach the shelter of their caves. Then, with a friendly wave at the grateful cavemen, you roar off - headed for new adventures!"

The first Prehistoric Times set had appeared in time for the previous Christmas, and was available for less than $5. The 47 pieces included plastic palms, ferns, and a rocky landscape made of thin, brittle plastic, with a simulated pool at its center. The set returned the next Christmas with 44 pieces, a form it stayed in for several years.

Through the rest of the Boomer period, Marx sold dinosaurs. They came on cards, in bags, and in play sets - including, in 1961-62, the Flintstones play set. In that set, dinosaurs were simply a part of the Stone Age suburban scene - much as they were in the Boomer suburban scene.

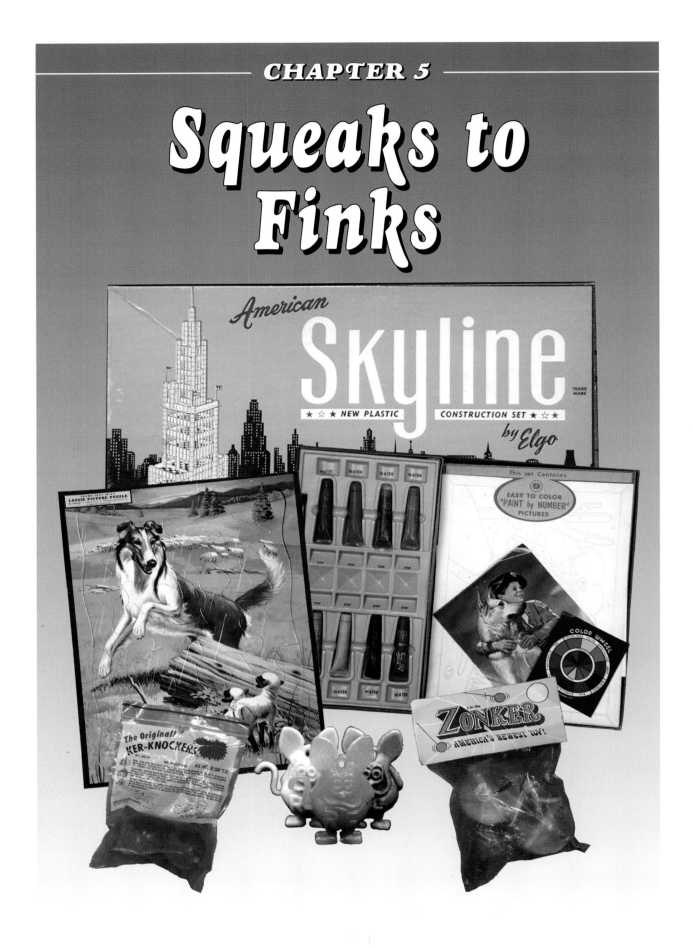

CHAPTER 5
Squeaks to Finks

SUN RUBBER SQUEAKER DOLLS

#31

Polka-dot charmer.
*Famed children's illustrator
Ruth E. Newton designed
several dolls for Sun.
Wearing the ever-present
polka dots of the time, this
girl doll, 8-1/2˝ tall, is made
of soft vinyl, with a squeaker
in her left foot. Sun Rubber,
1950s.*

Millions of children in the 1950s and '60s took for granted squeezable, shiny, highly detailed toys made of vinyl, available by the armload at Woolworth's and other dime stores.

Many of these toys were one-piece, doll-like figures, sometimes based on the works of famed children's artist Ruth E. Newton.

The company making these dolls started its successful toy-making business in the 1920s, when a man named Tom Smith came from Pennsylvania to sell off the unprofitable Avalon Rubber Co., and instead stayed to make the company a leader in the manufacture of rubber toys, under the name Sun Rubber. Its first toy hit, a rubber hot-water bottle for dolls, helped see the company through the Great Depression.

At the outbreak of World War II, Sun gave up toys and turned to production of wartime supplies, including gas masks for civilian use as a safeguard against possible coastal attacks. Having gotten to know the artist in the '30s, Smith consulted with Walt Disney about his company's masks. Gas masks were unappealing objects at best, and frightening objects at worst. How did kids see them? Would they understand that the masks meant potential safety when they looked so alarming? After their meeting, Sun Rubber started manufacturing its most unusual item: the Mickey Mouse Gas Mask.

As the years passed, Sun Rubber notched up a number of toy-making innovations. The company made the first cry-and-wet dolls, setting the stage for one of the doll hits for later Boomer kids, Ideal's Betsy Wetsy. Sun made the first black doll, named Amosandra, daughter of Amos and Ruby of the popular *Amos 'N' Andy* radio show.

Perhaps its most important contribution to the toy world was its development around 1953 of the rotational casting machine, which let the company produce dolls seven times faster than before, using a vinyl called Plastisol. The method and the material also allowed exceptionally good detail.

Sun Rubber may have over-invested in the new technology. It also over-extended in defending its patent in court, and went into bankruptcy, closing its doors in 1958. The company reopened in 1960, however, after the Ohio court ruled in Sun's favor.

Sun Rubber's Barberton plant was peremptorily closed by then-owner Talley in early 1974 during a labor-management dispute. While some operations were continued in Georgia, the rubber and vinyl toy giant's days were ending, after having provided well-loved playthings for the parents of the Baby Boomers and for the Boomers themselves.

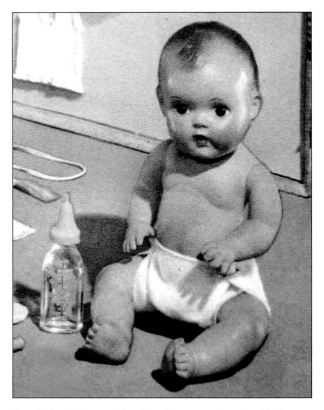

Sunbabe. *Many of the first Boomers played with Sun Rubber dolls as toddlers "Sunbabe Rubber Dolls ... They Drink ... Then Wet," this ad proclaimed. The baby dolls came with organdy dress, bonnet, knit cotton undershirt, soap tray and soap, hot water bottle, cotton slip, bath mat, two powder puffs, teething ring, booties, bottle, rattle and towel. The 1947 Christmas Book, Montgomery Ward.*

MOUSE TRAP GAME #32

The sensation of '63. *After its unprece-dented success in 1963, Ideal started advertising Mouse Trap on the* Magilla Gorilla Show, *which boosted the remarka-ble game, and Ideal, into a second surpris-ingly successful spring. Ideal, 1963.*

The ball rolls down the rickety stairs...

...the old man jumps for the barrel...

...and lands (sometimes on his feet!)...

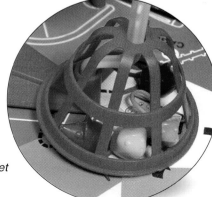

...and the basket descends over the mice.

Ideal was hitting its stride in the early 1960s. The designs of Marvin Glass were startling and new, and were being greeted with open arms by children and parents. In 1963, however, Ideal suddenly found itself with a mega-hit on its hands. It was, on the face of it, just another board game. It sold well for Christmas that year, as was expected. Strangely, however, it had already sold phenomenally well in the spring of '63. Observers in the business shook their heads. When did a board game do well in the spring? By that Christmas, it was a sell-out.

What was so different about it? Marvin Glass had given Ideal a board game whose object was not to earn millions, or even to emerge with the sense of "winning." His new game did involve the travel of playing pieces across the board, as was traditional, but it also involved the construction of a Rube Goldberg device consisting of carefully molded plastic pieces. These resembled ramshackle gutters, stairways, concatenations of pipes, a shoe, a bathtub, and an old man in his bathing suit.

The real aim? To get everything connected and put together - then to set the bizarre structure in motion.

Much like Glass's success for Ideal of just two years before (see #24, page 85), the Mouse Trap board game was a machine. The same delight children had long felt in setting dominoes on end in long rows, just for the pleasure of knocking one over and watching the chain reaction take place, came into play in Ideal's new board game.

This strange assemblage worked. You turned a crank and set in motion a process that had the feeling of inevitability, the same feeling evoked by those clattering dominoes. It took time for the whole mechanism to finish working. It was an utter delight watching it work through the motions. The old boot that kicked, the heavy steel ball rolling back-and-forth down the uneven stairs, the old man who jumped off a springboard (he jumped better if he stood backwards, we discovered in our household), the precariously perched hard-plastic net that clattered down over the hapless playing piece, which was a stylized, pear-shaped creature with a looping, long tail ...

For the first time in decades, in the minds of children, Mickey was no longer the #1 Mouse.

TV's ROY ROGERS CAP GUN

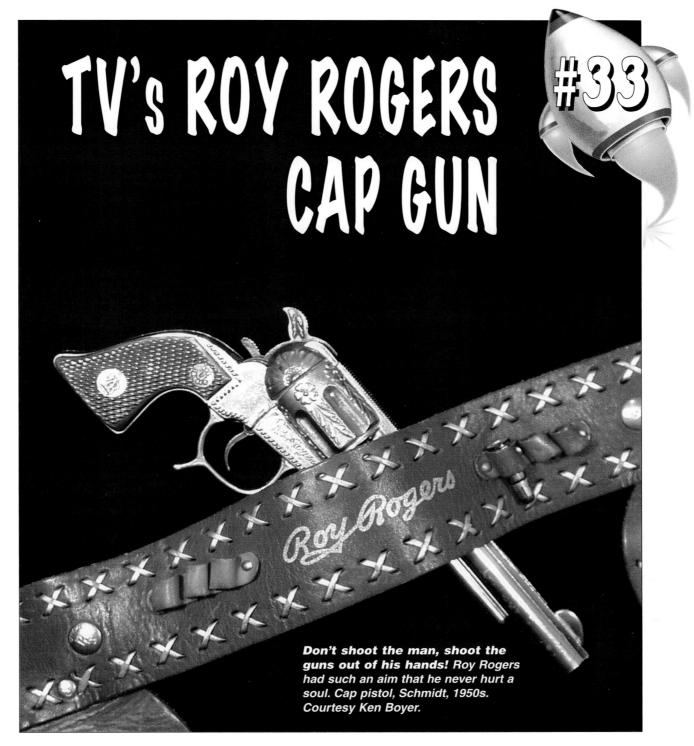

Don't shoot the man, shoot the guns out of his hands! *Roy Rogers had such an aim that he never hurt a soul. Cap pistol, Schmidt, 1950s. Courtesy Ken Boyer.*

While the career of Roy Rogers began in 1938 when he was cast as a last-minute replacement for Gene Autry by Republic Pictures, Roy and his onscreen family became a part of Boomer history through the usual medium: TV.

The man who would become Roy Rogers started a bit earlier - in Cincinnati, Ohio, in 1911, under the name Leonard Franklin Slye. After the family went west to California during the Depression, Leonard Slye started taking music jobs that paid little or nothing. Fame came slowly until his lucky break with Republic.

Movie theater operators ranked Roy Rogers as the top Western box office star from the years 1943 to 1954. By the end of this unprecedented run, the King of the Cowboys had ridden to the top of Western TV, beginning with *The Roy Rogers Show*, which originally aired 1951 through 1957. He returned for *The Roy Rogers and Dale Evans Show*, originally airing 1962 to 1963. He lent his name to restaurants, issued popular recordings, and opened a Roy Rogers museum in Apple Valley, California.

Most importantly, he hired a man named Art Rush for an agent. Rush was the man who made the childhood West what it was for millions of kids. He put together the contract that gave Roy and Dale full rights to their own names, voices, and likenesses for all commercial tie-ins.

Did this matter? Did it ever. Companies rushed to produce Roy Rogers, Trigger, and Dale Evans neckerchiefs, toy pistols, clothing, jewelry, games, novels, and song books. The contract probably made Rogers and Evans a little more willing to go along with it all.

Rogers' picture appeared on two and a half million cereal boxes from Post, and on the cover of comic books that sold at a rate of 25 million per year. Mutual Network's radio broadcasts attracted 20 million listeners a week, while the newspaper Roy Rogers comics reached more than three times that many fans. One year, Sears advertised more than 400 licensed Roy Rogers items for eager buyers scattered across America.

Rogers ranked second only to Walt Disney for the number of promotional tie-in items produced and sold. How did he do this? Just by playing

Two TV faithfuls. Dale Evans and Bullet, 60 mm. cream-colored plastic figures, Marx, 1950s. Courtesy Ken Boyer.

himself. Playing himself after he became Roy Rogers, that is. He legally changed his name to his screen name in 1942.

The Roy Rogers he played was consistently the easygoing, good-looking, good-singing, good-gunslinging Good Guy. And everyone thought: Good.

Singing cowboy. Roy Rogers was so famous for his singing that guitars bearing his name were still sought by youngsters in the late 1960s. Sears Toys, *1967-68.*

Not too hard - not too easy. Whitman made puzzles "for boys and girls who want REAL puzzles." Roy Rogers Jr. Jigsaw Puzzle, Whitman, 1950s.

In the face of overwhelming odds, run! *ABC-TV ran its spoof Western* Maverick *from 1957-62, featuring James Garner and Jack Kelly as Bret and Bart Maverick. The Maverick brothers found tongue-in-cheek trouble in such Old West towns as Apocalypse and Oblivion. Vinyl wallet, 1950s, and Hopalong Cassidy cap gun, 1950s.*

The other Good Guy TV cowboy of the times likewise had his start well before the war. Hopalong Cassidy was the invention of Clarence Mulford, who published his first Hopalong story in *Outing* magazine in 1906. Mulford followed it with dozens more stories and then novels about Hoppy, whose limp earned him his name, and the Bar 20 Ranch. Hoppy cussed, smoked, chewed tobacco, drank whiskey, and played cards. It might come as small surprise, then, to learn that Mulford cared little for the version that sprang to life on the silver screen. "Ludicrous," he said. Hollywood remade Hopalong just as it had remade so many other literary creations, with the help of William Boyd, who made a remarkable number of Hopalong Cassidy movies in the 1930s and '40s - 66 in all, with the last appearing in 1948.

Boyd's Hopalong became a true Boomer figure the following year when he hit the nation with not only a radio show but an NBC TV show, starting in June of 1949 and continuing through 1954.

The annual *Toy Fair* catalog advertised a great many popular items in 1951 including Monopoly ("Advertised in *Life*"), dish sets by Banner ("Advertised in *Life*"), Doepke's Heiliner Scraper ("Advertised in *Life*") and the Schoenhut Baby Grand Piano "with 18 true-pitch keys ... As advertised in *Life*."

Then it announced a set of puzzles. "Hard riding, fast-shootin' Hoppy fans, produce your own color TV show! Assemble these four puzzles and insert them into the realistic television screen. Watch Hoppy and Topper come alive in hard-hittin' action-packed scenes!"

They were just puzzles, but they were called the Hopalong Cassidy Television. Hoppy had arrived.

#34

DICK TRACY SQUAD Car #1

The Louis Marx Co. in the late 1940s and early '50s was still a happening company in the toy biz. It still knew how to bring out toys that were cheap, appealing, and appropriate to the times.

A good example of this is Marx's tin-litho Dick Tracy car, first issued, I believe, in 1949, the year Tracy and his patient fiancee Tess finally married.

Marx mined this toy idea deeply, issuing a small version called the Dick Tracy Squad Car No. 1, measuring about 7″ long, a medium-sized one also called Dick Tracy Squad Car No. 1, a little more than 11″ in length, and finally a large convertible called simply the Dick Tracy Squad Car, over 20″ long with no number.

The first two squad cars stuck to a basic pattern, with the smallest being the most simple of construction. It had three parts. The chassis was a bent piece of tin that held the axles and rear friction motor. This was held to the main body by a means not unusual in these postwar years: the body's lower edge folded out, then back in, making a lip into which the thin edges of the chassis slipped.

The body was a rounded, domed rectangle, shaped just enough to suggest the lines of the hood. It had an oval opening on top, where the roof fitted on. These toys had nothing fancy about them: just some metal with wheels. And nice lithography. The base color was green in both sizes of Squad Car No. 1. The smaller version had the words "Dick Tracy Friction Drive" on the hood and "Squad Car No. 1," "Police Dept.," and a yellow shield design with Tracy's profile on the sides. The trunk had a "305" license plate just below the round Marx logo.

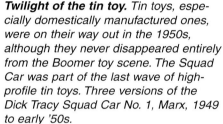

Twilight of the tin toy. *Tin toys, especially domestically manufactured ones, were on their way out in the 1950s, although they never disappeared entirely from the Boomer toy scene. The Squad Car was part of the last wave of high-profile tin toys. Three versions of the Dick Tracy Squad Car No. 1, Marx, 1949 to early '50s.*

The main attractions were the cartoon characters themselves, seen "through" the windows with the same flatness of the original comic strips: Tracy and Pat Patton in the front, while Tracy's ever-smoking sidekick Sam Catchem and yellow-haired Junior had the back. From the sides, you saw the sides of their faces. From the front, the fronts. From the back, the backs.

Simple toy? The experienced Marx workers threw these off at night while they were asleep. The toy market was entering a period of extremely intense competition, however. Even with Marx's long-standing prominence in the industry, the company had to make at least half an effort to do more than be bright and colorful. As a consequence, the larger version boasted a few more pieces: a separate grille, a rolled piece meant to represent a machine gun rising from the passenger side, and a plastic, nonfunctional spotlight on the roof. Tracy was still driving, while Sam now rode shotgun. Pat and another policeman occupied the back. More importantly, the friction motor was moved to sit beneath the hood. A slot in the tin beneath the gun let out sparks generated by the friction motor and a piece of flint. The original instructions were this simple: "1. Hold car firmly, push along floor and release. 2. Momentum set up in motor will propel it."

Did it work? Beautifully. Sparks spilled out abundantly over the hood, while the friction motor gave a satisfying grinding sound.

With all the distractions now available in catalog stores and dime stores, however, Marx had to keep improving the product. By 1951 the car was advertised as the Dick Tracy Siren Car, for a cost less than $2. "Siren wails, gun sparks, friction motor - Action-Noise Galore!" It now also came with an on-off switch on the back, since the rooftop searchlight now worked by battery power.

Two years later Marx, perhaps thinking the Dick Tracy car had run its course, introduced the G-Man Car. This had the features of Tracy's car - sirens, lights, and sparks - with the added attraction of a clockwork motor and option of going either in circles or straight ahead.

G-Man gave the car back to Tracy in 1954 when the Siren Squad Car returned a last time with the clockwork mechanism and the circle/straight option.

The mid-'50s saw many changes in the toy world. The passing of the simple tin Squad Car reflects the fact that it was part of the first wave of postwar toy innovation, and not one that would survive to rise with the next wave.

#35

BILLY BLASTOFF

America's First Boy in Space

Hybrid vigor. *While Eldon was best known for its slot cars, it made an important contribution to space toys with Billy Blastoff, a combination space-themed child doll and battery-operated toy. Although given relatively few accessories, Billy was the first successful fashion doll for younger boys. Eldon, late 1960s.*

In the second half of the 1960s, space action figures took over where plastic space people left off in the '40s and '50s. They came in all sizes and flavors. Moon McDare and his Space Mutt, produced by Gilbert in 1966, wore sterile NASA white tube suits with round space helmets. Unlike his real-life NASA counterparts, the 11″ McDare was billed as never being without his space gun, which shot soft pellets. Sears, in 1966, said of McDare: "Who knows what creatures he may find in outer space?"

In the same year, G.I. Joe also went into orbit, or at least came back from it in his "splashdown" set, with Mercury-style space capsule, rescue-party Frogmen, and zippered space suit of metallic plastic. A small 6″ figure, Major Matt Mason made a notable debut in 1967. He was a bendy, unlike other action figures. He appeared with his peg-wheeled Space Crawler and jet-propelled Space Sled. In the following year the Astro-Trac Space Missile Convoy, the eight-wheeled Space Mobile,

and Matt's double-sized friend Captain Lazer appeared.

Soon the semi-realistic space universe gained more dimension, with the addition of strange beings: the green, translucent Callisto ("transparent skull reveals his superior humanoid brain!"), and Scorpio, an insectoid alien. An even smaller figure than Major Matt went farther off the beaten path, fittingly enough for a space explorer. Billy Blastoff was "America's first boy in space," according to the ads. He wore a white, NASA-style suit with air tanks on the back that held batteries. These powered not Billy but his vehicles - a peg-wheeled crawler like Major Matt's, another crawler with treads, and a space capsule.

For a change, kids could play with a space figure that was not an adult make-believe character, but one they could imagine being right then and there. For with NASA's space efforts going full-bore by the end of the 1960s, they all wanted to go to the moon.

#36 AMERICAN SKYLINE

Builder of modern beauty. The American Skyline sets could be assembled into such wonders as the handsome "Elgo Apartments" or luxurious "Halsam Apartment Hotel." Sets were numbered from 1 to 96, with each one a progressively larger selection of the pieces. Set #93, for instance, contained about 800 pieces. Halsam/Elgo, 1950s.

Some kids were content to be frontier builders and got out their American Logs or Lincoln Logs. Others were content to be urban and suburban builders and got out their American Bricks. Yet others put their hands on their hips and went to Mom saying, "Listen, Mother. There have been modern skyscrapers in the United States since the beginning of this century. It's two generations and two World Wars later. So tell me. Where is my modern skyscraper building toy?"

Luckily for such architecturally sophisticated kids, a plastics company named Elgo teamed up with Halsam, a company best known as a maker of wooden blocks for tykes, and came out with a construction toy called American Skyline.

The toy must have seemed stunning to kids in the 1950s and '60s. As a mass-marketed architectural construction toy, in fact, American Skyline probably has never met its equal.

The building pieces were all an up-to-date antiseptic white. Posts fitted together for corners or vertical wall supports. Into slots in the posts, the pieces for the foundations, walls, windows, and doors slipped. The touch that made the buildings come alive was the use of plastic panes in the windows. The panes were separate sheets of translucent plastic, colored a deep sky-blue. With these panes inserted, the sky-reaching towers lost their

cathedral aloofness and seemed to breathe with life - with a distinctly Modern City life.

Other details were equally effective: stiff plastic sheets of checkerboard floor, flagpoles, flags, and - best of all to me as a child - staircases, wide and narrow. I could lay on my belly and watch tiny, imaginary feet going up and down those steps, hour after hour.

How To Build with American Skyline. *"Your American Skyline set is the most fabulous construction toy of its kind," the booklet trumpeted. Many young builders agreed. Since the building pieces were in HO scale, with 1/8 of a toy inch equaling one real foot, the sets also found favor among enthusiasts of HO trains, which were gaining in popularity in the postwar years.*

KLACKERS #37

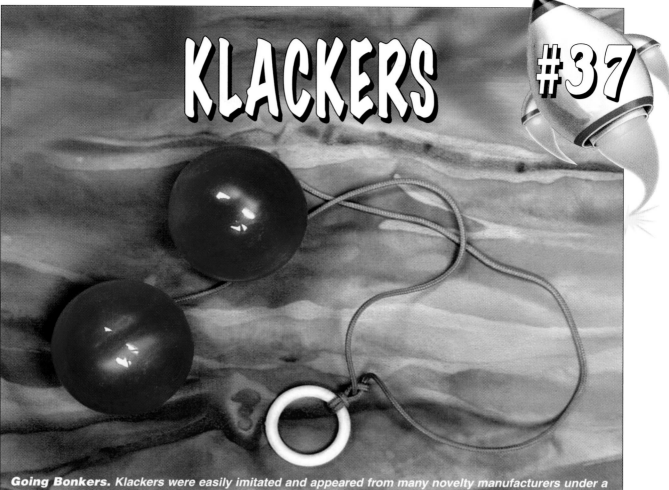

Going Bonkers. *Klackers were easily imitated and appeared from many novelty manufacturers under a variety of names. Pictured packaged are Zonker by C&K Novelty, and Ker-Knockers by the Ker-Knockers Corp. Loose is a pair of Klackers or similar brand item from the late 1960s to early 1970s.*

The thrill of the illicit, the banned, the black-listed: it still hangs over the mere word, "Klackers."

Klackers were simple toys designed for the irritation of parents, teachers, and other kids who were not allowed them. Consisting of a pair of hard-plastic balls connected by a yo-yo type string, with a tied-in ring at the middle for a grip, Klackers were excellently named: for they made noise, lots of it, sounding exactly like the name - clack clack clack - as the balls bounced against each other, perhaps gently at first, and then with increasing force, until the balls bounced not only against each other underneath the player's hand, but below, then

above, and below again, and above again, in rapid succession. This could be carried on for such a length of time, and with such force, that the balls cracked and went flying around in pieces, or simply detached from the strings, and went crashing through a window or into another kid's head.

In a time of anti-war protests, folk music, the Beatles, did kids protest when the ban came down? I don't recall myself. I only remember a greater sense of safety going down the school halls. So brainwashed was our entire generation with the notion of consumer safety that those of us already denied Klackers by our parents, for those same safety reasons, were mainly glad to see everyone else denied too.

#38 TV's RIN TIN TIN

Paint by Number

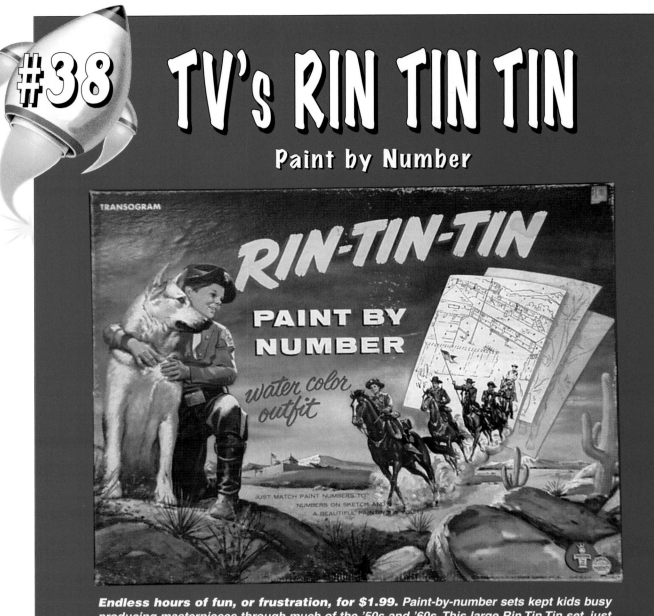

Endless hours of fun, or frustration, for $1.99. *Paint-by-number sets kept kids busy producing masterpieces through much of the '50s and '60s. This large Rin Tin Tin set, just over 16˝ x 13˝, included eight tubes of paint and nine "easy to color" pictures. Transogram, 1950s.*

Everyone, no matter if kid or adult, feels a touch of the miraculous when watching an animal show. The trained animals of showbiz, put onto the magic silver screen or rabbit-eared box, accomplished wonders. They saved people from fires, went to fetch the rescuing cavalry, or jumped on the Bad Man with the gun, diverting the bullet and making everything safe for the Good Guys again. They were champions of sweetness and light.

TV early embraced intelligent animal performers, from Zip the Monkey on *The Howdy Doody Show* to Trigger on *Roy Rogers*. The later Boomers

even ended up with a show centering around a trained porpoise named Flipper.

None could rival the dog heroes, however. Rin Tin Tin, a German Shepherd, was the greatly beloved leader of the pack, having started as a movie star in the 1920s. Although that Rinty died in 1932, his descendants included two of the dogs who played the role in the TV series, *The Adventures of Rin Tin Tin*, a Western that first aired in October 1954 and continued for nearly five years.

The Adventures of Rin Tin Tin was set in the Old West. An orphaned boy named Rusty and his

Rinty. *Among the many play sets issued by the Louis Marx Co. in the 1950s and '60s were Fort Apache sets, some equipped with small plastic figures of Rin Tin Tin. Marx, 1950s.*

The other dog star. *Later Boomers grew up knowing Lassie the way earlier Boomers knew Rin Tin Tin. Frame tray puzzle, Whitman, 1960s.*

trusty, heroic dog managed to get themselves adopted by a cavalry unit at Fort Apache, Arizona. In a violent world marked by gunfights and warfare against Indians, Rusty and Rin Tin Tin did their best to aid the cavalry and townsfolk of Mesa Grande.

Greatly beloved as a TV star, Rinty appeared on a variety of books, comic books, and activity toys. It was inevitable the animal star would be immortalized in art at last - art of the paint-by-number variety, of course. Paint-by-number sets sold in huge numbers through the Boomer years. While many now will deny having ever painted within the lines, these sets gave many youngsters hours of satisfying and no doubt artistic entertainment.

By the 1960s, many inexpensive paint-by-number sets gave budding artists the chance to work in more easily controlled acrylics. In the 1950s, however, youths attempting such kits as the Rin-Tin-Tin Paint by Number had to cope with more temperamental watercolor and tempera paints.

#39 ATOMIC MOBILE UNIT

Kids of the Boomer years grew up under a shadow new to history. The shadow grew from the fission of units of matter considered the building blocks of the universe: atoms.

Atom bombs flashed over New Mexico, then over Hiroshima and Nagasaki, ending the war in the Pacific and beginning a generation whose name, "Boomers," had an ironic reverberation to it.

The fission bomb that brought an already crippled Japan to raise the flag of surrender grew into a more powerful fusion bomb. At the same time, the ultimate weapon, as it was then seen, grew from being the proud result of consorted American ingenuity, sweat, and willpower, into a global fact of life:

for the Soviet Union soon tested a copycat device - only it was not a copycat. It was the real thing.

As the Cold War settled over the world, kept cold by the sun-hot temperatures the Bomb threatened, Americans found themselves faced with the prospect of global conflict, one that might come to their very doorsteps. Wendell Willkie promoted the idea of a small world, one in which people could travel from country to country in hours, and in which everyone's concerns were as one neighbor to another. Yet that same nearness and smallness could apply to war: for a bomber could just as easily drop an atom bomb in the middle of the Great Plains as above a museum dome in Hiroshima.

First-strike capability. Nothing less than atomic weapons empowered postwar children, who were born into a world capable, for the first time, of instant mass-destruction. The toy was renamed the ICBM Launching Truck in 1958. Ideal, mid-1950s.

Adults learned about making their own bomb shelters through the pages of *Popular Mechanics* and other handy-craft magazines, while children in schools went through regular drills to prepare for nuclear attack. "Duck and cover!" Those two

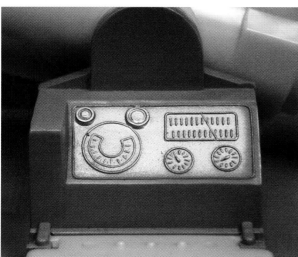

commands seemed sufficient, for a time. Black and white newsreels distributed through the school systems demonstrated the approach. All the children needed to do was get beneath their wood and steel school desks, with their heads beneath their hands.

How strange, then, that children thrilled to the word "atomic." It may have been that the best therapy for children was facing the threat directly. They could drive their Atomic Mobile Unit into the war zone, raise the rocket sites, set the trigger, and then launch the atomic missiles, striking decisive blows for Right and for Good, and for the American Way.

Children knew these concepts. They were featured in newsreels, in news programs, in their children's television programs, in their classroom history lessons. Best of all, they were featured in their toys.

"Best of all?" So it seemed at the time.

In the mid 1950s, Ideal was releasing a number of elaborate larger vehicle toys, with one of the best being its Atomic Mobile Unit, or Rocket Launching Truck, as it is called on its box. Measuring almost a foot long, the hard-plastic truck features a spring-loaded launcher that can be raised with a crank, red polyethylene rockets, and an ammo box beneath the nifty control panel at the rocket's side.

Why an ammo box? To store powder caps, which could be inserted into the "atomic" missiles, which then exploded when they struck their target.

#40 RAT FINK RINGS

Nastier than you - but cooler too. Rat Fink rings went onto the fingers of countless children who otherwise looked like normal suburban sorts. Store display card, 1960s.

Why did kids of the '60s respond so favorably to bulging blood-shot eyes, ratty shirts, and crooked teeth emerging from really wicked smiles?

We may never know. Maybe it had to do with the disillusionment of the 1960s. In one part of the adult world, an optimistic public watched the Kennedy Camelot spring into being, only to see it grow thin in its response to race riots, shudder beneath the threats of the Cuban Missile Crisis, and finally shatter with assassination. In another part, older brothers died in Vietnam or were returned strangely changed. In yet another, people dropped out and turned on, decried the War Machine and celebrated the plain old Human Condition.

Some of these last turned up occasionally with blood-shot eyes, ratty shirts, and ...

A connection might be drawn.

Whatever the origins and whatever the reasons for the attraction, kids shoved nickels into gumball machines for plastic Rat Fink charms, or shoved dimes across the counters of the new convenience stores springing up everywhere, to buy their Rat Fink rings. These rings were crazy to some, cool to others. To me, just as were the plastic Batman rings, they were Oh Wow Neat.

Who was Rat Fink? As a kid, I never knew. As a character, Rat Fink simply existed. I had no idea what he did. I had no idea, or at least no clear idea, what he represented. He was simply what he was. A rat. And a fink.

If I had ever given it thought, I might have perceived that Rat Fink was a kind of scummy guy. But that's just how he was. It was OK.

And even though the heyday of the dime store was quickly waning, this whip-tailed figure somehow rose into the Convenience Store Empyrean, to become a part of the magic pantheon already there.

It was quite the spectacle: Davy Crockett, Bullwinkle, Batman, Cat Woman, Wonder Woman, and... Rat Fink.

The face only a Mutha could love. Rat Fink charms, 1-1/4″ tall, 1960s.

CHAPTER 6

More Honorary Boomer Toys

The Honorary Baby Boomer Toys are toys that found their first measure of popularity before Boomers arrived on the scene. The top Honoraries, listed in Chapter Three, were Lincoln Logs, Monopoly, and Tinkertoys. The next three are equally famous.

THE GAME OF LIFE

The Road to Millions

Plastic people. *Players in the 1960s wandered the sinuous path through Life in pastel-colored plastic cars, filled with soft plastic people and their plastic children. The Game of Life, Milton Bradley, 1960s-70s.*

The great hit game of 1960 was in some ways brand-new, and in other ways, exactly 100 years old. In 1860 the young Milton Bradley took inspiration from an English board game and drew upon his skills as a designer and lithographer to create a new game he called The Checkered Game of Life. He made several hundred copies of the game and took a laborious trip in September from Springfield, Massachusetts, to New York City, where he found the stationery and department stores receptive.

He sold every example he had of this "highly moral game," and through the following winter sold 40,000 copies. When Milton Bradley revived the road-to-happiness game for its centennial year, it updated and revised it to include molded plastic landscape, a white plastic spinner, and plastic automobiles with plastic stick-people.

It revised the goal, too: It became the road-to-wealth game. Should it be surprising that Boomers now remember it almost as fondly as they do that other millionaire-making game?

The player with the most money Wins The Game! *The Game of Life had some of the best play money to be found. The face of Ransom A. Treasure graced the $500 note, and that of G.I. Luvmoney, the $20,000 bill. The face on the highest denomination bill, of $50,000? Bearded old Milton Bradley himself.*

VIEW-MASTER
The World's Fair Stereoscope

#5

Reel entertainment. *Most Boomers grew up with piles of View-Master reels such as this, with combinations of scenic and entertainment reels. This pile includes Sawyer's reels "Grand Canyon National Park" and "Mickey Mouse in 'The Brave Little Tailor'" alongside such new GAF reels as "Love Bug," "Bambi," and "Charlie Brown's Summer Fun." Reels from any period of View-Master history could be viewed through any viewer.*

Apopular parlor recreation early in the century involved stereoscopic viewers, through which photographic stereo images took on three dimensions. With people so accustomed to 3-D viewing, the advent of 35-millimeter filmstrips in the 1920s led naturally to stereoscopic filmstrips.

The first stereoscopic film viewer arrived from an unexpected source: the Rock Island Bridge and Iron Works in Rock Island, Illinois, which formed the Tru-Vue Co. around its new viewer and filmstrips, which consisted of 14 stereo frames.

Another unexpected source came up with the next: William Gruber of Portland, Oregon, who has been variously identified as a piano tuner or organ maker, two not incompatible professions. Gruber took his invention to Harold Graves, the president of Sawyer's, Inc., a company specializing in picture postcards. The two produced the first commercial View-Masters in time for a debut at the New York World's Fair in 1939, where they were sold as a tourist curio.

While Gruber's View-Master films featured only half as many stereo views as did Tru-Vue films, the films came in an incomparably convenient form: the frames were arranged in a circle, on a card easily popped in and out of the viewer. The cards had an appealing name, too, that evoked the glamorous film industry. Sawyer's called them "reels."

View-Master, sold through stationery and photo shops, appealed largely to the adult market, with Sawyer's reels providing 3-D images of national parks and other scenic wonders up into wartime.

Much as Walt Disney film makers found themselves busy with instructional films related to the war effort, View-Master photographers worked on educational and training reels for the government. Some reels, for instance, helped Army gunners train for anti-aircraft range estimation, and Navy personnel train for ship-to-ship identification.

Even if Tru-Vue came first, View-Master came to ascendancy after the war. Sawyer's issued color reels, forcing Tru-Vue to introduce "Stereochromes." Then, in 1951, it bought its competitor and moved Tru-Vue production from Illinois to Oregon. This allowed Sawyer's to move decisively into the children's market, Tru-Vue hav-ing already sewn up 3-D rights to Walt Disney Productions' animated characters. Sawyer's put Tru-Vue filmstrips onto cards, cutting the number of frames from 14 to seven, and eventually phased out the company.

Through the Boomer years, View-Master reels covered every desirable subject imaginable, from cartoon favorites to such TV pop figures as Pinky Lee, Captain Kangaroo, Rin Tin Tin, Hopalong Cassidy, the Lone Ranger, Roy Rogers, Flipper, the Munsters, the Green Hornet, and *Lost in Space* characters.

A particularly happy marriage of film media occurred in the early 1950s, when Sawyer's produced promotional reels in cooperation with the National Screen Service. The reels naturally promoted the new and fabulously hip 3-D films of the times. The films and View-Master reels included Warner Brothers' *House of Wax* with Vincent Price, Universal's *It Came From Outer Space*, and Metro-Goldwyn-Mayer's *Kiss Me Kate* of 1953; Columbia's *Jesse James vs. the Daltons* of 1954; and R.K.O.'s *Son of Sinbad*, another Price film of 1955.

General Aniline and Film Corp. (GAF) bought View-Master in 1966 and introduced such innovations as the Talking View-Master and the View-Master Projector.

I remember as a child being a little frustrated at these reels. They were fascinating and fun - yet they ended so quickly. Then you had to put in another one. This must have worked in Sawyer's and then GAF's favor. Kids always needed new reels and Sawyer's and GAF were always happy to provide them.

Also working in their favor was the long-lived utility of Gruber's original View-Master. Sawyer's never changed its fundamental design, which meant that if a child in 1969 was given a new reel, but only had a Bakelite 1939 Model A viewer handy, the two would still match.

Unlike much of the rest of the toy industry, which relied on constant change for survival, View-Master at its core never changed. That saved it, and made it a fixture in the childhoods of not only the Boomers but of their own children and grandchildren.

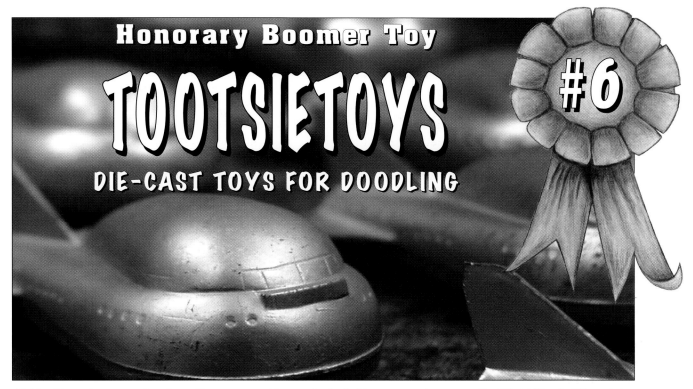

Honorary Boomer Toy
TOOTSIETOYS
DIE-CAST TOYS FOR DOODLING

#6

Old-fashioned space adventure. *These spaceships are typical of toys appearing soon after World War II. Although in a sense "futuristic," the 3-1/4″ long toys were made of a heavy die-cast zinc alloy instead of plastic, and evoked the 1930s even in design, which was modeled after Buck Rogers vehicles, although unlicensed. Midgetoy, late '40s.*

Sometimes toys need no gimmicks. After all, kids start out with one power that puts all the rest to shame - the power to imagine things.

Thus the toys that left room for the imagination - that didn't drive away every instinct toward creativity and invention - sometimes proved the most rewarding to children, especially when they had to play, as most children did, with the same toy day after day, week after week, month after month.

At the Dowst Co. in Chicago before World War II, the company president decided that already famous die-cast Tootsietoys were "for doodling, not collecting." The company focused on simple, sturdy toys that conjured up the adult life of driving cars and trucks, flying airplanes, and riding trains, which all kids yearned for. In the 1950s and '60s, being adult meant being a part of a world of transportation options of every kind.

Sandboxes and sidewalks and driveways: Tootsietoys went everywhere. An archaeologist 100 years from now would be able to find this out from looking at the toys themselves. An overwhelming number of them today are not just rubbed and worn - but heavily worn down, often to the point of having only residues of the original paint left in the cracks and corners.

Tootsietoy's parent company Dowst had roots in the 1800s. More importantly, it was in the prestig-ious position of being the inventor of the die-cast toy car, which it introduced in the 1920s. It prospered in the toy world and was well positioned in 1945 to hold onto its popularity.

Other prewar die-cast toy companies survived and sometimes thrived in the postwar era, including Hubley and Manoil. One small company, Midgetoy, entered the fray just after the war and offered yet more stylized, Deco-inspired vehicles. It gave Tootsietoy serious competition for two decades.

Tootsietoys gradually grew smaller through the Baby Boomer years, so that older Boomers fondly remember playing the hell out of 6″ cars and trucks, while middle Boomers ground down the tires of a nice mixture of 6″ and 3″ cars. The tail-end Boomers found themselves offered the Jam Pacs, which were collections of 1″ toy cars and trucks. They played with them happily, no matter the size.

Road favorites in miniature. *Tootsietoy specialized in providing inexpensive models of contemporary cars and trucks for floor-level motorists. Ford pickup, 3″, first introduced in 1949.*

CHAPTER 7

Flip Your Wig!

THE BEATLES FLIP YOUR WIG GAME

GEORGE

JOHN

RINGO

PAUL

ROLL AGAIN

PUT BACK BEATLE CARD

TAKE A BEATLE CARD

THE **BEATLES**
FLIP YOUR WIG GAME

Totally flipped! *With such lyrics as "I want to hold your hand" available, Milton Bradley might have come out with a hip version of poker. Instead it gave the nation's infatuated millions a relatively simple board game they could play and sigh over. Milton Bradley, 1964.*

In 1964, the first Beatles song entered the U.S. singles charts at number 35, only ten days after its release. "I Want To Hold Your Hand" was the fastest-breaking, fastest-selling record in Capitol Records history. The Beatles swiftly became a major force in making kids throw aside their toys in a rash rush to grow up - albeit in a Mod kind of way.

Even so, the Beatles became an influence in toys through the remainder of the '60s - not only toy instruments but dolls, Yellow Submarine toys, puzzles, and games.

Milton Bradley lost no time in bringing out The Beatles Flip Your Wig Game promptly in 1964. The game itself was fairly sedate, as board games go. The pieces went around in a circle and the cards in the center determined the progress of each player. The magic was in the art, which was nothing more - and needed to be no more - than color photography of the young Beatles themselves.

The magic was also in the role-playing, for each player could choose a piece that represented an individual player: John, Paul, George, or Ringo. Each player had to accumulate the cards that matched the character: a portrait, a signature, a hit record, and a musical instrument.

Of course, only four could play.

Meanies Invade Pepperland. *Only a few years after their bright-eyed, youthful beginnings, the Beatles introduced the world to psychedelia. The Beatles Yellow Submarine Picture Puzzle, Jaymar, 1968.*

1968! *German poster artist Heinz Edelmann created the stylistically diverse yet unfailingly appealing images of the Beatles'* Yellow Submarine. *In this detail from the 1968 Jaymar puzzle, a realistic girl weeps at the oppressions of the cartoonish Meanies.*

ETCH A SKETCH #42

Doodle Dialing

Etch A Sketch MAGIC SCREEN

MAGIC Etch A Sketch SCREEN

HOURS OF fascinating FUN FOR THE ENTIRE FAMILY

PRINT! write! DRAW!

Just SHAKE TO ERASE

DOODLE DIALING IS FUN FOR ALL

unlimited design possibilities

SKETCH · ERASE AND SKETCH AGAIN

Everything but dot the i. *When Ohio Art released its "family-tested toy," it promised that "Etch A Sketch does everything but dot the i," an acknowledgment of the fact that everything drawn on the toy had to be connected by the single, roving line. A properly dotted i was an impossibility. Ohio Art, 1960s.*

Of all the companies that attempted a toy that looked like a TV, none succeeded the way Ohio Art did with its Magic Etch A Sketch Screen.

"Hours of fascinating fun for the entire family - Doodle Dialing - unlimited design possibilities!" Ohio Art raved on the packaging of its toys.

Paul Chasse, a garage mechanic and general tinkerer who lived near Paris, invented his L'Ecran Magique (Magic Screen) in 1958. It used a mixture of aluminum powder and plastic beads with a metal stylus guided by twin knobs. Since it was clever, needed no batteries, and had no loose parts to be lost, he figured it might be worth a tidy sum.

Most toy companies thought otherwise - including Ohio Art - the first time around. When successive levels of Ohio Art executives were later won over by a prototype, they took it to the boss, not realizing the boss had already said no to Chasse once.

This time he said yes. Ohio Art issued the toy as being "As New as 1960." It seemed new for years to come.

#43 TV's THE MAN FROM U.N.C.L.E. GAME

Imprisoned in THRUSH head-quarters! The Ideal Toy Corp. capitalized on the super-spy phenomenon with its The Man from U.N.C.L.E. Game. "The word is out," Ideal told its apprehensive players. "THRUSH is planning something big. Quickly, U.N.C.L.E. is alerted and counters by assigning men to capture the THRUSH chiefs!" Players, beset by THRUSH agents at every point, were given their missions: "You must battle your way back to U.N.C.L.E. headquarters through overwhelming odds!" Ideal, 1965.

"'Let me get out of this lei and into something more comfortable,' was what she'd said. And then abruptly she was dead. Napoleon Solo stood immobile, staring at the bewitching corpse without a face. Deceptively slender, no more than of medium height, he had the smart appearance of a young intern, a Madison Avenue account exec. He looked like anything except what he was: a diamond-hard, exhaustively-trained enforcement agent for perhaps the most important secret service in the world, the United Network Command for Law and Enforcement. His jacket and slacks were impeccably tailored with a Brooks Brothers quality, but the disarming cut concealed a strapped-down Berns-Martin shoulder holster housing its hidden U.N.C.L.E. Special, 37 ounces of deadly weapon, including silencer."

Harry Whittington's opening for one of the Man from U.N.C.L.E. books of the mid-1960s captures much of the bizarre, tangled and far-fetched nature of television's greatest spy series. Running from September 1964 through January 1968, NBC's answer to the popular James Bond movies combined to good effect the high-tech thrills and essential silliness that seemed intrinsic to the super-spy genre. Far more than the TV series I Spy or Get Smart, The Man from U.N.C.L.E. balanced its spoof element with an intense fantasy world of danger and intrigue.

Part of its success came from the light-and-dark main characters of dark-haired and calmly urbane American agent Napoleon Solo, played by Robert Vaughn, and the blond, quiet, and mysterious Russian agent Ilya Kuryakin, played by David McCallum, who together combated the evils of the international crime syndicate THRUSH.

While most kids played being Napoleon and Ilya by simply pretending they were handsome and incredibly cool (or incredibly beautiful and cool, if The Girl from U.N.C.L.E.), others were lucky enough to have plastic guns, badges, or Marx plastic figures to evoke the colorful and wonderfully weird show.

In some ways games were the best ways of returning to favorite TV shows, for they could be played again and again.

And, as on TV, the good guys could always win.

WHEE-LO

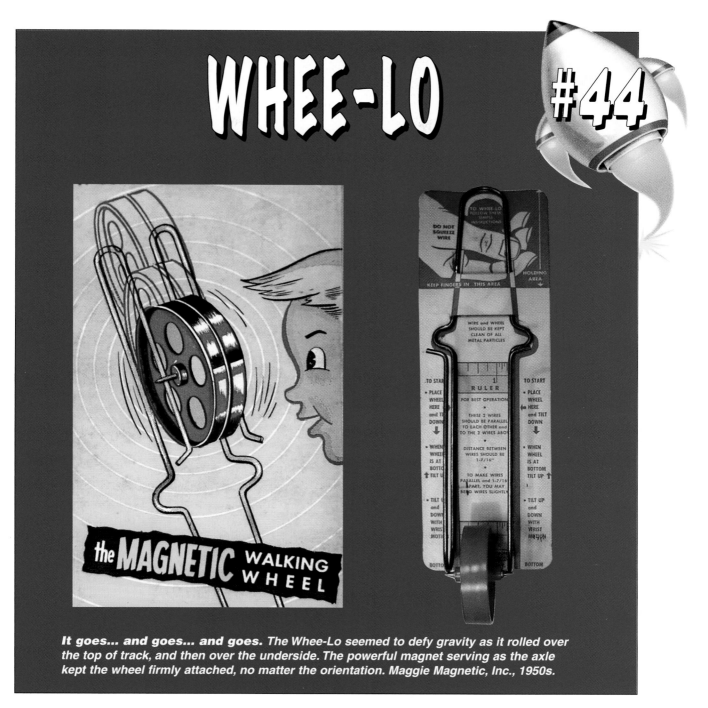

It goes... and goes... and goes. *The Whee-Lo seemed to defy gravity as it rolled over the top of track, and then over the underside. The powerful magnet serving as the axle kept the wheel firmly attached, no matter the orientation. Maggie Magnetic, Inc., 1950s.*

Not every toy that made a hit during the Boomer years received huge promotions in *Life* magazine or on TV. Some simply appeared, were accepted, did their job - which was to entertain someone for a while - and then disappeared.

Maggie Magnetic, Inc., of Paterson, New Jersey, produced one such toy that turned into a minor hit of the late 1950s: the Maggie Whee-Lo, consisting of a thick wire track, a plastic wheel, and a heavily magnetized spoke that ran through the wheel and connected it to the contorted track.

It amused people, watching the wheel roll rapidly up and down. The wheel turned and rolled along the top of the track, looped over the bend, even if it was upside-down, and then passed around to the other side. It went back and forth, and up and down, for as long as the person cared to stand playing with the toy. The wheel hummed as it went more quickly.

In seeming to defy gravity, it easily absorbed a child long enough for a storekeeper to make the sale.

Maggie Magnetic issued a more complex version of the toy to capitalize on American furor over Russia's having been the first to launch an artificial satellite into Earth orbit. With its

The space race brought home. *America's astonishment at Russia's satellite program, which included the launch of a living passenger into orbit around Earth, found its way down to child level with this toy. Sputnik, Maggie Magnetic, Inc., late 1950s.*

Sputnik, the Magnetic Satellite, the company turned the hand-held track into a circle on the outer side of which the magnetized wheel, representing an American satellite, could run. On the inside of the track, Maggie Magnetic placed a hollow plastic ball, representing Russia's satellite. Inside was a flat plastic dog, one of Russia's animal cosmonauts. The child's hand fit over the handle in the center of the circle, where it was hidden by a plastic hemisphere painted to look like the Earth. The Americas were showing, of course.

"Run your own exciting Space Race! Watch our Satellite chase the little traveller 'round and 'round the Outer Space Orbit!"

Maggie Electric knew exactly what nerve it was striking with those words: America's rawest one.

The first Twister. *This exceptionally enjoyable spinning toy incorporated, for no doubt the first time in toy history, the Moebius strip. The "spinning mystery wheel" whirls first inside the track, then outside. Maggie Magnetic, Inc., 1958.*

AURORA MONSTER KITS

The Models of Midnight

#45

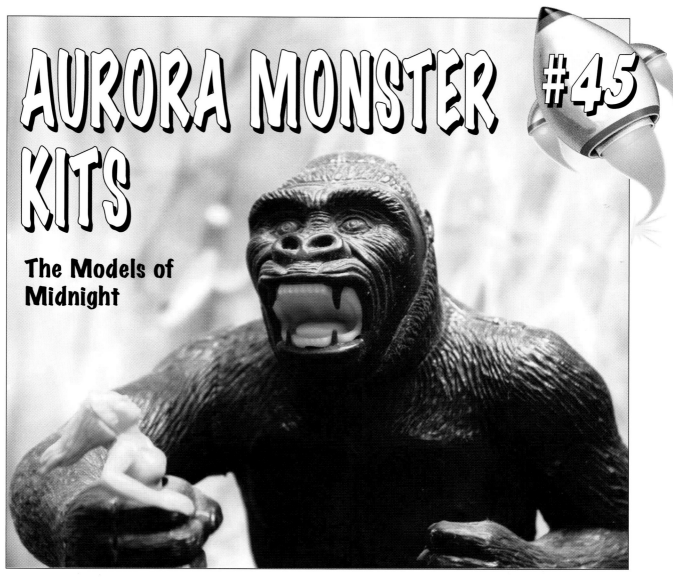

Lord of Skull Island. *King Kong found renewed popularity in the 1960s, helped in no small part by a dynamic model kit. Aurora, 1967.*

Model building went through a boom through the 1950s and '60s, thanks to modern plastics - and thanks too, to Friday late night and Saturday afternoon TV.

Monster movies, as old as movie-making itself, proliferated in postwar years, spurred by 1950s mass fears about the Bomb, atomic radiation, and Red infiltration. By the 1960s, the same low-budget parade of the bizarre and ugly helped fill the gray air times around the last weekday midnight and the sleepy downslide from Saturday noon. Kids must have sensed that these monsters and fright films reflected something important about the world in which they were growing up. They attached themselves to the monsters as they would to friends. They wanted them in their lives, in their houses, in their rooms.

Monster madness. *Monsters of every kind were in vogue during the 1960s. Makers of low-end toys made sure the supply never stopped. Monsters, Palmer Plastics, 1960s.*

Monster rods! *Monsters and hot-rods went hand-in-hand in the 1960s, with everyone from Rat Fink to Godzilla burning rubber in model kit form. Some of the weirdest were Aurora's Mummy's Chariot, Dracula's Dragster, and Godzilla's Go-Cart. Aurora Plastics Corp., 1966.*

Model companies did the best job of responding to that desire - especially Aurora, an enterprising and adventurous company that not only gave kids models of TV figures from *The Man from U.N.C.L.E.*, *Lost in Space*, and *Star Trek*, and such superheroes as Batman, Superman, and Spider-Man, but hordes of horrors: the Forgotten Prisoner, the Bride of Frankenstein, the Hunchback of Notre Dame, Dr. Jekyll as Mr. Hyde, Godzilla, Salem Witch, the Mummy, the Frankenstein Monster, Wolf Man, the Creature from the Black Lagoon, Dracula, Rodan, the Phantom of the Opera.

And then the goofy stuff: The Munsters, Dracula's Dragster, the Mummy's Chariot (a hot-rod with ancient Egyptian snakes writhing from the engine block), and Godzilla's Go-Cart.

I'M THE NEW TRUCK INSPECTOR.

Toy fancier. *Monster card, 1960s.*

Millions of kids grew up spending hours with Aurora's Fireproof Styrene Plastic Cement, One Hour Humbrol Plastic Enamel, and the Monster Paint Package ("Look for the package with the Haunted House!").

Model-building also created a social division among kids: those who sniffed "airplane glue" and those who said they never did.

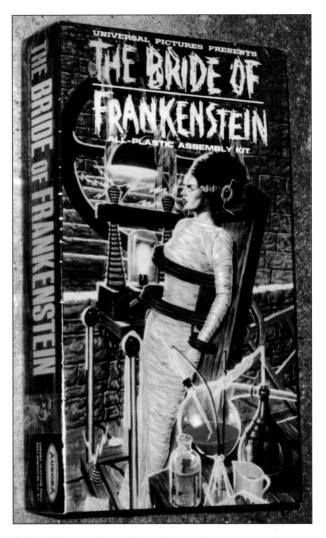

Scientific marriage. *One of Aurora's more complex monster model kits, the Bride of Frankenstein included such rewarding details for the modeler as "discarded body parts," "severed hand," the bandaged Bride herself, and even a plastic "electric bolt." Aurora Plastics Corp., 1965.*

COLORFORMS

They stick like magic!
The Malibu Barbie Dress-Up Set arose from the happy marriage of fashion doll and accessory toy. "Barbie, Francie and Skipper have their own wardrobes and enjoy trading certain outfits," says the instruction sheet. "Just press down the Colorforms. They stick like magic." The Malibu Barbie set appeared in time to charm the last of the Boomers and the first of the post-Boomer children. Colorforms, 1972. Photo courtesy Sharon Korbeck.

Dancing Dolls. *While Colorforms was a pioneer in the use of vinyl in toys, it did acknowledge tradition in such sets as Dancing Dolls, which used heavy cardboard figures of ballet dancers with a wardrobe made of coated paper. The clothes attached to the plastic-surfaced dancers with adhesive tabs. Suspended from elastic bands, the figures could be made to dance on the stage hidden behind the striped panels. Colorforms/United Productions of America, 1950s.*

Girls not playing with a Barbie in 1959 may have been too busy anyway with a different kind of fashion toy: Colorforms. They may even have had the new Sleeping Beauty set, released to coincide with the Walt Disney animated movie.

While paper dolls never died out in popularity, even enjoying a renaissance of sorts with the regular releases of Betsy McCall paper dolls in the pages of *McCalls* magazine, Colorforms were the true Boomer incarnation of paper dolls. The pieces were all flat - and usually vinyl. The sets came with a backing board, usually decorated with figures who could be dressed and accessorized, and the colorful vinyl cutouts themselves. Better than paper dolls, the vinyl tended to cling, which eliminated worry about folding and tearing tabs, as happened with paper dolls.

A New York City couple, Harry and Patricia Kislevitz, invented the toys after receiving a fortuitous (if odd) gift from a friend of a roll of pliable vinyl. Their simple observation that cutout pieces stuck to the semi-gloss paint in their bathroom made toy history.

The idea of packaging candy in toy-like containers was nothing new in the 1950s. For decades, candy makers had made attractive glass animals, boats, and cars to hold sweets.

In the late 1920s, Austrian Eduard Haas III created an intense peppermint candy, which he called Pez as a kind of shortening of the German word for peppermint, "pfefferminz." Eventually it came to be sold in a package not toy-like at all: it resembled a cigarette lighter, which helped sell the mints as anti-smoking aids.

When the company tried to market the product in the United States, it failed to attract much attention. Haas changed the candy to fruit flavors, even while retaining the peppermint-evocative name, and changed the containers. In some cases the entire Pez dispenser was reshaped, as was the case with early Santa Claus and Space Robot dispensers. More often the company simply changed the top of the dispenser, which retained its cigarette-lighter thinness.

Those tops made the dispensers immensely attractive, for they featured the heads of famous cartoon characters, fanciful animals, and such miscellaneous oddities as whistles and eyeballs.

Kris Kringle. *From the late 1800s well into the Boomer period, candy containers often appeared from manufacturers in the guise of toys. While glass was the material of choice for most of the century, the postwar rise of plastic led to an increasing number of toy-like candy containers in the new material. The most famous of these were Pez dispensers. Pez, made in Austria, 1950s. Courtesy Mindy Borchardt.*

TV's THE ADDAMS FAMILY GAME

Altogether ooky. Composer Vic Mizzy wrote lines that vied with toy jingles in the minds of the TV-bound children of the 1960s. "They're creepy and they're kooky, mysterious and spooky, they're altogether ooky: The Addams Family." Former child star Jackie Coogan, here peeking from behind the chair, was turned down for the role of Uncle Fester until he showed up bald and dressed to resemble the crazed man of Charles Addams' original cartoons. Ideal, 1964.

While many of the names everyone came to know and love were not to come until later, the characters who were to become TV's Gomez, Morticia, Uncle Fester, Wednesday, Pugsley, Grandmama, and Lurch first appeared in the sophisticated pages of *The New Yorker*.

Charles Addams stood out among the cartoonists of that often witty and usually elevated magazine. His cartoons, many of them set within a moldering, many-spired mansion, took a distinctly grotesque and often morbid turn.

John Astin, Carolyn Jones, Jackie Coogan, Ken Weatherwax, Lisa Loring, Blossom Rock, and Ted Cassidy played in the starring roles when the cartoon inspired the 1964-66 TV show. Cassidy also played the role of the helpful hand named Thing. Felix Silla occasionally turned up as the all-hair Cousin ITT.

The Addams Family and its competitor *The Munsters* fit neatly into the burgeoning interest in all things monstrous on the part of America's youth.

Ideal's The Addams Family Game gave kids of the time the chance to wander a little deeper into America's most morbidly funny mansion.

"The moon, half hidden behind dark gray clouds, casts weird shadows around the Addmas Mansion," the 1964 game tells players. "It is a perfect night for the Addams Family to go on their annual midnight picnic at the nearby cemetery. The only trouble is that the family is scattered all over the house. You must have them meet in front of the house so that they can all leave together."

A house with a carnivorous houseplant, Wednesday's headless doll, a dashing and debonair gentleman in love with a pallid but beautiful witch, a wide-eyed lunatic capable of lighting light bulbs with his ears...

In a world gone half crazy anyway, it made its own kind of sense.

Thing. *While mechanical banks had played an important part in pre-Boomer childhoods, relatively few came to prominence after the war. An exception was a plastic battery-operated bank that took advantage of the popularity of the Addams Family's most helpful hand. Thing Bank, 1964. Photo courtesy Krause Publications.*

Astronaut's dream girl. *TV comedies involving the fantastic also included* Bewitched *and* I Dream of Jeannie, *the latter being especially interesting for featuring the U.S. space program in its back-story.* I Dream of Jeannie Game, Milton Bradley, 1965.

#49 SPEED KING

Dime store King. One of Renwal's dime store hits was its series of hard-plastic versions of the Speed King race car. Renwal, 1949 to mid-1950s.

Plastic toy cars started rolling out of factories a few years before the war from toy companies including Kilgore and Lapin. Those in the plastics industry saw this as a sign of things to come. Plastic was a happening medium. It had a versatility that made it a perfect match with the toy industry.

Plastic remained only a vision until the end of the war. Soon thereafter, hard-plastic airplanes, ships, trucks, cars, trailers, and helicopters started filling dime store bins and even appearing in Christmas catalogs. Plastic became so popular and useful a material that even pressed steel and cast metal outfits such as Wyandotte and Hubley made use of some plastic vehicles in their toy assortments.

One of the first companies off the postwar starting block was Renwal Manufacturing Co., which had operated out of a factory on Broadway in New York City since 1939, originally as a manufacturer of glass knives. It leapt into plastic toy making in 1945, when the company turned out hard-plastic World War II airplanes. In the following years a wide variety of plastic vehicle toys appeared, some of them complex affairs with multiple movable (and easily breakable) parts, others no more than hollow shapes of cars with wheels beneath.

Renwal's "Motorcycle with Sidecar Construction Kit," for instance, appealed to the kids with a can-do attitude. The kit's eight pieces of colorful hard plastic snapped together into a toy. "You be the mechanic," the package exhorted the child. "Build it - fix it - take it apart - put it back together again!" Competing companies Ideal and

Marx also made multi-piece fix-it and take-apart toys, perhaps as a challenge to the patience of parents.

Few plastic toys captured the imagination as well as a more simple toy made by the company: the Speed King. This racing car had a blunt nose, tires covered with prominent, swept-back, teardrop-shaped fenders, and a small, forward-placed covered cockpit. While the smaller versions came in only one color, the larger sizes had different colors for the bodies and fenders, and often simple paint applications.

Speed Kings offered everything an imaginative kid could want. Shiny and bright, they evoked the excitement of the race track. They were made of that wonder material, plastic.

And they were something else, too: cheap.

Released in a variety of sizes from 1949 into the mid-1950s, these breathtaking baubles sold, at tops, for $.79 which bought the biggest version, more than 10″ long. It came with the bonus of a whining friction motor.

What if you didn't have $.79? How about a nickel? For that, you could have the smallest version, a little over 3″ long.

Dime stores aisles had plenty of companies to fill them with bright, colorful, hard-plastic toys. Venerable toy makers Marx and Ideal produced more complex toys, sometimes costing as much as $2 or $3, while Thomas, Acme, Banner, Wannatoy, Pyro, and Renwal fought to fill the $.10 to $.39 bins.

SPACE PEOPLE #50

Triumphant science! Space would be conquered, many Americans believed in the early 1950s, despite dismissive noises often made in many governmental and scientific circles. These dime store best sellers helped bring the future thrillingly near for countless children. Space People and vehicle, Archer Plastic, early 1950s.

The early days of plastic had several surprise best sellers hidden among the dime store aisles.

At least in part because of the saucer craze, space-adventure movies, and the growing popularity of pulp science fiction magazines, when Archer Plastics released its colorful, 4″ Space People in the early 1950s, they were an instant hit.

The Space People were stylized people in angular space suits and clear plastic dome-helmets. With wide faces and Modigliani features, the Space People held heroic positions reminiscent of social-realist Eastern Bloc statuary.

Why such triumphant postures? America had just emerged victorious from a war won, to a large degree, through technological innovations. Even if Germany had developed rockets to send over London and had initially beaten the Allies senseless with its advanced armored tanks, America's victory came thanks to the quick growth of a military industry at home.

The dream of space was steadily gaining in popularity - and if people were ever to go to space, Americans knew it would have to be, as many writers of the time put it, a "conquest."

In those years just after the war, conquest was something Americans thought they knew something about.

CHAPTER 8

The Life-Size Kitchen & Electric Football

THE LIFE-SIZE KITCHEN

All the conveniences. *Not all the kitchens of Boomer youth were made of lithographed metal. Some were made of even cheaper board, with plastic handles and faucets. The Life-Size Kitchen, however, was a deluxe five-piece set of metal appliances for young homemakers. Wards, 1960s.*

America's love affair with "convenience" intensified in the 1930s, becoming so obsessive it led some to observe that everyone was working too hard saving up for labor-saving gadgets.

Convenience was important nowhere more than in the kitchen. Partly through the influence of catalog stores, kitchens rose in prominence from closed-door, my-eyes-only rooms to the gathering place for friends and neighbors. For kitchens were starting to fall subject to house-decorating whims. As catalog stores spread their vision of what Middle Class lives could look like, kitchens increasingly became sources of pride within the household.

The modern kitchen remained utilitarian - but now it was beautiful in its usefulness, with shiny surfaces, linoleum floors and counters, and color-coordinated appliances.

Just as real-life kitchens turned this corner, so did play ones. Catalog stores gave the same care and attention to younger homemakers, issuing child-size, color-coordinated kitchen sets. These were not the foot-high tin versions suitable for larger dolls, such as the ones made by Wolverine. These were large appliances, three and four feet high. Children could stand at them without crouching down. All sets had the same components - cupboards, refrigerators, ovens, and sinks. Children could store canned and dry goods, open the fridge for a Coke, cook in the stove, and do the dishes. Many times the insides of the doors, especially of the refrigerators and freezers, had beautiful lithography depicting foodstuffs.

Never again were children embarrassed to have a friend step into their kitchen.

It worked out well for the catalog stores, too. What better way, after all, for those stores to prepare young homemakers for the responsibilities of adulthood?

Which would include the purchasing of identical appliances, only now scaled for adults, not children.

#52 SNOOPY AND THE RED BARON

Marbles, for Peanuts. *In Snoopy and the Red Baron, one child tried to sneak marbles down the plastic raceway, while the other tried to catch only "his" color inside the doghouse, the roof of which opened for catching, or closed for blocking marbles. The number of* Peanuts *toys and games greatly increased in the last years of the Boomer period. Snoopy and the Red Baron, Milton Bradley, 1970.*

Intelligent and well drawn, the *Peanuts* comic strips by Charles Schultz attracted readers young and old from the time of their debut in newspaper funny pages of the 1950s. Yet they never reached their full measure of popularity until a series of specials on TV featured the same characters. Slowly *Peanuts* toys began to appear: vinyl dolls, games, puzzles, and tin tops and drums from Chein.

The strip changed through the years, introducing new characters and sometimes letting others slip away. The basic cast, however, remained the same: Charlie Brown, Lucy, Linus, Schroeder the musical genius, and Pig Pen.

Increasingly through the years, the *Peanuts* strips focused on the imaginary life of Charlie Brown's dog Snoopy, who from the beginning was the jolt of lightning, laughter, and occasional lunacy in that child-high world.

A true postwar child, Snoopy lived in a world deeply affected by the fact of World War II. In his mind, he "relived" his days in the war, sometimes as foot soldier, and often as pilot of his airborne doghouse, which he flew against the dreaded Red Baron.

In this he was no different from the millions of boys in their sandboxes, who even by the 1960s were still playing with plastic soldiers colored green

and gray, to depict the Americans versus the Germans. In some ways, Snoopy was a child Walter Mitty, living a life detached from the ordinary one, sustained by illusion. In this, he may have helped the generation see itself.

For eventually we grew and learned, and discovered that the romantic picture we cradled in our minds of World War II was illusory. Daily in the 1960s, radio announcers gave us body counts, as if quietly relating the changing score of a years-long ball game. Increasingly we saw war as a disturbing and incredibly repellent reality - especially for those of us growing up and truly, deeply not wanting to grow up, because growing up meant facing the draft.

Snoopy had just been playing us all along. We were the ones atop those flying doghouses, our fists raised against the comic-book enemy.

The number of *Peanuts* items rose gradually through the end of the Boomer years, so much so, in fact, that they may actually be more characteristic toys of the post-Boomer generation. Even so, a great many Boomers grew up feeling the *Peanuts* gang, and especially Snoopy, belonged to them, helped in no small part by games such as Snoopy and the Red Baron, a marble game that submerged kids in the beagle's world of wartime fantasy.

TV's CAPTAIN VIDEO PREMIUMS

DuMont, the company that offered the world its first all-electronic television receiver, operated a pioneer broadcasting network in the late 1940s and early '50s. The flagship of the network's programming was aptly named *Captain Video and His Video Rangers*, which started off as a daily, radio-style children's program. Greatly popular among children for its futuristic adventures and props, and among parents for the Captain's regular Ranger-to-Ranger talks to his viewers, Captain Video inspired the other space-opera TV serials of the '50s, *Space Patrol* and *Tom Corbett*.

The Captain was played by Richard Coogan in the show's first year, 1949-50, and thereafter by Al Hodge, who had reached radio fame before the war as the Green Hornet. Teen actor Don Hastings, 15 years old when the series started, played the onscreen Ranger and was one of the first TV-created teen idols of the Boomer generation, if not the first.

DuMont, always in financial difficulties, had a budget of $25 per week for the daily series. Captain Video, who was broadcasting from a secret mountain fortress at some time far in the future, would use super-advanced space gadgets constructed from Wanamaker's items, since DuMont was renting from the department store at the time. The controls of the good ship *Galaxy* were painted on cardboard. Especially in the early years, producer James Caddigan would fill out the program with breaks to view the Rangers themselves in action. Viewed via "Remote Carrier Beam," they were often cowboys in clips from old Westerns.

The show soon turned into a full-fledged science-fiction TV serial, however. The Captain set out to save the universe from such adversaries as Dr.

They came from out of the Raisin Bran. In the 1950s, Raisin Bran cereal issued Captain Video Space Men premiums. The 2″ aliens, robots, and space people were made of a shiny hard plastic by Superior, a Brooklyn-based maker of plastic toys. Superior also packaged the figures in small play sets, together with small space vehicles. In soft plastic they reappeared as premiums, in dull, gray-black colors, in the 1960s. Another plastics company, Lido, made larger Captain Video figures in the 1950s. Superior, 1950s.

Clysmok, Heng Foo Seeng, Kul of Eos, Mook the Moon Man, Nargola, and the beautiful Atar and her unstoppable mechanical robot slave, Tobor.

Captain Video invented a long run of wonderful gadgets, including the Opticon Scillometer, which saw through anything, the Atomic Rifle, the TV-like portable viewer called the Discatron, the palm-held Radio Scillograph for communications, and the Cosmic Ray Vibrator, which made villains vibrate and shake into surrender.

Evil scientist Dr. Pauli, played by Hal Conklin for most of the show's run, fought against the Video Rangers with his Astroidal Society, wielding his Barrier of Silence and Cloak of Invisibility.

DuMont was not fated to survive as a network. The intransigence of Paramount Studios, which had bought a controlling interest and was doing its best to keep down the threatening monster of TV, and the barrier of FCC regulations played into the network's end. DuMont's leadership team was made up of innovators brilliant at devising new technology for a new medium, but poorly prepared for leading a major corporation in the mid-20th century.

Competition from companies better poised in the industry, even if they were less innovative than DuMont, certainly played its role, too. Who was Dr. Pauli, really? Was he RCA? Was he NBC or CBS, or the Paramount Theaters-ABC nexus that formed in 1953? Whoever Dr. Pauli was, he won in the end.

Signal siren. In 1953, the Tom Corbett Space Cadet Kit included the Tom Corbett ring, badge, compass, the Planet Distance Guide, an Interplanetary Weight Chart, and the lithographed 7″ steel flashlight called the Signal Siren. "Flashlight throws 500-foot spot beam," boasted catalog ads. "Red plastic head lights up around rim for danger signals. Flasher button for signalling!" Tom Corbett Signal Siren close-up, 1953.

Faces of the future. Perhaps because the world was growing ever smaller through air flight, television, news-reels, and photo-magazines, children had to turn their hopes for utterly strange beings to outer space. Aliens, Tom Corbett Play Set, Marx, 1950s.

DuMont's doors closed in 1955. The Captain's show, by then known as *The Secret Files of Captain Video*, last aired April 1, 1955.

While the Video Rangers disappeared into the telecasting oblivion from which they had saved the universe for almost six years, the Captain Video name survived in toy boxes and play rooms across the country. One of the most popular promotions, through Raisin Bran cereal, put small Captain Video figurines in the hands of children across the country - no doubt including many who never had the chance to see the original Captain on TV.

JOHNNY ASTRO #54

Pretending to be at the controls of jets, space-ships, missile systems, and rocket launching pads became easier in the later Boomer period, thanks to De Luxe Reading Corp., also known through the years as De Luxe Topper and Topper Toys.

The company produced large, plastic, battery-enhanced dashboards of cars, with steering controls and endless dials. The equally large Jimmy Jet had the U-shaped steering control of an aircraft cockpit, firing plastic missiles, and a screen that lit up to reveal the shadow of the army-style jet traveling across the landscape.

Best of all may have been Johnny Astro, which De Luxe Topper announced as "The Most Exciting Toy Ever! Johnny Astro really flies!" Relatively simple in concept, it used the same principal that appeared in the 1958 toy Satellite Train, in which the "satellite," much like a ping-pong ball, lifted over the train, held up by a cone of moving air created by a small fan.

In the Johnny Astro, a larger fan could be guided by a pair of control levers. The suspended spacecraft were simple balloons with markings on the sides such as "Luna 3 USA" and "Mars 2," weighted on the bottoms with small landing platforms.

The plastic control unit came with a cardboard landing field where the spacecraft could land after extraordinary adventures several feet above the ground.

Space-age balloon launcher. De Luxe Topper admitted ordinary balloons would work, but "may not perform as well." It offered to send six extra balloons for $.50, postpaid. Johnny Astro, De Luxe Topper, 1960s.

#55 NUTTY MADS

Weird Waldo. *The larger Marx plastic figures, made in single-color plastics, invited painting, especially in a time when everyone was accustomed to assembling plastic model kits and then painting them. The Nutty Mads, like models, were more display pieces than toys. The original clay-green hue of this Waldo the Weight Lifter peeks through some child's vivid paint job. Louis Marx Co., 1963.*

Marx made a new reputation for itself through the 1950s and '60s as a maker of plastic play sets and plastic figures. Many were Western toys, farm toys, military toys, and space toys. A fair number were cartoon oriented. While the popularity of many such sets declined in the 1960s after their heyday in the 1950s, they remained a source of pleasure for many children.

While no longer among the most creative of toy companies by the 1960s, the Louis Marx Co. still stayed hip to happenings in that most happening of decades. Never was this made so vividly clear as in the years following 1963, when Marx started its weird and wacky Nutty Mad series.

The Nutty Mads were all popping eyeballs, jutting teeth, and taut, contorting bodies. They fit

perfectly with the other counter-culture freak images - Rat Fink from Ed Roth and the Weird-ohs from Hawk Model Co.

Nutty marbles. *Bagatelles retained their prewar popularity through the Boomer years. Clear plastic covers, instead of glass or no cover at all, made the toys more portable and versatile by the 1960s, and made losing the marbles next to impossible. In the 1960s, bagatelles often used attractively decorated tin backboards - in this case, with Nutty Mads: Manny the Reckless Mariner, Dippy the Deep Diver, Waldo the Weight Lifter, Donald the Demon, Rocky the Champ, and Roddy the Hot Rod. Louis Marx Co., 1960s.*

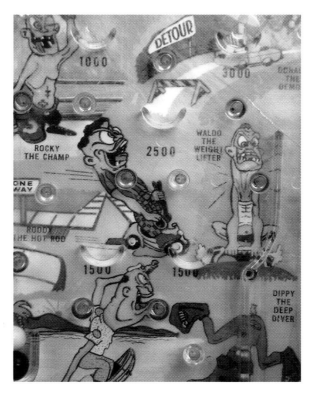

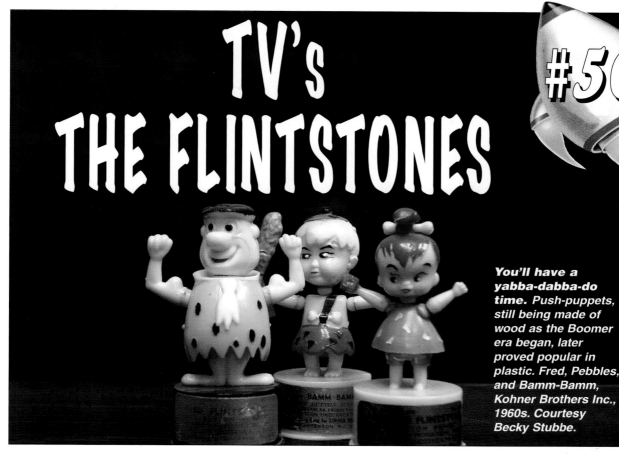

TV's THE FLINTSTONES

#56

You'll have a yabba-dabba-do time. *Push-puppets, still being made of wood as the Boomer era began, later proved popular in plastic. Fred, Pebbles, and Bamm-Bamm, Kohner Brothers Inc., 1960s. Courtesy Becky Stubbe.*

A parody on the suburban life so many families of the Boomer years were living, Hanna-Barbera's *The Flintstones* was television's first prime-time television cartoon, making its debut the evening of Sept. 30, 1960. Lasting through 1966, it was also the longest running prime-time animated series of the Boomer years.

The Flintstone family of Fred and Wilma, later joined by baby Pebbles, experienced all the joy and turmoil of modern suburban life in a campy prehistoric setting. They drove rock-wheeled cars, played a record player with a bird loaning its beak for the stylus, and kept a buzzard beneath the sink for garbage disposal. They kept pets, including a dinosaur. They quarreled, made up, had barbecues, and went on outings with their friends and neighbors, the Rubbles.

Until the cartoon showed up on their televisions, people never knew how far they hadn't come since the Stone Age.

Alan Reed provided the voice for Fred, Jean VanderPyl for Wilma and Pebbles, Mel Blanc for Barney Rubble and Dino the Dinosaur, Bea Benaderet for the first Betty Rubble and Gerry Johnson the second, and Don Messick for Bamm Bamm.

Numerous cameo characters spoofed famous TV personalities, including Perry Masonry and Ed Sullystone.

The Flintstone family entered the play room through games, battery-operated toys and plastic figures. Perhaps the most enduring fun through the years came from a series of simple but entertaining toys from the Kohner company. Based on the wooden push-puppets the parents of the Boomers had enjoyed before the war, Kohner's plastic push-puppets were figures that could bend, wave their arms, nod, and bow.

Dancer. Even less famous Hanna-Barbera characters made their way into toy form. "I'm Dancer the Dog Push-Button Puppet," the label of this one reads. Kohner Brothers, Inc., 1960s.

#57 SUPERBALL

Jewels of rubber. *Colorful Superballs bounced their way into, and often out of, children's hands and hearts. Wham-O or unknown manufacturers, 1960s.*

Among the few toys absolutely every child played with at least once during the later 1960s was the Superball, a hard-rubber hyper-bouncer introduced by Wham-O and subsequently issued in countless colors and sizes by unknown numbers of companies.

I remember having one particular Superball - fairly opaque and whitish, with reflective sparkles imbedded inside. I guarded it carefully. Superballs were so lively on hard surfaces that living in the midst of so much suburban pavement made me cautious.

Most of the early Wham-O Superballs were completely opaque, either in solid colors or in attractively swirled combinations of the same solid colors. The largest was a heavy black ball, and intimidating in its weight, solidity, and bouncing power. I felt intimidated, at least. Maybe it was because that was the Superball wielded by the bigger boys and by the school yard bullies. You remember the ones. If they ever got hold of your Superball, over the school building it went.

And Superballs didn't have to be thrown very hard to be lost forever.

TV's FURY

Frame Tray Inlay

Fury. *Television's black stallion, starring figure of a late-1950s TV show, inspired story books, comic books, and toys such as this puzzle, which proved a good seller for the company when released in the 1950s. Fury was the second media horse to bear the name. The golden palomino of radio's 1948-51 Straight Arrow series was given the same name by children, who selected it through a mail-in promotion sponsored by Nabisco Shredded Wheats. Fury tray puzzle, Whitman Publishing Co., 1950s.*

Horses moved from also-starring to featured roles as TV matured as a medium. Such popular series as *The Adventures of Champion* in 1955-56, *My Friend Flicka* in 1956-58, and *National Velvet* in 1960-62 moved hooved heroes and heroines closer to the main limelight.

None proved as popular or long-lived as *Fury*, aired Saturday mornings from 1955 through 1960. The only show to center primarily on the horse, it featured a Missouri stallion originally named Highland Dale. Ralph McCutcheon, famed at the time for training animal motion-picture stars, discovered Highland Dale at age 18 months and moved him to Hollywood where he appeared in not only his own TV series but also in movies including *Black Beauty*, *Gypsy Colt*, *Wild Is the Wind*, and *Giant*, the last one costarring Elizabeth Taylor. Through her hundreds of appearances on film, Fury earned a reputation as the smartest horse in Hollywood.

In the TV show on Saturday mornings, renamed *Brave Stallion* when syndicated from 1960-66, Fury's costarring human characters were Peter Graves as Jim, Bobby Diamond as Joey, and William Fawcette as Pete.

Horse toys had long proved popular with children, with wheeled riding toys, cast-iron horse-drawn vehicle toys, and small lead horses popular early in the 1900s. In the Boomer era, Marx, Stuart, MPC, Ajax, Archer, Tim-Mee, and Lido,

147

Grazing beauty. *Even though cowboys rode horses, horse toys were often seen as girl toys in many households. Glossy hard plastic proved to be the material of choice for many horse toy manufacturers. Hartland, 1960s.*

among other plastics manufacturers, turned out a wide variety of toy horses to fill Western play sets and plastic "header bags" for dime stores. Many of these inexpensive toys were detailed and attractive, often having cast-in saddles and reins and sometimes coming with loose accessories.

Besides the Wonder Products Co., which produced countless spring-suspended riding horses for tots, two toy companies rose in the Boomer years to cater to children with equine infatuations. Hartland Plastics, Inc. had its origins before the war outside of the toy industry, producing miscellaneous acetate items for domestic and wartime use. The company started as the Electro Forming Co., founded by Ed and Iola Walters in 1941. After the war, as Hartland Plastics, it started producing a variety of horses and Western figures familiar to children. Such horse-riding figures from history (and history-flavored movies) as Annie Oakley, General George Washington, Jim Bowie, and General Robert Lee joined characters more typical of the times - Dale Evans, the Lone Ranger, Matt Dillon, Roy Rogers, and Tonto.

In contrast, the Breyer company, founded late in the 1950s, emphasized stallions, mares, mules, ponies, and colts to exemplify different breeds,

largely passing over their riders. For TV's most popular horse, Breyer produced both Fury and Black Stallion figures.

The Aurora Plastics Corp. issued a Black Fury model for the rubber cement set and reissued it in the late Boomer years. Kenner produced Give-A-Show reels, and publishers including Dell, Whitman, and Grosset & Dunlap made sure Fury's hooves sounded as loudly during reading time as during TV time.

But everyone started with Frame-Tray Inlay Puzzles made by Whitman Publishing. These puzzles provided most Boomers with their earliest problem-solving exercises while giving them outlet for their earliest hero worship. They could assemble and disassemble and reassemble Fury and Rin Tin Tin hour after hour.

I had no idea how deeply embedded these puzzles are in our minds until I was talking with a friend, who remembered more clearly than I do those covers bent over the Frame-Tray Inlay.

But once he started describing how many pieces of these puzzles were different shapes - bells, ships, people, planes - it all came back to me, with the vividness of having just put down the puzzle after a play time.

AURORA SLOT CARS #59

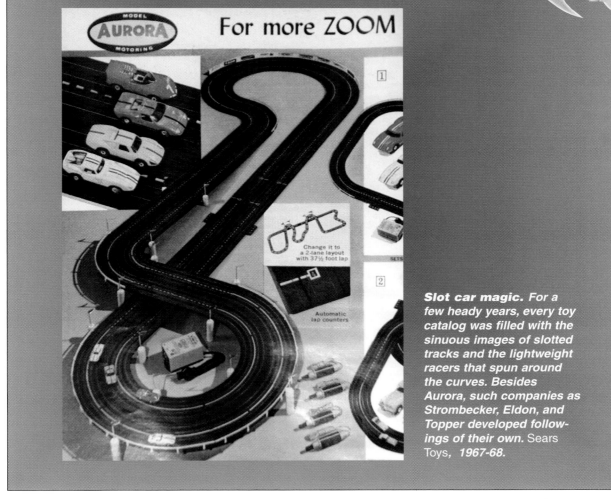

Slot car magic. *For a few heady years, every toy catalog was filled with the sinuous images of slotted tracks and the lightweight racers that spun around the curves. Besides Aurora, such companies as Strombecker, Eldon, and Topper developed followings of their own.* Sears Toys, *1967-68.*

In the middle of the 1960s, HO-scale motoring appeared to be the wave of the future. Suddenly every kid, and probably every father, wanted grooved track sets, down which wedge-nosed cars whirred and raced.

Train sets had struggled to maintain the popularity they had enjoyed before the war. One of the best strategies for survival had been the move toward the smaller, HO-scale tracks and trains. Slot cars, however, threatened to take the place of even HO railroads, since they occupied the same place on the den floor a toy train might otherwise take and had an unbeatable advantage: friends could visit and take the controls for the second track and actively race against one another. If a train took a corner too quickly, it just fell over. If a racing car took a corner too fast and leapt off the track, it meant losing the race.

As huge as the phenomenon was, it proved to be short-lived. By the late '60s kids were ready for something even more exciting, quicker to set up, and more portable. Mattel gave it to them in spades, in the form of Hot Wheels.

CLUE

Mr. Green, with the Wrench? *While the playing pieces representing Professor Plum, Colonel Mustard, Mrs. Peacock, and their friends and enemies were represented by simple wooden markers, the die-cast weapons were morbidly realistic. Parker Brothers, 1960.*

Your Detective Notes: It was Colonel Mustard with a Lead Pipe in the Conservatory. Or it was Mrs. Peacock with a Revolver in the Billiard Room. No, no, no: it was Miss Scarlet, who used a Rope in the Kitchen. But no! Surely it was Professor Plum, yes, wielding that wicked Candlestick in the Library!

Clue, which arrived in living rooms and dens across the country in the 1950s, gave every member of the family the chance to be a detective.

Or villain.

DREAM PETS

#61

Quick Draw McGraw. *The popular comic character was made in Dream-Pet-like form by one of the many smaller companies that imported toys from Japan. Herman Pecker & Co. and other manufacturers, 1960s. Photo by Martha Borchardt.*

Dakin's Dream Pets, among the leading stuffed animals of the 1950s, were anything but soft and cuddly. They were tightly stuffed with "wood byproducts," a term accepted by the toy industry in lieu of sawdust. The outer materials were likewise usually on the stiff end: while often it was felt or a similar material, leatherette vinyls were also used.

Yet they were among the most charming toys of the time. Dakin was one of several companies importing stuffed animal toys from Japan, with others including Circle Importers (Treasure Pets), Animal Fair (Animal Fair Pets), Kamar, Takara, and Herman Pecker & Co. The manufacturers in Japan took a decidedly whimsical turn with these toys, issuing pink rhinos, rose-colored wiener-dogs, beret-sporting skunks, and fire-engine-red reindeer.

#62 GIVE-A-SHOW

Projecting childhood dreams. *Bedrooms became movie houses with the flick of a switch. Kenner sold film strips with the battery-operated projectors, and offered more in separate boxes. Almost any animated character might appear on bedroom walls: Dick Tracy, Space Ghost, The Flintstones, Deputy Dawg... Give-A-Show Projector and slide strips, Kenner, 1960s.*

Kenner had several hits in the early 1960s, including the somewhat strange sell-out hit of 1963, the Flintstones Building Boulders, which looked much like Block City or Lego pieces at a considerably larger scale, made of lightweight Styrofoam.

Besides the Girder & Panel sets, Kenner devoted much of its TV advertising budget to a toy that proved to be a steady source of enjoyment for kids through the decade: the Give-A-Show Projector.

While Kenner would later have a more innovative idea of what to do with light bulbs, with the Give-A-Show it found a fairly traditional but still solid way of working wonders in the playroom. The projector was a sturdy plastic affair. It was battery powered to avoid the hazards of electrical cords.

The films it showed were simple too: the short sets of cels, with written narration, were set in strips of cardboard which slipped easily in and out of the projector.

Projectors typically came with a dozen or so strips, each one featuring a different cartoon star. Kenner stayed away from nature and live-action shows - which hardly limited its choice of subjects in the TV cartoon heyday of the early '60s. If children tired of the ones that came with the projector, they could always buy more.

While projectors for children had appeared before, the convenience of Kenner's Give-A-Show, Kenner's timing in releasing the toy at a time of ferment in the world of TV animation, and, not least, the extensive TV advertising made the toy truly memorable for many Boomers.

TV's THE LONE RANGER

and the Plastic Old West

Hi-Ho Silver, and away! *It only took two accessories - a hat, and a mask - to make any child one of the great Western heroes. Lone Ranger and Silver plastic figures, 60 mm., Marx, 1950s. Courtesy Ken Boyer.*

*T*he Lone Ranger was among the first wave of television serials, first appearing in September 1949, and having a remarkable run lasting nearly a decade, with the show ending in September 1957.

Unlike Roy Rogers, who started in movies, or Hopalong Cassidy, who had his origins in pulp magazines, the Lone Ranger was a child of prewar radio. The Lone Ranger began his days as John Reid, a young member of a posse of Texas Rangers chasing desperadoes. The bandits lured the Rangers into a canyon and ambushed them. Left for dead, Reid managed to crawl to the safety of a water hole where he was found by a friendly Indian whom Reid had once helped. Tonto, the Indian, said to Reid, "You kemo sabe. It mean 'trusty scout.'" Vowing vengeance on the outlaws, Reid became the Lone Ranger and set out in pursuit of his enemy, Butch Cavendish.

Clayton Moore played the Lone Ranger for much of the TV show's run, first in 1949-52 and again 1954-57, with John Hart playing the masked man in the middle years. Jay Silverheels, by blood partly Mohawk, played Tonto.

The Lone Ranger was originally created for radio before the war by George Trendel and Fran Striker, who also created yet another masked crime-fighter, The Green Hornet. The mask itself was a genetic trait: the Green Hornet's father was John Reid's nephew.

While playing the Lone Ranger was commonplace before World War II - a mask and cowboy hat were easy to come by, after all, and Lone Ranger cap pistols were made even in the cast-iron toy days - young Boomers in the 1950s saw a new world open with the Marx Western play sets. While the tradition of playing Cowboys and Indians never entirely vanished from school playgrounds and backyards, a new tradition was born on playroom floors based on plastic figures. Marx released Lone Ranger sets through much of the 1950s, in addition to many other Western sets.

Other companies including Tim-Mee, Stuart, MPC and Lido helped Marx insure the Boomers spent hours at a time with bellies flat to the floor, surveying their vast but miniature Old West dominions.

#64

AUBURN VINYL CARS

That unbeatable, hot-roddin'
Number Two. Auburn Rubber Co.
turned increasingly to vinyl toy
production through the 1950s.
Toward the end, some toys from the
vinyl molds even appeared in
cheaper polyethylene. Auburn
Rubber Co., 1950s-60s.

The Auburn Rubber Co. of Auburn, Indiana, was the largest rubber toy manufacturer in America from 1935, when it first issued rubber toy soldiers, into the 1950s.

The company stopped issuing exclusively rubber toys early in that decade. It turned more and more to vinyl, which allowed the company to put greater detail in their toy figures and vehicles.

From 1953 through the '60s, Auburn Rubber released motorcycles, trucks, construction vehicles, and automobiles made of the new, flexible material. The last vehicles made of the old, thick rubber appeared in the 1950s.

Auburn's vinyl cars and trucks probably appeared in every sandbox in America. Not only were they inexpensive toys, they were safe, sturdy, and attractive.

Perhaps because Auburn largely sold its goods through dime stores and made little in the way of high-profile playthings, it stayed away from the TV limelight and saw its fortunes dwindle in the 1960s. By the end of the decade it had moved production to New Mexico, where the company faded from view by 1969.

TRU-ACTION ELECTRIC FOOTBALL

#65

Players out for a rumble. *The vibrations of the rumbling, shaking game surface kept the players moving in the Tru-Action Electric Football Game. This set cost $6.95 in the mid-1950s, a price it stayed at for the remainder of the decade. Tudor Metal Products, 1954.*

Tudor's 1949 Tru-Action Electric Football Game was as strange and unlikely as a game could be. It was large, arriving in a box measuring roughly 17″ by 27″. The game board was a raised platform with a flat metal sheet lithographed to resemble a football field. The players were pieces of metal cut in a shape that more or less resembled football players. On their undersides were two small tin strips, the only part of the football players that touched the metal field when they were set down for the game. With these strips bent so that they pointed slightly backwards, the football players moved forward.

Why? Because the whole board vibrated. Once you set up the players, you plugged in the game, flicked the switch, and watched the fast-jiggling guards and tackles have at it.

Strange as it was, the game did well for Brooklyn's Tudor Metal Products Corp. By the 1960s the players were realistically molded in plastic, with four plastic hairs on the underside taking the place of the earlier strips of tin.

The game was no less strange than before, yet somehow kept winning over new kids who loved to watch the players run around the board as if alive.

CHAPTER 9

More Honorary Boomer Toys

The Honorary Baby Boomer Toys are the ones Boomers played with that their parents, too, had enjoyed. The other Honoraries, listed in Chapters Three and Six, are Lincoln Logs, Monopoly, Tinkertoys, The Game of Life, View-Master, and Tootsietoys. Some of these toys changed steadily through the years, while others remained virtually unchanged. A few were radically changed with the introduction of the new plastics of the Boomer years.

Honorary Boomer Toy
DUNCAN YO-YOS
Butterflies and Tournament Tops

#7

Jeweled splendor. Duncan Jeweled Tournament Yo Yo Tops, 1950s, and Beginner's Yo-Yo, 1960s, both in wood.

Some are surprised to learn how old the yo-yo is. String-wound, up-and-down wheel toys apparently inspired fads among the populations of Europe and Asia for decades, perhaps even centuries, before the toy found its way to America.

The first large-scale American fad for the toy took place in the decade that saw the revival in this country of table tennis, the worldwide Mah Jong craze, and the arrival of the Charleston: the 1920s. Companies including Flores, Duncan, and Cheerio started at that time, followed by dozens of other companies, making yo-yos of wood and tin.

The Baby Boom, coupled with innovations in plastics, revitalized the world of yo-yos. Duncan took the lead with a variety of wooden yo-yos, including the innovative Butterfly versions, and by introducing solid-plastic yo-yos of new weight and durability. The material also gave the manufacturer greater freedom: the toys could now be translu-

cent, opalescent, transparent, colored, plain, glitter-flecked, and molded with new imprints and designs.

The toys themselves were only half the phenomenon in the '50s and '60s. Corner competitions sprang up everywhere among kids eager to compare skills at fancy and fanciful tricks. Duncan and other companies sponsored many such competitions, giving out embroidered badges that yo-yoists prized above anything.

Walking the dog, round-the-world, making it play dead... I could do that last one.

Yo-yoing was not automatic with many children, just as Frisbee-flying skill proved elusive to many. Me, I mainly remember trying to untangle the string on a wooden yo-yo that I was sure didn't work.

It was fun anyway.

#8 GILBERT ERECTOR SETS

Nickel-Plated Girder Builders

Spanning generations. *The Gilbert Erector sets satisfied the building urge for children from early in the century through the entire Boomer period. Erector set building, 1950s-60s, with 1954 advertisement from* Boy's Life *magazine.*

Metal construction sets were a growth industry in the 1910s, when such companies as A.C. Gilbert, of New Haven, Connecticut, and Structo, of Freeport, Illinois, issued sets of electroplated steel girders and die-cast pulleys, gears, axles and wheels that could be assembled into almost anything the child could desire.

Structo started giving more emphasis to its Auto-Builder Toys in the 1920s, eventually developing a line of large and sturdy vehicle toys that would take it safely through the Great Depression and land it in a position of strength when World War II arrived. After the war it remained one of the leading toy manufacturers, with its heavy construction vehicle toys consistently strong sellers through the 1950s and earlier '60s, when Tonka more aggressively marketed its increasingly diverse line.

A.C. Gilbert hewed to the construction toy line, however, with its popular Erector Sets. As with other companies, Gilbert's postwar offerings initially repeated prewar toys, including its famous Ferris Wheel. In the late '40s and early '50s, some of its sets were made with aluminum girders, due to the combined effects of a steel strike and the beginning of the Korean War. By the late '50s, Gilbert adapted to the times, issuing sets to build rocket launchers, robots, and space vehicles.

Structo 66. Structo started in the construction toy business in the 1910s, as its name suggests. By the Boomer years, having sold the construction toy part of its business, Structo was known for its fine line of pressed-steel toy trucks. Oddly, by entering into a distribution deal with American Flyer, Structo found itself allied with its old competitor, Gilbert. Tin bank, Structo, 1952.

#9

Coloring Within the Lines

Forty-eight colors... and all forty-eight tasted the same. Advertising blotter, 1940s.

In the late 1800s, the Binney & Smith Co. moved gradually deeper into the educational market, progressing from slate pencils to dustless chalk, and from there to wax crayons, which previously had been available only in expensive European versions.

Alice Binney, wife of company co-owner Edwin, devised the Crayola name. The beginning was based on the French word for "chalk," while the ending suggested "oil."

Crayons proved of immense importance to most childhoods thereafter, especially in the Boomer period - for Crayola Crayons did for books what Winky Dink Magic Crayons had done for TV: they turned a nontoy into a toy.

Coloring books covered every possible subject during Boomer years, issued by publishers including Whitman, Saalfield, and Lowe.

Project Book. Binney & Smith did its best to plant activity ideas in the heads of kids. One idea, to make an Indian headdress from a brown paper bag, was used in various forms in every elementary school across the country. Playing Indian in the Boomer years would have been different without those cardboard packs of color. Crayola Crayon Project Book, Binney & Smith, 1958.

KRAZY IKES

A Thousand Funny Things

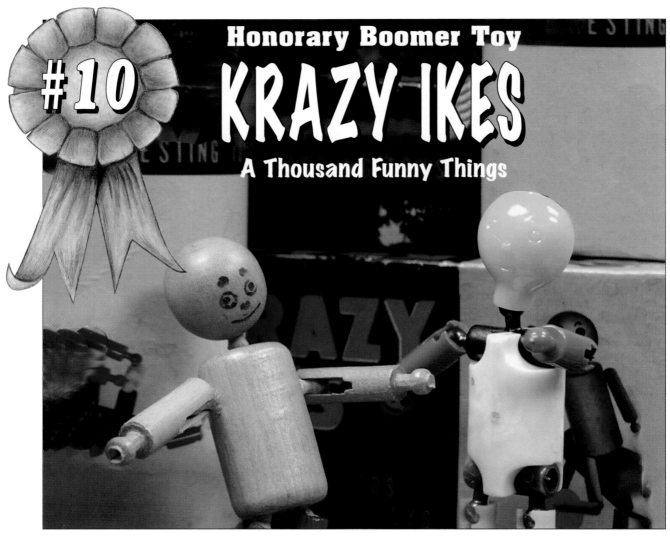

Plastic Ike meets wood. *Whitman publishing oversaw the Ikes' transition from wood to hard plastic in the 1950s. The phrase, "Makes Hundreds of Interesting Toys," remained a constant through the Boomer years - a significant toning-down from Knapp Electric's "A Thousand Funny Things." Whitman Publishing Co., 1950s-60s.*

Introduced in the late 1920s by Knapp Electric Co. of Indianapolis, Krazy Ikes was a construction toy from which, Knapp promised, children could "build a thousand funny things, all different."

The toy remained the same through World War II, having the good fortune to be made of a material with no rationing restrictions. It was one of the first toys to greet young children in the heady days ending the war.

Whitman Publishing Co., better known for a long and illustrious line of children's books, purchased the Ikes, and by 1960 or so saw it through the inevitable conversion into plastic, the form in which most Boomers came to know the toy.

Krazy Ikes consisted of miscellaneously shaped pieces that could be assembled into people, animals, and things best just called "Ikes." The slender connector pieces were of about pencil thickness, 1-1/2″ in length. These could attach to knobs on the body pieces or to the head or feet pieces. The people heads, which were spherical in the wooden versions with printed faces, were slightly flattened and hollowed and had raised features in the plastic versions.

The strange and wonderful beings and things to be made from Krazy Ikes remained unchanged in the transition from wood to plastic: the Kangarike, the Bucker-Ike, the Ike-Hopper, the Ikeville Flier, the Ike-Cycle, the Ikabird, the Crocodike, the Ikosaur, the Gooner-Ike, the Shmike, and the Lazy-Ike.

In the 1950s and '60s, following Schaper's lead, Whitman issued Ike-A-Doo, in which children could assemble their Ikes with a spinner instead of the Cootie's dice.

CHAPTER 10

Bash!

FLATSY

Flower child. *When she appeared, Flatsy seemed a symbolic return to the origins of the style doll. Although not as thin as a paper doll, she was a flat figure for dressing and undressing. Her costumes often played off styles of the time, as did this 5˝ Flatsy flower child. Ideal, 1969.*

Girls of the 1960s had a wealth of fashion dolls that were small and easy to lose, from the Kiddles and Hasbro Storykins to the Trolls and Pee Wees.

When Ideal applied the bendy concept to the idea of the miniature fashion doll, the results were the Flatsys. Unlike the space bendy toys of the more boy-oriented Major Matt Mason line, Flatsys took the Gumby approach. Looking as though Ideal had used cookie-cutters on vinyl slabs to make them, the dolls, in a sense, represented a

return to the beginnings of the style doll. They were essentially thick paper dolls, only made of new and more durable materials.

With changeable clothes, plastic vehicles, and the seemingly obligatory vinyl townhouse, the dolls appeared in 2˝, 5˝, and 8˝ sizes. Definitely children of their time, their hair was long and their outfits hip and trendy.

Ideal issued the Flatsys in 1968-70 for the last children of the Boomer years.

BASH!

#67

Bash! By mid-decade, games relying on keeping things on even keel, in even balance, were transforming the games market. Milton Bradley, 1967.

OH FOOEY!

FOR AGES 5 to 12

The trend that started in 1961-62 reached its crest a few years later. Games, once designed for family enjoyment, fairly quiet for the most part, and often dependent on mental agility and knowledge, gave way to bright, brilliantly designed, fast-paced, and noisy games of impulse and chaos.

Many gained their feeling of mounting tension by creating an imminent disaster, which one player would set off. No one could tell at the beginning who that player would be - who could be the winner or lower, depending on how you felt that day.

In Ker-Plunk, a 1967 Ideal game, players sat around a clear plastic tube filled with marbles held from falling by plastic straws. The players had to pull out the straws, without letting the marbles fall. In The Last Straw, Schaper's 1966 hit, players kept adding plastic straws to the camel's basket, wondering whose would be the one to tip the balance and break the camel's back. In the same company's Don't Break the Ice, players took turns hammering out chunks of ice, trying to leave just enough to keep the hapless ice-fisherman from falling through.

The games came out in profusion: 1965's Booby-Trap, a wooden spring-bar game from Parker Brothers; Operation from Milton Bradley in 1965; Tip-It, a balancing game, Hands Down, "the slap-happy game," and KaBoom!, a balloon-popping device from Ideal in 1965; Don't Spill the Beans and the Voodoo Doll Game from Schaper in 1967; Careful - The Toppling Tower Game from Ideal in 1967.

Bash! was another Milton Bradley game issued in 1967. The Bash! man was a stack of plastic disks, with the man's head looking agonized on top, and his large feet at bottom. Equipped with a plastic hammer, players took turns knocking pieces out of his body, making him progressively shorter, or else making him totter over, sending the pieces flying, clackity-clack.

Which was what all the games were about.

Time Bomb, issued in 1965 by Milton Bradley, may have touched at the heart of the matter. Anything connected to the word "bomb" was connected to a notion new on Earth, which was made vivid in America by events in Cuba a few years earlier: Everything hung in a delicate balance.

Duck and cover.

Kids had to learn it somehow.

#68 TV's FAMILY AFFAIR

A wholesome face at the end of a weird and wacked-out decade. *Why a doll should take so much of the limelight may remain a mystery to future generations. To the people there at the time, it was utterly natural. In the last years of the 1960s and early '70s, Mrs. Beasley appeared in both hard-plastic and cloth forms. Photo courtesy Krause Publications.*

Late Boomers watched the situation comedy *Family Affair* from 1966 through 1971. The toy industry watched as well - not just because the show as a whole was enjoying great popularity and the toy industry always watched popular shows, but because of one character in particular.

Siblings Buffy, Jody, and Cissy unexpectedly entered the life of their well-to-do bachelor uncle named Bill Davis. Davis, who was used to flying around the world and living the finest life the city could offer, was even tended in his daily life by a modern-day butler, the dapper Mr. French.

Buffy stuck out in the minds of children because she carried with her a doll named Mrs. Beasley, a simple cloth doll distinguished by her polka-dot dress and wire, square-rimmed glasses. Buffy rebuffed the fancy playthings offered her by her reluctant guardian and clung to her dependable stuffed friend.

Buffy was played by Anissa Jones, her twin brother Jody by Johnnie Whitaker, older sister Cissy by Kathy Garver, Davis by Brian Keith, and French by Sebastian Cabot.

Mrs. Beasley played herself.

The line of analysis on the part of the toy industry was quite simple: Young *Star Trek* fans wanted pointed ears. Young *Family Affair* fans wanted Mrs. Beasley. Simple, and accurate. But while *Star Trek* fans bought a few ears, *Family Affair* fans bought Beasleys by the thousands.

THE GYROFRICTION CAR #69

Powerful screaming car! By later toy standards, the car with its "powerful screaming siren" was tame and quiet. In the early to mid-1950s, however, it was the latest thrill. It appeared with a variety of paint schemes. Irwin, 1950s.

Irwin Corp. of Fitchburg, Massachusetts, started in the 1920s as a manufacturer of novelties - probably the sorts of things you would pick up at carnivals and five-and-dimes: celluloid pinwheels, rattles, dolls, and general whatnots.

Novelty companies tend not to develop much of a profile within the industry, even if they are dependable suppliers, as Irwin was for decades. Or maybe it's exactly because they are dependable suppliers. The novelty market has little need for brand names or the kinds of toy innovations that can make a brand name famous. It just needs stuff good enough to attract the eye for a few seconds or to satisfy some lucky mark at the midway shooting gallery.

Irwin was not entirely a bit-part player, however, as it did its best to prove in the years after the war. One such effort came in 1953 with the copyrighted "New 'Gyrofriction' Motor." Friction motors were not exactly news by this time. Louis Marx had popularized them with its early versions of the Dick Tracy Squad Car No. 1, which had gone to children across the country thanks to Marx's presence in catalog stores. To give it credit, Irwin's Gyrofriction Motor was a smoothly running mechanism attached to the rear axle that made enough of a pleasing whirring sound during operation to lead the company to claim its cars had a "powerful screaming siren." Toy claims at the time could stretch truths at least a little. The "siren" was neither powerful nor screaming. Yet it was a good sound to a child's ears.

Irwin also claimed that the Gyrofriction car "travels a long distance" - again, a bit of a stretch. If rolled forward and released, the friction of the motor's turning parts soon brought the toy to a halt. An example I have with a dysfunctional Gyrofriction Motor rolls much, much farther. Yet kids could figure it out: if they never removed their hands from the toy, they could, indeed, make it travel a long distance. After all, it had come all the way from Fitchburg.

The Irwin Hard Top Convertible, with its sheet-metal under-chassis and two-piece plastic top, turned out to be a good toy. It had several features to speak for it. For one, it used a clear plastic dome over the seats. Surface black paint covered the "hard top" part, which could either be depicted as pulled all the way forward or partly pulled back. The part of the top meant to be windshields, of course, Irwin left unpainted. The company saved money on the ones with the top pulled forward, leaving out the attractive interior seats and steering wheel found in the others.

More fun than the sounds made by the Gyrofriction Motor were the working wipers - yellow plastic rods that waved together and apart in front of the windshield. The front, free-turning wheels powered these. So they never stopped.

The Hard Top Convertible was a car always in the rain. That must have puzzled at least a few of the children who owned the version with the pulled-back top.

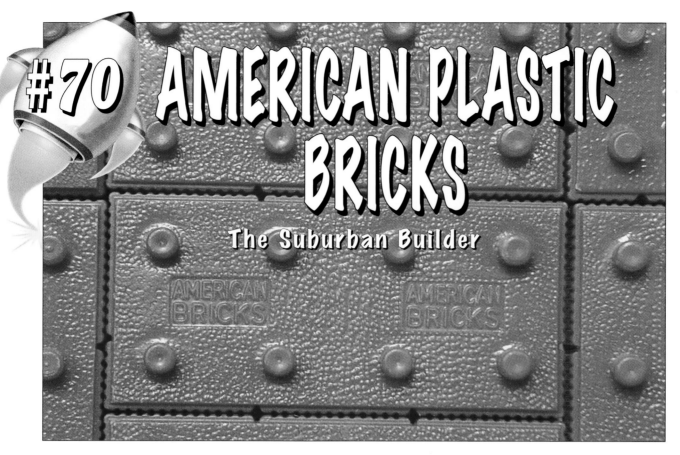

#70 AMERICAN PLASTIC BRICKS

The Suburban Builder

Child's-eye view. Much of the attraction of the Plastic Bricks came from their highly detailed, brick-like texture.

During the same period Lego was developing its building blocks in Europe, Halsam in America was selling a set of wooden bricks that would interlock to create buildings very much like the brick houses springing up in the spreading American suburbs.

Halsam changed the building pieces to plastic by the 1960s, making them a bright red, and issued them as Halsam's American Plastic Bricks. The sets featured pieces that allowed the placement of a roof, and doors and windows that opened and closed. Part of their charm was the extreme ease with which they went together to form attractive toy buildings: perfect, neat, and tidy, just as all suburbia was supposed to be.

Another part of their charm came from the nature of the building materials themselves. The lightweight hard-plastic pieces were more durable than the easily chipped American Skyline pieces, and greatly more attractive than Lincoln Logs.

Plus they mixed together in the box after the building was taken down with a clattering sound that was strangely pleasant - a sound that, minor as it is, remains clear in memory to all the millions who played with the toy.

Red-brick construction. American Plastic Bricks were the plastic building blocks of choice for the generation raised before Lego came to America with its more versatile but less detailed construction toys. American Plastic Bricks, with plastic pickup truck by Irwin, 1960s.

BUGS BUNNY'S #71

MAGIC RUB-OFF PICTURES

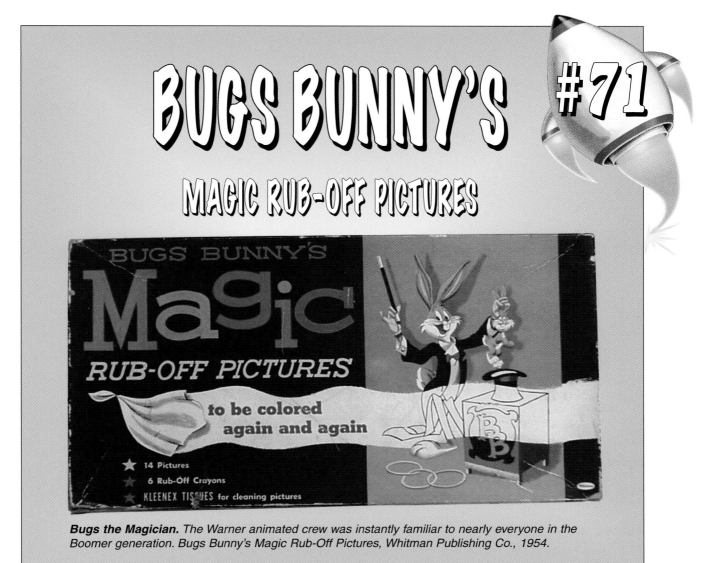

Bugs the Magician. *The Warner animated crew was instantly familiar to nearly everyone in the Boomer generation. Bugs Bunny's Magic Rub-Off Pictures, Whitman Publishing Co., 1954.*

Warner Brothers created a star a few years before the war. Its cartoon department had come up with a new character with a voice by Mel Blanc. The character, a rabbit, responded in his opening scene to a hunter pointing a gun: "Eh, what's up, Doc?"

When the first audiences roared with approval, director Tex Avery figured the line had better stay.

Bugs Bunny's star kept rising as he appeared in new Looney Tunes and Merrie Melodies films each year. Unlike Mickey Mouse at Disney, Bugs showed no signs of retiring from the theatrical stage after the war, and continued taking starring roles until Warner closed down its cartoon department in 1963.

Bugs' fellow animated stars were also constant companions to the Boomers: Porky Pig, Daffy Duck, Elmer Fudd, Pepe LePew, Tweety Bird, Sylvester, Foghorn Leghorn, Roadrunner, and Wile E. Coyote, and many others.

The cartoon stars made ideal subjects for coloring books. Cheaply printed by companies including Whitman and Saalfield, and distributed through every dime store in the nation, coloring books were the artistic teethers for the Boomers.

Bugs Bunny's Magic Rub-Off Pictures were a kind of ultimate - the coloring book that never ran out of pictures, for you could color and erase, and color and erase, and...

And then you could get out a real coloring book and get in some satisfyingly permanent scribbling.

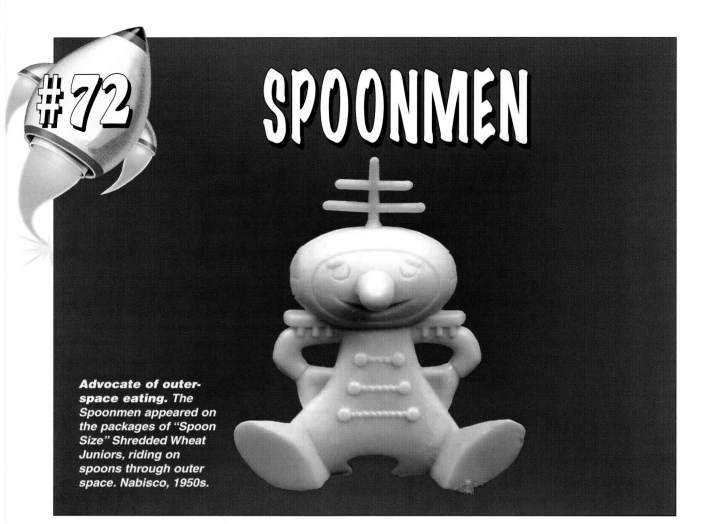

#72

SPOONMEN

Advocate of outer-space eating. The Spoonmen appeared on the packages of "Spoon Size" Shredded Wheat Juniors, riding on spoons through outer space. Nabisco, 1950s.

In the late 1940s, Nabisco was looking for a way to move into the lucrative children's cereal market, which was dominated by Post, Kellogg's, and General Mills. Deciding on Shredded Wheat as the cereal to promote, the company hired an advertising company to create a new radio show, which led to the Mutual Network's *Straight Arrow*, featuring an Indian hero. Soon, "Injun-Uity Cards," carrying tidbits of American Indian know-how, appeared in Shredded Wheat as a premium.

In the 1950s Nabisco hit on a new way of winning its way into children's fancies, and their cereal bowls. Included in packages of Spoon Size Shredded Wheat were the Spoonmen - a trio of plastic spacemen whose heads looked like the Nabisco logo and who had slots in their seats that would fix them to the handle of the average cereal spoon. They even had names: Munchy, Crunchy, and Spoonsize.

The cereal, like the Spoonmen, took off.

Sitters and hangers. Winnie the Pooh spoonsitters were issued as premiums in boxes of Wheat Honeys and Rice Honeys in the mid-1960s. Packages featured Nabisco figure Buddy Bee promising, "Inside! One of seven Breakfast Buddies!" The Breakfast Buddies could not only sit on spoons but also hang onto the edges of cereal bowls. Nabisco, 1960s.

TV's BEN CASEY #73

M.D. Game

BEN CASEY M.D. GAME

©1961 BING CROSBY PRODUCTIONS   MANUFACTURED BY TRANSOGRAM COMPANY, INC., N.Y.

X-Ray Report - Positive! With a handful of diagnostic cards and a few cardboard stand-ups representing their favorite TV doctor, kids re-created the "drama of life in a big metropolitan hospital." Ben Casey M.D. Game, Transogram, 1961.

Even though the TV networks in the early 1960s were moving toward sitcoms and generally goofy programming, several series focused on serious topics, including the medical drama *Ben Casey* from ABC, the same network that would release the top-ranking TV medical series of the end of the Boomer period, *Marcus Welby, M.D.*

Ben Casey won audience loyalty not only through realistic depiction of the daily life of a doctor in a busy, demanding metropolitan hospital environment, but also through the visual charisma of its star, Vince Edwards.

Young women enjoyed the show. So did kids who had always gotten a kick out of playing doctor and nurse. They suddenly had a more focused character in mind for their role-playing.

Knowing the show's popularity, toy manufacturers produced doctor bags, play hospital sets, and games. The doctors visiting ailing patients in play houses no longer needed be anonymous.

Ben Casey aired from 1961 to 1966, a run matched by *Dr. Kildare* on NBC, which starred Richard Chamberlain as Dr. James Kildare.

#74 THIMBLEDROME

Best of two worlds. *The Prop Rod by Thimbledrome had the sleek body of a racer, and the clear-plastic, covered cockpit of an airplane, plus the spinning spectacle of a rear propeller. It burned real fuel while friends looked on, burning with jealousy. L.M. Cox Manufacturing Co., 1960s.*

For the technically oriented, miniature vehicles with working gasoline engines were part of the exciting toy scene immediately after the war. A variety of companies worked with such engines, including Dooling Brothers of Los Angeles, who produced an open-cockpit racer cast of magnesium. Riding on semi-pneumatic wheels, its two-cycle gasoline motor could move the 8-1/2 pound car at speeds up to 90 miles per hour.

To go even faster, another company called McCoy issued a teardrop-shaped car of the same weight with a ram-air-intake gas engine. In tests it clocked over 115 miles per hour. For powering toy planes and boats, Minijet Motors created a "real jet motor, not a toy" that produced three pounds of thrust.

The Minijet Motors warning hit the problem on the head. These were designed for adults, not children. Their cost was similarly adult-scale: the Dooling Bros. and McCoy racers cost $70 or more, and the Minijet Motors jet cost $35. In contrast, a 19″ car from Buddy L, still made of hardwood due to wartime materials restrictions continuing into postwar times, cost only $6 in 1946.

The company to bring gas-powered toys more within the reach of children was L.M. Cox Manufacturing Co. of Santa Ana, California, whose Thimbledrome racers, dune buggies, and "Red Hot Drag Racing" Buicks and Corvettes went buzzing and causing havoc down the streets of their lucky owners.

MYSTERY DATE #75

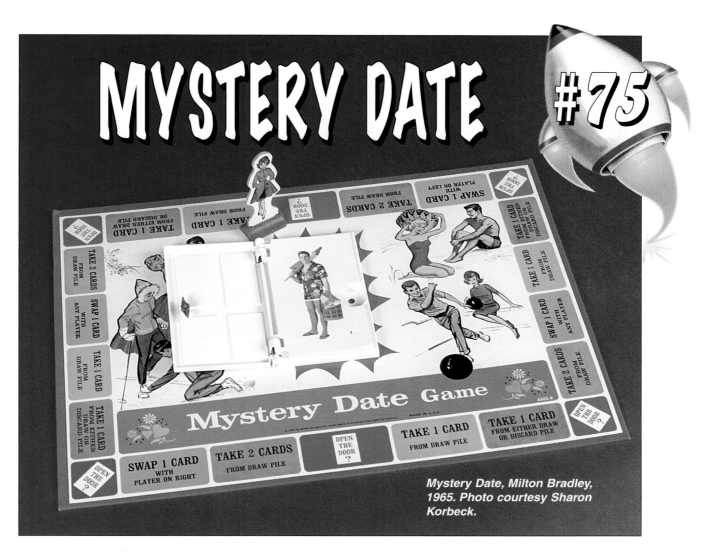

Mystery Date, Milton Bradley, 1965. Photo courtesy Sharon Korbeck.

If Milton Bradley, with its long history, had simply rested on its laurels during the Baby Boomer years, that in itself would have been newsworthy. The company remained a dynamic presence in the business, as demonstrated by such entries as Mystery Date in 1965.

At that point in the decade, every game manufacturer, including Milton Bradley, was emphasizing action-oriented games that threatened players with collapses, explosions, or general breakdowns of some variety. Mystery Date, aimed at girl players, offered a different kind of general breakdown.

The player might luck out and get the cool ski dude, wearing a turtleneck sweater and exuding wealth and confidence.

Or she might not.

Ski bum, or just bum? *Girls responded to the mock thrill and dismay of opening the plastic door at the center of the game to reveal their date. Mystery Date, Milton Bradley, 1970s.*

#76 RENWAL DOLL HOUSE FURNITURE

Treadle machine. *Renwal's sewing machine was its most complex doll house accessory, having a moving treadle, a lid that lifted to become a work surface, the machine that could be hidden in the cabinet or raised out, and a moving control wheel that caused the sewing needle to raise and lower. Renwal, 1950s.*

Hard plastic proved to be an ideal material for making doll house furniture, toy makers discovered immediately after the war. At the time, doll houses of a traditional nature were still popular playthings. The houses themselves aspired to realism, with windows, shutters, tiled roofs, realistic wall decorations and floors inside, and the semblance of bricks outside. Usually they were multi-story and evocative of upper middle-class style.

The children either lived in this style themselves, or aspired to it, having seen it on TV. Children spent hours of imaginative play time with these houses, with or without dolls, arranging and rearranging the contents in the various rooms. The accessories seemed as real as the houses.

Companies including Marx, Banner, Irwin, Plasco, and Ideal produced plastic miniatures during the early Boomer years, with the result that every household item, from telephone and vacuum cleaner to toilet and claw-foot bathtub, became available for tiny household use.

None rose to the same level of excellence Renwal achieved with its couches, chairs, dining room sets, cabinets, chests of drawers, and bathroom sets, however. Renwal's careful attention to detail, its consistent use of moving and movable parts, and its solid production values made it the doll house furniture of choice in the early Boomer years.

SILLY PUTTY

Nothing Else Is

Silly Putty®

SILLY PUTTY MARKETING

New Haven 10   Connecticut

Silly Putty ad. Playthings, *March 1964.*

"As Seen in *Life*," some toy packages said. "As Seen on TV," said a lot of others. "As Seen in the Pages of *The New Yorker*," a very few might have read.

You would think Silly Putty would be the last item to have benefited from an appearance in that august weekly. Yet mention in a 1950 "Talk of the Town" column of the rubbery curiosity, which was then available through Doubleday book stores in the city, made the unlikely toy bounce high from obscure novelty to nationally embraced plaything.

A formulation made of boric acid and silicone oil, sold in plastic eggs, Silly Putty stretched, flattened, rolled into a ball, bounced, and picked up images off newsprint. Although it ended up performing no useful function that anyone could determine, the substance came into existence through a government contract to develop an inexpensive synthetic rubber.

James Wright was working in New Haven at General Electric's labs when he happened to combine the necessary materials. The results surprised him. Not only did the rubbery stuff bounce higher than rubber, and stretch farther, but it retained its properties over a wide range of temperatures. By the end of the war, however, the U.S. War Production Board had dismissed it as being of no interest as a rubber substitute. Since Wright and others found his bouncing putty entertaining, it became the center of attention at New Haven cocktail parties, where it caught the attention of a toy store owner, Ruth Fallgatter, and an ad man, Peter Hodgson.

The bouncing putty sold well through the catalog Hodgson produced for Fallgatter's store. While the shop owner decided to let the substance go, Hodgson persevered, hiring Yale students to shape pieces to put in multicolored plastic eggs. Selling the new product was an uphill battle before the mention in *The New Yorker*. Within days afterwards, Hodgson's orders topped tens of thousands of dollars.

And then hundreds of thousands, surpassing a quarter of million dollars in half a week.

TV's YOGI BEAR DOLL

Smarter than your average bear. *Knickerbocker made its Yogi Bear, 18˝ tall "with two-tone real bear markings," the company boasted. "All the fun of a college cut-up!" Yogi, one of many stuffed, plush toys with vinyl heads made by Knickerbocker and its competitor Rushton, originally cost less than $5. Knickerbocker, 1960s. Photo by Martha Borchardt.*

In 1957, the team of Bill Hanna and Joe Barbera left behind MGM superstars Tom and Jerry and started pitching simple, original cartoons to the TV networks. Their first was *The Ruff and Reddy Show,* starting that year in black and white and lasting through 1964 in color, followed in 1958 by their first TV hit, *The Huckleberry Hound Show.*

Huckleberry Hound featured a half hour of the Southern-talking blue hound dog, voiced by Daws Butler. In his onscreen life, Huckleberry went through every occupation possible, from sheriff and farmer to mailman and lumberjack. In his offscreen life, he was an Emmy Award winner, as of 1959. Besides Huckleberry's own cartoons, the show included segments for Pixie and Dixie, both voiced by Don Messick, and Yogi Bear, voiced by Butler. When Yogi and his college-style, pork-pie hat proved popular enough to spin off into his own series, a new duo, Hokey Wolf and Ding-A-Ling, took his place.

The Yogi Bear Show made its debut in 1961, with a cast of Yogi Bear (Butler), Boo-Boo the bear cub (Messick), and Ranger John Smith (Messick), and with two additional segments, one featuring Snagglepuss (Butler), and the other Yakky Doodle (Jimmy Weldon) and the bulldog Chopper (Vance Colvig).

Among the most popular toys of the early 1960s was the Knickerbocker Famous Plush TV Characters line, a selection of television's best in "DuPont crush resistant plush," feather foam stuffing, and, with the exception of the mice, vinyl faces: Ba Ba Looey, Snooper Sleuth, Blabber Detective, Quick Draw McGraw, Mr. Jinks, Doggie Daddy, Augie Doggie, Huckleberry, Yogi, Pixie and Dixie, none measuring much more than 20˝ tall.

The series reigned supreme in the playroom, surrendering their hegemony only when Mattel's plush figures turned talkers.

ARGO ACTION CARS #79

Simple toy, simple appeal. *Small tin toy cars, some with free-running wheels and others with friction motors, were commonplace. Most were imported from Japan. In the early Boomer years, the American-made Action Cars were among the few that had a brand identity. Argo, early 1950s.*

While shiploads of tin-plate toy cars flowed into this country from Japan in the 1950s, a few American companies made similar products.

The only fleet of small, tin-litho cars to be played with by a large segment of the Boomer generation, in fact, was made by an obscure domestic company named Argo. Sold through catalog stores and known as the Action Cars or Action Fleet, Argo's 4″ cars had simple but clever mechanisms that were set in motion by rolling them across the floor.

The Fire Chief car had a tin profile of a bell protruding from the hood, going back and forth as the car rolled, with a real bell ringing inside. Passenger cars had tin windows that raised and lowered, or windshield wipers that moved back and forth. The Taxi kept a rolling tally of the fare. The detective car's machine gun went in and out, rattling.

The Action Cars remained available from the early to mid-1950s, when the combination of cheap imports from abroad and changing toy-market conditions at home hastened their demise.

#80 HONEY WHEAT DINOSAURS

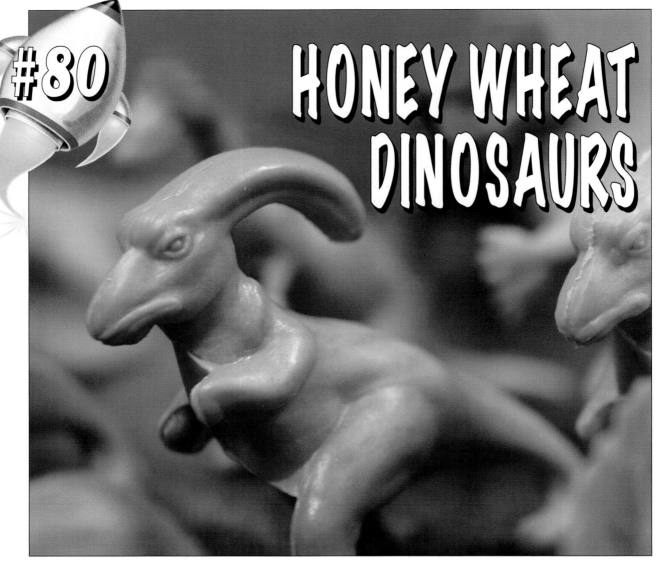

Prehistory, Honey Wheat style. *Dinosaur premiums appeared in boxes of Honey Wheats and Rice Honeys in the late 1950s, making children dig into their cereal with paleontological fervor. Nabisco, late 1950s.*

Was it that the best things come in small packages, or that the small things come in the best packages?

A kid growing up in the late 1950s had trouble with this axiom, especially when trying to convince mom to buy yet another ("You haven't finished the last one, kid!") box of Nabisco Honey Wheats, just to get another Honey Wheats Dinosaur.

When mom finally gave in, the dinosaur inside turned out to be one the kid already had. Of course.

The colors of the dinosaurs, issued around 1958 in Honey Wheat and Rice Honey cereal boxes, were glorious: a swirled, honey golden color, a swirled, cranberry-relish red color, or a swirled, yellowish green.

The dinosaurs themselves were small - 2˝ long or less - and stylized, a bit chubby, and just the slightest bit cute, even though they were dinosaurs: Brontosaurus, Tyrannosaurus, Stegosaurus, Triceratops, Trachodon, Ankylosaurus, and Parasaurolophus, as well as the Plesiosaur, the swimming reptile.

The slightly later group of kids being raised in the 1960s had their chance at the same creatures, in darker and duller black and gray plastic, in packages of corn chips from Frito Lay.

CHAPTER 11

From Pogo to Play-Doh

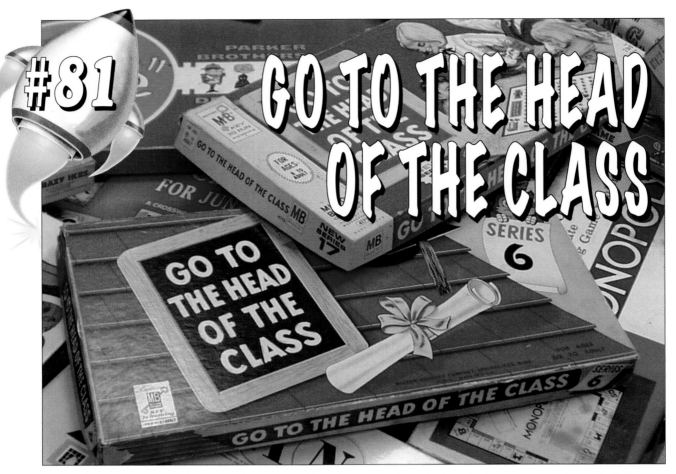

#81 GO TO THE HEAD OF THE CLASS

Not just skill. *The aim of Go to the Head of the Class is to move from desk to desk, grade to grade, and win by graduating first. You move not just by answering questions, but with the help of "Luck" cards. "You are a general nuisance," says one. "Go Back 7 Desks." Although simple in conception, the board is an attractive one, evocative of the one-room schoolhouses that were disappearing in the early Boomer years. Milton Bradley, mid-1950s and '60s.*

An apocryphal story goes this way: A pious man of the cloth stopped Milton Bradley on the street. The clergyman had heard disturbing gossip.

"I hear you're making a game of cards," said the horrified clergyman.

"It's true."

"But Bradley - you're a Methodist!"

Bradley then showed the clergyman his game: Curious Bible Questions. "A sure-fire thing for a Sunday afternoon," he said. "I think it will stimulate Bible reading, don't you?"

Many "educational" cards of the time simply had snippets of information or religious patter on otherwise normal playing cards, which made them more palatable for those who professed to have religious beliefs counter to card playing. Milton Bradley's Curious Bible Questions, however, was simply a trivia game, without suits and numbers. It pretended to be nothing but what it was.

Abashed, the clergyman tried to communicate that perhaps Bradley had indeed produced a posi-

tive and maybe even uplifting game, albeit with cards.

Soon thereafter, Bradley introduced another version with a brazen name aimed directly at churches: Sunday School Cards.

Trivia games kept appearing through the years. During the middle Boomer years, the trivia quiz game of choice was Go to the Head of the Class, produced in the 1950s and '60s by the same Milton Bradley Co.

The board was designed to look like a school room. It showed desks occupying the bulk of the space, with the teacher's chalkboard at one end. The playing pieces were cardboard images of children and adults, set in wooden bases in the '50s and in plastic ones in the '60s.

The trivia quiz was broken down into Junior, Intermediate, and Senior sections, which allowed people of all ages to struggle forward to the head of the class.

Or slip back to the dunce's chair.

Go to the Head of the Class Trivia Quiz

from the *New Triple Quiz Book*, 1955

1. Complete this line: Little Polly Flinders ...
2. Complete this line: A Dillar, a Dollar ...
3. What is the name of Dixie Dugan's little niece?
4. Who is Joe Palooka's little friend who can't talk?
5. A young hare is called ...
6. Which letter of the alphabet do Bridge players often use?
7. What royal comic strip character never talks?
8. What comic strip character agrees with everyone?
9. TV Slogan: What gives you "No unpleasant after-taste?"
10. TV Slogan: What "Guards against throat scratch?"
11. TV Slogan: What is "Look sharp, feel sharp, be sharp?"
12. TV Slogan: What fights headaches three ways?
13. TV Slogan: What does L.S.M.F.T. stand for?
14. TV Slogan: "What'll you have?"
15. Automobile: My model name is Land Cruiser, but what is my real name?
16. Automobile: My model name is Firedome 8, but what am I usually called?
17. Automobile: My model name is Hornet, but what is my common name?
18. What is the popular name of the F4U made by Chance Vought?
19. What is the popular name of the F80 made by Lockheed?
20. How big a crew does a B-36 bomber have?
21. What is the popular name of the C-119 manufactured by Fairchild?
22. Who led the American League in hitting in 1951?

23. Who was the top pitcher in the National League in 1951?
24. What is the number one U.S. magazine in both circulation and advertising revenue?
25. What is the number two U.S. magazine in advertising revenue?
26. Within 105,000, what was the circulation of Life magazine in 1951?
27. In playing Easy Money, how much money does each player start off with?
28. What company makes Lux toilet soap?
29. What company makes Mobilgas?
30. What company makes Crayrite crayons?

The Dunce's Chair (Answers)

1. Sat among the cinders
2. A ten o'clock scholar
3. Imogene
4. Max
5. A leveret
6. W (double you)
7. The Little King
8. The Timid Soul
9. Chesterfield
10. Pall Mall
11. Gillette Blue Blades
12. Bromo Seltzer
13. Lucky Strike Means Fine Tobacco
14. Pabst Blue Ribbon
15. Studebaker
16. DeSoto
17. Hudson
18. Corsair
19. Shooting Star
20. Fifteen
21. Flying Boxcar
22. Ferris Fain - .344
23. Preacher Roe, 23-3, for Brooklyn
24. *Life*
25. *Saturday Evening Post*
26. 5,297,000
27. $2,000
28. Lever Brothers
29. Socony-Vacuum Oil Co., Inc.
30. Milton Bradley Co.

#82 GRIPPIDEE GRAVIDEE
Down the Battery Track

Slow motion. *Like slot cars and HO train sets, Grippidee Gravidee combined the construction toy with the vehicle toy, with the difference that this spaceship had its own battery power. The move away from plug-in power pleased many parents. The ship measures 4-1/4˝. F.E. White Co./Tomy, 1960s.*

Contemporaneous with the fad for HO and 1:32 scale model racing was a less heralded but still popular series of vehicle toys that relied equally heavily on tracks.

Where little slot cars were zipping along, these larger vehicles were slow and sometimes even ponderous. Also unlike the slots, half the fun of these was in the moving-around of the more versatile tracks into different configurations and to different places, even outdoors. Being battery-powered, with the power packs located in the vehicles themselves, kids were no longer restricted to the reach of the power cord.

Batteries were admittedly expensive. Even so, the toys won a welcome from parents, who had long been nervous about the idea of their children putting anything into electrical sockets. With households moving away from the easygoing pace of prewar times, too, parents had less time to play along with their children and to supervise the use of wires, plugs, and transformers.

Switch 'N Go vehicles, which included a Ford racer, Batmobile, Lost in Space crawler, and dump truck, had the most flexible of tracks, in that it consisted of a simple plastic tube that could be placed anywhere, over almost any terrain. A grooved wheel on the vehicle's underside kept it on track.

Unlike the Switch 'N Go Lost in Space, Grippidee Gravidee was a contemporary Space Age toy, using a more realistic design that looked forward to the space shuttle. The track, which came in segments, could be built into various three-dimensional configurations, with the spacecraft equally able to travel right-side-up or upside-down.

TV's UNDERDOG MASK

When Polly's in trouble I am not slow! Brittle plastic masks were a vital part of childhood in the Boomer years. Even kids whose mothers made their costumes would go to school for the Halloween parade and be surrounded by countless images from contemporary TV and ageless fairy tales including Cinderella, Batman, Zorro, Wonder Woman, and the Lone Ranger. Underdog mask, Ben Cooper, mid-1960s.

One of the most important TV cartoons of its time, *Underdog* ran from early October 1964 through early September 1973.

Many of the phrases of the rhyming and bumbling superhero filtered into the talk of young children during the heyday of the show. Underdog, whose voice was provided by Wally Cox, was the most understated of heroes. In the cartoon's opening sequence, in which a crowd looks up and delivers a spoof version of the opening lines from the TV Superman show, Underdog responded, "Not bird, nor plane, nor even frog. It's just little ol' me, Underdog."

The hero spent his nonheroic time as "humble, lovable Shoeshine Boy," who needed only slip into a phone booth at a call of alarm. Troubles frequently centered around his girlfriend, TV reporter Sweet Polly Purebread, voiced by Norma McMillan.

"When Polly's in trouble I am not slow," cried out Underdog, his voice was never strident - never even quite heroic, for that matter. "It's hip, hip, hip and away I go!" Usually he took off into the air in pursuit of villains Riff Raff, a gangster, or mad scientist Simon Bar Sinister.

Underdog's show proved a useful vehicle for other cartoons. In its initial NBC TV days it featured The King and Odie, originally aired 1960-63 as King Leonardo and His Short Subjects, with the King of Bongo Congo, his skunk advisor Odie Cologne, the King's brother Itchy, and Itchy's ill-meaning friend Biggy Rat.

When *Underdog* moved to CBS TV in 1966, it included animated shorts such as *The World of Commander McBragg* with wildly embellished tales of Baron Munchausen-style adventure, and *Go Go Gophers* with the buck-toothed Native American denizens of Gopher Gulch.

Animated characters provided rich mining grounds for companies specializing in Halloween costumes in the later Boomer years. Underdog, who like Superman had a daily, hum-drum character and a superhero alter-ego, appealed to the millions of young Boomers who knew, deep in their hearts, that they, too, had secret identities.

BUZZY BEE

The steady drone of progress. *Fisher-Price, long the bastion of all-wood toys, introduced plastic to its toys in 1950. Buzzy Bee, the standard-bearer for plastic at the company, was later crowned for her effort. Fisher-Price Toys, 1950.*

Fisher-Price Toys of East Aurora, New York, was not caught sleeping in 1950. In that year, the venerable toy maker, an industry leader in the 1930s and '40s, introduced plastic. It released one of its most famous toys, Buzzy Bee, Fisher-Price No. 325.

Buzzy Bee rolled forward on standard wooden wheels and had wood-tipped spring antennae. She also had wings that spun rapidly when she rolled, made of a bright yellow acetate.

Buzzy Bee was a successful addition to the Fisher-Price line. After being produced for three years, she was briefly retired, only to reappear in 1956 with a polyethylene crown and a new name - Queen Buzzy Bee, No. 314.

For preschoolers 1-4 years. For much of the Boomer period, preschooler toys often combined paper-litho-graphed wood and plastic. "Enormous bill flaps open and shut - fascinating 'craw-aww, craw-aww' sound!" says the box for this toy. "Flipper-like feet rotate with comical paddling motion. Unbreakable polyethy-lene bill holds toy fish. Solid wood body, nontoxic finish. Preschoolers 1-4 years." Big Bill Pelican, Fisher-Price Toys No. 794, 1961-64.

POGO PREMIUMS #85

Okefenokee friends. *Pogo and pals Albert, Beauregard, and Churchy spoke loudly to both children and adults at a time when many other creative voices were being stifled, censored, and blacklisted. Proctor & Gamble detergent premiums, 1969.*

The quizzical 'possum of the Pogo strips made his debut in the first issue of *Animal Comics* in December 1941. The character's creator, Walt Kelly, was working for Dell Comics after a stint at Disney, where he had worked on *Snow White, Fantasia,* and *Dumbo.*

Not until after the war did the 'possum and his fellow Okefenokee Swamp critters take on their most characteristic forms, however. The first funny-pages strip, on October 4, 1948, featured a turtle, a worm, and the round-headed 'possum with his upswung nose and vertically striped shirt. It appeared in the *New York Star,* where Kelly had a gig as political cartoonist.

Pogo's talky and intelligent misadventures, together with Albert Alligator, Beauregard Montmingle Bugleboy III, Churchy La Femme, Porky Pine, Howland Owl, and other memorable figures, soon became mainstays of newspapers across the country, with the daily adventures giving rise to a widely popular series of books.

As happened with *Peanuts,* the paperbacks, printed in sizes larger than standard mass-market editions, gave the characters and their comic commentaries a permanent place in Boomer culture. Issued from 1951 through the cartoonist's death in 1971, they established Kelly and Pogo as much-needed voices of reason, even fearlessly taking on the McCarthy witch trials and black-lists.

While Pogo toys that combined vinyl with fake fur appeared the year before, the 1969 premiums from Proctor & Gamble were the form in which they entered the most late Boomer households. All vinyl, they effectively evoked the original comic-strip figures - and they seemed free, coming as premiums in boxes of detergent.

They were good, clean fun.

CAPITOL'S BOZO
The Clown Doll

Bozo, the recording star. *The television presence of Bozo grew strong enough in the 1960s that eventually few Boomers remembered the clown's origin in a recording studio. This early doll is marked "A Genuine Bozo, 'The Capitol Clown,' Capitol Records, Inc." Renall Dolls, Inc., late 1940s or early 1950s.*

While some characters of the Boomer era entered TV from newspaper cartoons, Hollywood, or radio, one of the most durable entered from vinyl.

Bozo the Clown was the creation of Larry Harmon, who provided the voice, and Alan Livingston, a Capitol Records executive who not only helped create the clown for Capitol's line of children's records but wrote the lyrics of the "Bozo Song" of 1948.

In the early days of television, Bozo was no one particular person. Local stations had local talent play the clown, using the official Bozo music and Bozo costume. In 1959, WGN-TV in Chicago started airing a regular Bozo show featuring Bob Bell, who would continue playing the famous clown for a quarter century.

Livingston enjoyed other hits in his life, being the person to sign the Beatles to Capitol and bring them to the United States for the first time.

Bozo the Clown dolls, which would remain available in various forms throughout the Boomer period, were probably born as soon as the original recordings were pressed. Early dolls were released by Capitol, while later dolls and Bozo-related toys were issued by other companies under license. For many Boomers the most familiar version is the 1960s Mattel Bozo, proud possessor of a Chatty Ring.

GIRDER & PANEL #87

Industrial High Rise.
Kenner's Girder & Panel sets were to building toys what Structo and Doepke construction trucks were to vehicle toys. Girder & Panel and Bridge & Turnpike combined set, Kenner, 1959.

Quite different in concept from other architectural toys, Kenner's Girder & Panel and Bridge & Turnpike construction sets of the 1960s combined a variety of materials. It had thin, brittle plastic for angular braces, building panels, and road sections. Then it had heavy cardboard for foundation panels. Polyethylene was the material for the vertical and horizontal girders.

The Girder & Panel sets created play spaces evocative of the world of heavy construction and urban industry. Lacking the elegance of American Skyline or the suburban simplicity of American Plastic Bricks, the Kenner structures had in their favor that they could rise quickly from the floor, easily achieving heights that could only be reached through dedicated, piece-by-piece assembly of the other construction toy sets.

The Bridge & Turnpike sets also included roads, which could spread across the floor below, or rise into the air held aloft by red plastic beams.

These held a special attraction for kids during those Matchbox years, since they provided two-lane networks of the proper size.

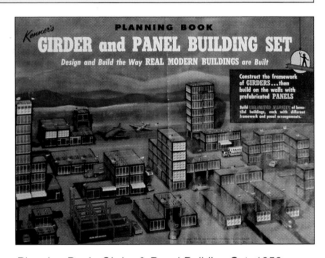

Planning Book, Girder & Panel Building Set, 1958.

TV's DASTARDLY AND MUTTLEY

In Their Flying Machines

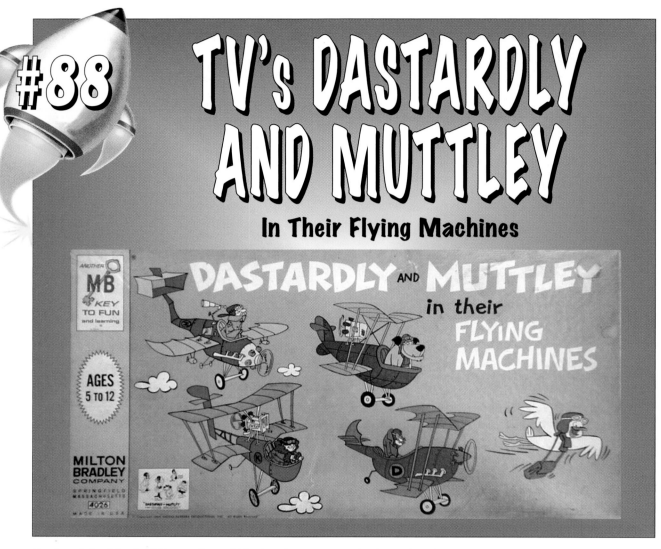

Drat and double drat! *Dastardly and Muttley vie to capture the bugle-blowing Yankee Doodle Pigeon. Milton Bradley, 1969-70.*

One of the late hits for Hanna-Barbera Productions in the 1960s was *Dastardly and Muttley in Their Flying Machines,* featuring an animated duo given voices by Paul Winchell and Don Messick. The characters had already gained fame in the simple yet popular *Wacky Races,* which had its debut in 1968.

"Once upon a time there were four great pilots who flew their beautiful, specially built flying machines in great precision formations," Milton Bradley told kids who played their tie-in game. "They were called, for their daring, Vulture Squadron. Their mission, to knock from the air Yankee Doodle, a carrier pigeon who flew a mail-bag full of enemy secrets." The other two pilots, Klunk and Zilly, never quite stuck in memory the way Dastardly and Muttley did.

The popular *Wacky Races,* with its large cast of cross-country racers designed by Jerry Eisenberg and Iwao Takamoto, had been inspired by such similarly wacky movies as *The Great Race* and *Those Magnificent Men in Their Flying Machines.* *Wacky Races* also led to the spin-off series *The Perils of Penelope Pitstop.*

FUNNY FACE! #89

The magnetic man. *"Dapper Dan is a secret agent, chosen because of his easily disguised face,"* the back of the Dapper Dan card says. *"Alter his appearance to help him carry out his investigations."* Pictures show him as Scientist, Detective, Counter Agent, Dictator, and Magician. Dapper Dan, 10-1/2˝ by 14˝, Smethport Specialty Co., 1950s.

The vacuum-forming devices developed by the plastics industry in the late 1940s and early '50s gave rise to Smethport Specialty's hit toy of the Boomer years.

Smethport had been a maker of tops, horseshoe magnets, and other playthings since before the war. One idea for a toy had never quite gotten off the ground in the prewar, early-plastic years. It featured a line-drawn face, over which whiskers and other facial hair made of metal filings could be moved around with a stick magnet. The metal filings always leaked.

Once manufacturers were able to create airtight containers of transparent plastic, Smethport Specialty released a series of toys that proved perfect for rainy afternoons and back-seat entertainment on long road trips.

Funny Face, Brunette Betty, the larger-scale Dapper Dan, and Wooly Willy: all were essentially the same. First sold on a test basis through the G.C. Murphy dime store chain, they performed well enough to attract the attention of the nationwide chain Woolworth's.

After that, time went quicker for all of us sitting in the back seats of the family car on summer trips.

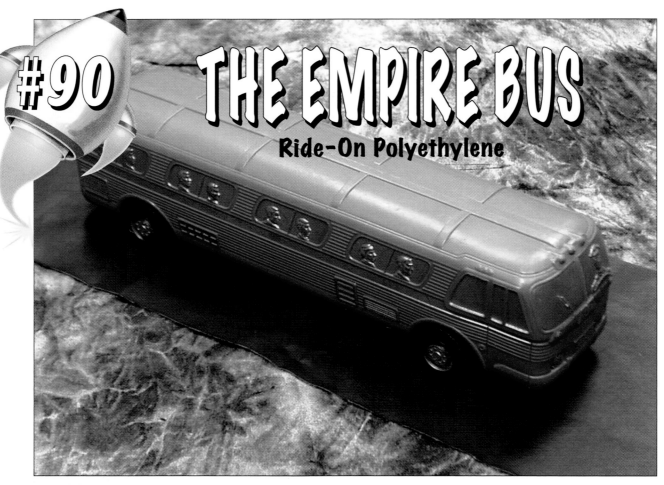

#90 THE EMPIRE BUS
Ride-On Polyethylene

Greyhound Bus, 17˝ long, Empire Plastics Co., 1960s.

The rise of soft plastics in the 1950s and '60s changed many toys, not least ride-on toys, which previously had to be made of sturdy steel or wood.

Many companies tried their hands at soft-plastic ride-ons. Marx issued a single-piece, black plastic railroad engine that whistled when squeezed, and that was big enough for only the smallest to straddle and ride.

Empire issued some of the most popular ride-on soft-plastic toys, including a long, blue Greyhound Bus for smaller kids, and the sturdy green farm tractor for larger ones. Both became backyard and sidewalk staples.

The face in the windshield. In common with Auburn's vinyl cars, faces sometimes appeared in raised relief in the windows of soft-plastic ride-on toys. Greyhound Bus, Empire Plastics Co.

MAGIC ROCKS #91

The Mountains of the Moon

Educational - Fascinating - Exciting! Packages of Magic Rocks boasted the contents produced "all the colors of the rainbow in fantastic shapes and sizes." Despite the additional claim of being educational, the composition of the growing salts and their dyes were tightly-kept secrets. Magic Rocks Co., 1971.

Novelties were important to every child of the Boomer years, whether they were such oddball items as Mexican Jumping Beans, kits of a vaguely scientific nature such as Uncle Milton's Ant Farm, or game-like question-and-answer devices such as the Magic 8-Ball.

One of the most interesting of novelties was Magic Rocks, originally called the Magic Isle Undersea Garden when first introduced in California in 1945 by brothers James and Arthur Ingoldsby. They consisted of colored salts that "grew" quickly - in the space of roughly a half hour - when put in water and the "Magic Growing Solution." Aside from the fun of watching them develop in glasses and fish tanks, Magic Rocks were not so much toys as decorator items, and accessories for the "far-out" lifestyle.

#92 THE BOP BAG

Picking on someone their own size. A child could punch Hanna-Barbera's Pixie on one side, who holds a book entitled "Diary by Pixie Mouse." Tiring of Pixie, she could turn it around to Dixie, who holds a sling-shot and a rock. Around the rock is tied the message, "To Mr. Jinx from Dixie Mouse." Standing 18″ high when inflated, the "Puncho" was made by Kestral Corp. of Springfield, Mass., as part of its Air-line Inflatable Toys line. Early '60s.

In 1947, parents could encourage a child's natural inclinations to hit things in one way only: They could buy a leather punching bag.

Ward's offered the classic sheepskin striking bag in a six-panel pattern, double-stitched in the seams, with hardwood frame, steel platform, and leather hanger. Then it offered its Jack Dempsey Boxing Gloves, endorsed by the great pugilist with his signature over the knuckles. These gloves had backs of wine sheepskin, palms and cuffs of tan sheepskin, and padding of selected goat hair. They came with a Jack Dempsey Boxing Chart. Three sizes were available: 8-ounce for youths 10 to 16; 6-ounce for boys 7 to 12; and 4-ounce for boys 4 to 8.

Since the wise souls at Ward's knew the kids didn't really want a punching bag for an opponent, they sold these gloves only in sets of four. Children should have a chance at some head-battering well before kindergarten, after all.

The onset of plastic toy production changed a great many things. It may have changed childhood boxing most of all. Suddenly it became a sport suitable for everyone, girl and boy alike. This happened not through a change in punching bags, gloves, or even the number of gloves. It happened through the invention of the bop bag. Kids could now have an opponent who never fought back. One they could hit with their bare fists too. Since their opponent was made of sand-weighted ("for roly-poly action"), air-filled vinyl, fists and the bop-bag could go boppity-boppity-boppity with no one emerging the worse for wear. Even if the bags had a tendency to spring leaks, no one bled.

One of the best-loved of the bop bags was Bobo, a clown figure made by Doughboy Industries. Built of "Forti-Plyed" vinyl, it featured a squeaker nose - irresistibly punchable.

Through the latter Boomer years a wide variety of bop bags made by different manufacturers rebounded to the punches of young pugilists. Usually classed as "inflatable toys," they came under such names as Punch-Me's, Punchos, and even Bop Bag.

Toy manufacturers always put kids' favorite characters on these bags - Flipper, Gumby, Bozo - as though they imagined the kids really wanted to take it out on the Good Guys.

TV'S CAPTAIN KANGAROO

Accessories

CAPTAIN KANGAROO ®

©1962 RKA

Puffy sticker. *As was true of the television show, Captain Kangaroo toys and games were designed to appeal to the youngest children. Most Boomers played with them at so young an age they have few or no memories. Many who had vinyl stickers such as this one would stick flower or Weird-Ohs stickers on their notebooks in a few years. Robert Keeshan Associates, 1962.*

Bob Keeshan, the original Clarabelle Clown of Doodyville, had the distinction of being twice fired from NBC's flagship children's program, the second time in December 1952.

In the summer of the next year, he managed to land another clown job, this time as Carny the Clown on ABC. A formerly struggling station, ABC was undergoing a facelift and revitalization after being acquired by United Paramount Theaters, which had been separated from Paramount Pictures due to an antitrust ruling.

Unlike Clarabelle, Carnie the Clown talked on camera, showing a more easygoing and gently humorous side of the actor. In 1954, a new show made its debut after Keeshan convinced network execs at CBS that television needed a program for the very youngest.

Tinker's Workshop went on against NBC's *Today* and CBS's morning *Jack Paar* show. It soon put ABC neck-and-neck with NBC for early-morning ratings.

The watershed year proved to be 1955. October was the watershed month. Not only did Walt Disney's *The Mickey Mouse Club,* aimed at older children, begin airing in the early evening, eating into the *Howdy Doody* time slot, but Bob Keeshan's new show for young children began airing in the early mornings on CBS.

Captain Kangaroo began in 1955 and remained a daily television fixture for 29 years, making Keeshan a legend in the industry and a familiar, favorite-uncle figure for millions of Boomers.

While Captain Kangaroo cloth dolls were popular playthings, the majority of Boomers played with the smallest of toys, usually accessories that identified the child's allegiance to the Captain, or simple, preschool card games.

These Captain Kangaroo items were vitally important to millions of Boomers, even if few remember that to have been the case.

If they were still young enough, it would all come back.

FISHER-PRICE SAFETY SCHOOL BUS

The bus of 1965. Instantly recognizable to the last Boomers, the most popular version of the Safety School Bus rolled from the mid-1960s into the '70s. Fisher-Price, 1965 and on.

At the beginning of the Boomer years, Fisher-Price was known for its inventive, colorful, and charmingly noisy pull-toys and push-toys, which the company had been making since the 1930s. Many of the toys were quite large, with some being a foot or more in length. While a few measured only a few inches, they were in a distinct minority.

In some early toys, particularly vehicles, Fisher-Price used figures made from small wooden columns and spheres, with simple smiling faces painted on. The people were always firmly affixed to the toys, and so were never lost. When the company decided to let some of these simple miniature figures be free-standing, it unknowingly created a new category of toy for its own catalogs, one that would become a major reason for Fisher-Price's considerable success in the later Boomer years.

The first of the loose "Little People" appeared with the Safety School Bus, issued in several forms from the end of the 1950s to the middle of the 1960s, when the most characteristic form was introduced and subsequently kept in constant production.

The Little People themselves changed through time, starting as all wood and ending as all plastic. Since their round bodies fit into round holes inside the Safety School Bus, they were reminiscent of the pegs every child in the 1950s and '60s hammered into wooden benches made by Playskool and Halsam.

But these pegs had heads, with charming expressions: freckles, smiles, frowns. One was even a dog. In a sense, Fisher-Price had learned what other companies learned during the Boomer years - the toys with the best chances of acceptance and longevity were toys with accessories. In every other toy line, figures of people were the main toy. In the case of Fisher-Price, the Safety School Bus, with its rattling noises, rolling eyes, and turning-head driver, was the toy. The passengers were the accessories.

And just like Barbie, who often reappeared years later in shoe boxes and sock drawers without clothes or wigs, or G.I. Joe, who always lost his weapons, hats, uniforms, and boots, the Safety School Bus emerged from closets without people.

MEGO'S SPIDER-MAN

Web-head. *Starting in 1972, Mego issued some of the best-received superhero toys of the late Boomer period. Smaller than G.I. Joes, while still larger than the action figures that would be made popular by Kenner's Star Wars line a few years later, the 8˝ World's Greatest Super Heroes series represented the twilight of Boomer fashion dolls with their jointed, hard-plastic bodies and removable clothes. Spider-Man, Mego, 1974.*

Spidey, one of the most important superheroes of the Marvel Comics line, first appeared in the early '60s. He was given his own comic book in 1963, when *The Amazing Spider-Man* started its long and popular run, facing such foes as the Terrible Tinkerer, Morbius, Daredevil, and, most importantly, the Green Goblin, who first appeared in 1964.

Spider-Man toys gained in importance through the last years of the Boomer years, hitting their stride in the late 1960s and early to mid-1970s when the last Boomers were in their comic-devouring early teens.

The company poised to capitalize on this growing interest was Mego, a company making a new, smaller-size action doll. Mego's 1974 Spider-Man stood at the generational crossroads, being one of the last toys that would have appealed to the last of the Boomers as they moved into their teen years.

GUND MUSICAL TEDDY BEAR

Swiss movements. *In an earlier age, only the wealthiest would have owned moving automatons with Swiss-quality music boxes and movements. Boomer children owned them as a matter of course, through quality plush animal manufacturers. The Gund Musical Toy line was a useful one to parents. The slow, hypnotic motions of the head and the music-box lullabies made countless bedtimes easier. Teddy bear, 8˝ tall, puppy dog, 9˝ long, Gund Musical Toys, 1950s.*

While the Gund Manufacturing Co. of New York City made a variety of rag dolls and hand puppets through the 1950s and '60s, stuffed animals were its most typical toys. Of those, the pride of the line were the musical teddy bears.

These bears had Swiss-made music boxes inside, which could sustain the constant use imposed by children. They also moved as the music played. The head would slowly, peacefully turn. While the motion seems slight and inconsequential compared to the clattery and elaborate tin windups and battery-operated toys that brightened Christmases through most of the Boomer period and before, the quality of the gear action made these bears more akin to European automata, the playthings and novelties of the wealthy from another age, than to the clever, skittery baubles that tumbled over playroom floors.

The teddy bears are emblems in their own way of the wealth that flooded America in the postwar years. Toys that once would have graced the parlor of only a Marquis and Marchioness could now be found in nurseries of the American middle class.

Box art from toy packaging. Gund, 1950s.

HOPPITY HORSE

Bouncing innovation.
The Sun Rubber Co. intro-
duced a new kind of riding
toy when it released its
Hoppity toys in the late
1960s. Hoppity Horse, Sun
Rubber, 1968. Photo by
Martha Borchardt.

Much as the doll form of Barbie came from Germany, or as the massive Tiddly-Wink fad of the mid-1950s came from England, the last hit toy for the Sun Rubber Co. came from abroad.

On a trip to England, Sun Rubber executive Richey Smith found his eye caught by a kind of toy he had not seen before. On his return to America, he quickly developed a new line he called Hoppity Toys, including a horse, Donald Duck, and Mickey Mouse.

The simplest of riding toys, the Hoppities were inflatable balls of heavy rubber with heads on them, which served as handles for the small rider. A child wrapped legs around the toy, hung on tightly, and then bounced.

Sun Rubber introduced the toys to the last of the Baby Boomers in 1968 with an advertising budget of $40,000. Hoppity Horse and his fellow Hoppity toys soon brought Sun Rubber two and a half million dollars in sales.

Makers of trampolines, moon-shoes, and pogo sticks had long known this about kids: bouncing was all it took.

#98

TV's LAMB CHOP

The sock who upstaged everyone. *Children had good excuse to be sassy when they played with their Lamb Chop hand puppet. Vinyl and cloth Lamb Chop, (right) 8″ tall, Tarcher Productions, 1960; vinyl Hush Puppy, Alan Jay Clarolite Co., Tarcher Productions, 1962.*

Who was the only character in the world with the guts to gush over the Queen of England and tell her how much bigger she was than her postage stamp?

Lamb Chop, the endearing sock-puppet creation of ventriloquist and musician Shari Lewis.

Lamb Chop was born as a result of the suggestion to Lewis, before she appeared on *Captain Kangaroo* in 1952, that she use something smaller than the large, wooden, McCarthy-style dummy she brought with her. With the success of ever-smiling, ever-sassy Lamb Chop, the characters Charlie Horse and Hush Puppy soon followed.

Shari Lewis studied piano and violin and attended the New York High School of Music and Art. Following her well-received appearances on *Captain Kangaroo*, she was given her own show on NBC, *The Shari Lewis Show*, which aired from 1960 until the conversion of daytime children's programming completely to animation in 1963.

After NBC's cancellation of her show, Lewis took her performances to England, where British Boomers welcomed her with open arms.

PLAY-DOH

Colors blend. *Play-Doh came in packs of four colors, which, although not pure primary colors, still mixed together under the kneading fingers of the patient child. Play-Doh Modeling Compound four-pack, Rainbow Crafts Inc., 1963.*

In the mid-1950s, Joe McVicker invented a compound for his father's soap and cleaning products manufacturing company. Its purpose?

Cleaning wallpaper.

He had created a nontoxic, putty-like substance that was easily shaped and kneaded. And it did clean wallpaper.

When McVicker's school-teacher sister-in-law mentioned that the school's modeling clay was difficult for her children to shape, he mailed her a sample and started a chain of events that would result in stores across the country carrying millions of canisters of a colored substance called Play-Doh.

The family business changed its name to Rainbow Crafts, perhaps thinking the name Kutol Chemicals had an odd sound for a toy maker.

Fun Factory. *Devices to help shape the modeling compound came almost as soon as the compound itself. Rainbow Crafts package, 1963.*

#100 THIS LITTLE PIGGY

Pull Toy

Went to town. *Fisher-Price's This Little Piggy marked the company's entry into all-polyethylene toys. A plaything that almost no one remembers, buried as it is beneath memories of more vivid toys that arrived in later childhood, the squeaking pull-toy was popular and long-lived, going through three versions in the 11 years following its introduction in 1956. 16" long, Fisher-Price, 1960s.*

Soft polyethylene toys ranked among the most played-with toys of the Boomer years - and also among the most forgotten. Why? We were too young at the time.

Fisher-Price, which had long specialized in toys for the youngest children, rightly realized that polyethylene presented endless possibilities for the future. Not only was it easy for the company to manufacture, it had the advantage of being a soft, nontoxic material - perfect for crawlers and toddlers.

It launched itself, and the rest of the toy-making world, firmly on the road to softening the world of toddler toys with This Little Piggy, a pull-toy entirely of soft plastic, in 1956.

Fisher-Price reached even more children - maybe even all the children of the late Boomer years - with its squeezable sets of take-apart soft plastic beads.

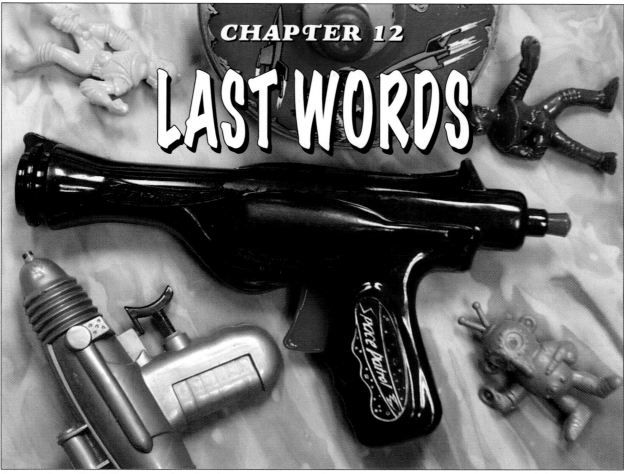

CHAPTER 12

LAST WORDS

I zapped you first! Prewar toy favorites in metal, ray guns changed to plastic in the Boomer years. Space Patrol dart gun and other space toys, 1950s-60s.

Birthrates peaked in the mid-1960s for the Baby Boomers, then declined rapidly enough that by 1969 the nation had about as many preschool children as it did in the early 1950s - a little more than 17 million, as opposed to the high of 20-plus million from 1959 through 1964. The lowering birthrate would take longer to be felt among school-age children. The peak in the nation's population of children ages five to 14 came in 1969 - only a few hundred thousand short of 41 million kids, or roughly twice the number of kids filling schools as before World War II.

By this time, Boomers had already lived through three distinct periods in terms of their toy-playing years. The first extended from the dropping of the atom bombs in Japan to the testing of the first hydrogen bombs by the U.S. and Russia in 1952 and '53. Toys of the time were an odd mixture of the old and the new. Domestically manufactured tin toys and new plastic toys sold in store aisles side-by-side. Old-fashioned Western toys, great favorites before the war, continued in popularity, while toys inspired by new wartime technologies gained on them rapidly.

You bet your bippy! Hassenfeld Brothers' cardboard pencil boxes were a thing of the past by the time manufacturers were dreaming up tie-in items for the number one show of 1968-70, Rowan & Martin's Laugh-In on NBC. Shiny vinyl appealed to the image-conscious kids of the times. Laugh-In vinyl pencil case, late '60s or early '70s.

Sometimes the two combined, as in perhaps the strangest toy of the period: the Lone Ranger Atom Bomb Ring, a premium found in 1947 boxes of Kix cereal.

Dare-devil motorcyclist. *Hero to many later Boomers, Evel Knievel jumped his ever more elaborate motorcycles to glory. Ideal 7″ bendy, 1972.*

Winning consumer affections. *New promotional toys took the place of the old in the last Boomer years. Especially successful in winning consumer affection were the Funny Faces. Walker toy, Pillsbury Co., 1971.*

The Space Age was also gathering steam, although usually in terms of the images developed in the 1930s, with Art Deco and Futurism remaining important influences. Plastic space people, space ships and futuristic cars became standard dime store fare.

Most importantly, TV became an element in everyday life, a fact that attracted the increasing notice of toy manufacturers.

During the second period of Boomer toys, from roughly 1952 to 1962, the postwar bloom of optimism was shrinking. The Korean War, Cold War, and McCarthy witch-hunts cast a pall over much of American culture. Boys grew up reading *Boy's Life*, learning how satellites would circle the earth, then tuned in their homemade receivers to hear the beeps of Sputnik a few years later. Space and technology-oriented toys took a turn toward the realistic. Disney toys acquired their most characteristic forms as the Disney entertainment empire spread into TV, live-action movies, and a fantasy-oriented family park. By the time Barbie appeared in 1959, TV had completely altered the American cultural landscape.

In the third period of Boomer Toys, from roughly 1962 to 1969, animated cartoon characters took over the roles played earlier by puppets and marionettes. Toy manufacturers made toys to match the new TV stars, using not only cartoon characters but also the cartoon style. New toys were bright, loud, and absurd. With the escalation of the Vietnam War, war toys proliferated, as did anti-war sentiments. G.I. Joe made his debut the same year students protested in Washington against the bombing of North Vietnam. The Beatles, who had changed rock and roll when they arrived the year before, helped usher in psychedelia. First people, then toys, started to let it all hang out.

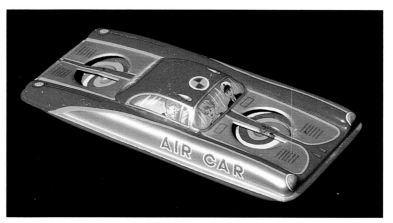

Japanese tin Air Car, 1960s.

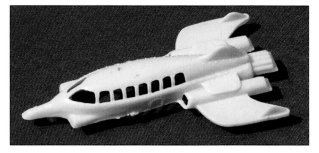

Hard plastic space ship, Premier, 1950s.

The change of space fashions. *While some toys of the 1960s, such as Melvin the Moon Man, retained a fanciful approach to outer space themes, space toys increasingly took a realistic turn as the decade progressed. Remco, 1960s.*

Hard plastic sweetheart. *For much of the 1950s, hard plastic provided the toy-making material of choice. Valentines toy, manufacturer unknown, 1950s.*

The toy years of the last Boomers continued through about 1976 or '77, as the kids born in the mid-1960s were entering their teens. Many toys stayed true to trends set in the 1960s. Yet many of the successes and innovations of that and the prior decades were forced to change or retreat in 1969 and subsequent years. The epitome of safe indoor toys, the Nerf Ball, conceived by Twister inventor Reyn Guyer, made its debut. The sharp-pointed pieces that attached accessories to Gumby and Mr. Potato Head fell victim to child safety laws. For the same reason, the Cootie bug lost much of its rangy bugginess, Klackers were banned, and the lead-based paint jobs of the early Hot Wheels and Johnny Lightnings lost their glitter.

In perhaps the surest sign of the end, Barbie, who changed through the 1960s from a perfectly poised and utterly sophisticated model to a Tammy-like Wholesome American Teen, lost her calm and started, albeit hesitantly, to smile.

Things would never be the same.

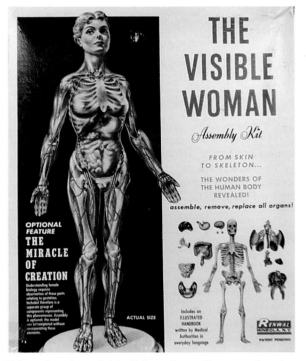

Educational model-building. *Some Boomers less into monsters or latest-model cars were fascinated by the educational kits issued by Renwal in the 1960s, including the Visible Man and Visible Woman. Renwal, 1960s.*

BOOMER TOY VALUE GUIDE

To give an idea of today's collector values for Boomer toys would take another book at least as long as this one. The following list consists of examples, which may help you as a guide.

Note that the values given are for examples in complete, undamaged, and overall excellent condition, unless designated otherwise. The abbreviations MIB and MOC mean "Mint in Box" and "Mint on Card," respectively, and presume an excellent-condition box.

These values are meant as guides only. They are meant to indicate the price a dedicated collector might pay for a toy, if the collector happened to desire ("need" is the usual word) that particular toy. I urge you to consult specialized collecting books, such as those mentioned in the bibliography, as well as current magazine ads, Internet sources, and experienced dealers for current values. Remember, too, that all values are highly provisional and always approximate. The antique toy market is simply a mass of miscellaneous collectors and dealers, all of whom disagree, to greater or lesser degree, about how much their toys are worth.

The prices listed here come from a variety of sources: collector books, dealer price lists, achieved auction prices, and dealer's tables at toy shows. The prices assume excellent condition. Games are assumed to have boxes in the same condition. All are listed by manufacturer.

Archer
Cars of Tomorrow Pickup Truck, 10″ . . . .$75-$100
Robot . . . .$20-$25
Space man . . . .$8-$10
Space woman . . . .$45-$50

Argo
Action Cars set, MIB . . . .$90-$125
Action Cars, loose, each . . . .$10-$15

Auburn Rubber
Cadillac Convertible, 3-1/2″, vinyl $10
Hot Rod, 4-1/4″, vinyl . . . .$15-$20
Jeep, with cannon, vinyl $25
Telephone Truck, 7″, vinyl . . . .$25-$30

Aurora
Frankenstein, built-up kit, 1961 . . . .$30
King Kong, built-up kit, 1964 . . . .$75
King Kong, Glow Kit, built-up $75
Mario Andretti GP International Challenge, in box $55
Odd Job, built-up kit $200
Thunderjet, Dune Buggy, slot car, red $30
Thunderjet, Hot Rod Coupe, slot car $40

Automatic Toy Co.
Hopalong Cassidy Automatic Television Set $100

Breyer
Fighting Stallion, 1961-71 . . . .$150
Lassie, 1958-65 . . . .$40
Running Foal, glossy gray, 1963-73 . . . .$45

Colorforms
Bugs Bunny Cartoon Kit, 1950s . . . .$75-$85
Huckleberry Hound Cartoon Kit, 1962 . . . .$100-$125

Dillon Beck
Wannatoy Coupe . . . .$15-$20

Eldon
Power 8 Road Racer Set, 1960s, in box $75
Billy Blastoff Space Base, MIB . . . .$100-$150
Billy Blastoff Space Scout Set, MIB . . . .$200-$250
Billy Blastoff's Robbie Robot, MIB . . . .$70-$80

Elgo and Elgo/Halsam
American Plastic Army Bricks . . . .$110-$120
American Plastic Bricks #715 . . . .$100
American Plastic Bricks #725 . . . .$75-$150
American Skyline, #92 . . . .$50-$125
American Skyline, #93 . . . .$115-$125
American Skyline, #94 . . . .$300

Fisher-Price
Buzzy Bee, #325, 1950-56 . . . .$40-$50
Queen Buzzy Bee, #314, 1956-59, blue crown . . . .$35-$40
Queen Buzzy Bee, #444, 1959-62, red body . . . . .$30-$35
Queen Buzzy Bee, #444, 1962 and on, honeybee .$10-$12
Safety School Bus, #983, 1959-61 . . . .$350-$450
Safety School Bus, #984, 1961 . . . .$225-$300
Safety School Bus, #990, 1962-65 . . . .$85-$100
Safety School Bus, #192, 1965 and on . . . .$15-$25
This Little Pig, #900, 1956-9, all pink pigs . . . . . .$15-$20
This Little Pig, #905, 1959-1963, different colors . .$10-$15
This Little Pig, #910, 1963-1966, wood ball inside .$10-$15

Hartland

Davy Crockett on horse $550
Paladin and horse, MIB $250
Roy Rogers, walking, MIB $250
Tonto and horse, miniature series $75

Hasbro

Batman and Robin Game, 1965 . . . .$50-$60
Jumpin' Mr. Potato Head SEt, 1966, in box . . . .$25-$40
Laugh-In's Squeeze Your Bippy Game, 1968 . . . .$75
Leave It to Beaver Rocket to the Moon Game, 1959 . . .$45
Little Miss No Name, doll, 1965 . . . .$75
Mr. & Mrs. Potato Head Set, 1960s $50
Mr. Potato Head on the Moon, MIB $200
School Days Potato Head Pencil Case . . . .$35-$40

Ideal

Addams Family Game, 1965 . . . .$75-$100
Atomic Rocket Launching Truck, with fair box . . . . .$75-$95
Batman, hand puppet, 1966, cloth with vinyl head $45
Davy Crockett and his Horse, plastic figures,
　　with box . . . .$150-$175
Flatsy doll, Dale Fashion Flatsy, hot pink maxi . . . .$40-$50
Flatsy doll, Baby $10
Howdy Doody Sand Forms, 1953-55, on card . . . .$60-$70
Ker-Plunk, 1967 . . . .$10
King Zor, 1964 . . . .$150-$250
Luxury Coupe, 10˝, early 1950s, with tools
　　and box . . . .$100-$125
Mouse Trap, 1963 . . . .$45
Mystic Skull, 1965 . . . .$50
Robert the Robot, opening tool box, 1954 . . . . .$200-$225
Robert the Robot, no opening tool box, 1955 . . .$150-$175
Robert the Robot, no glassy eyes or antenna,
　　1956-59 . . . .$100-$125
Roy Rogers Fix-It Stage Coach, with box,
　　mid to late '50s . . . .$125-$150
Tammy, doll . . . .$35-$60
Tammy's Dad, doll, MIB . . . .$65-$75
Tammy's Mom, doll, MIB . . . .$65-$75

James Industries

Slinky, 1948, in box . . . .$75-$100
Slinky Dog, 1950s $35

Jaymar

Bullwinkle & Rocky, frame tray puzzle, 1960s $30
Red Ryder, frame tray puzzle, 1951 . . . .$10
Winky Dink, frame tray puzzle, 1950s . . . .$25-$30

Kenner

Easy-Bake Oven, turquoise . . . .$15-$40
Girder & Panel, #3, 1958 . . . .$50-$60
Girder & Panel Constuctioneer Set, #8 . . . .$85
Girder & Panel Hydro-Dymanic Single Set, #17 . . . . . .$150
Girder & Panel Skyscraper Set, #72050 . . . .$50
Give-A-Show Projector Set, 112 slides, 1963 . . .$100-$125
Roy Rogers Give-A-Show Projector, with slides,
　　1960s $50
Sky Rail Girder & Panel, 1963 . . . .$125

Knickerbocker

Huckleberry Hound, plush and vinyl . . . .$50-$75
Yogi Bear, plush and vinyl . . . .$50-$75

Kohner

Atom Ant Push Puppet $40
Howdy Doody Push Puppet, 1950s, wood and plastic .$150

Pebbles Push Puppet Push Puppet $35
Fred Flinstone Push Puppet $30
Bamm-Bamm Push Puppet $20

Lesney Matchbox

Alvis Stalwart, #61, 1967 . . . .$30-$40
Bedford Dunlop Van, #25 . . . .$50-$60
Boat and Trailer, #9, 1967 . . . .$10
Hillman Minx, #43 . . . .$40-$50
Leyland Tanker, #32, 1968 . . . .$20-$25
Rolls Royce Silver Cloud, #44 . . . .$25-$30
Safari Land Rover, #12, 1965 . . . .$20-$25

Lowe

Jack Barry's Twenty One, 1956 . . . .$30
Yahtzee, 1956 . . . .$10

Lowell Toy Manufacturing

What's My Line? game $45

Maggie Magnetic

Sputnik . . . .$75-$100
The Twister $45
Whee-Lo, with box $15

Marx

Alamo Play Set, #3530 . . . .$300
Davy Crockett Frontier Rifle, 1950s, 32˝ long $75
Fix-All Wrecker Truck, with tools and box . . . . . .$100-$125
Fort Apache Carryall, #4685, play set $75
Nutty Mads Bagatelle, 1963 . . . .$45
Nutty Mads Target Game, 1960s $70
Plastic figure, Davy Crockett, on stand, 60 mm $15
Plastic figure, Jackie Gleason, 60 mm $50
Playset figure, Bullet (Roy's dog) $10
Playset figure, Dale Evans, 60 mm $10
Playset figure, Fred Flintstone $10
Playset figure, Howdy Doody, 60 mm $35
Playset figure, Lone Ranger, 60 mm $20
Playset figure, Prince Valiant, 54 mm $20
Playset figure, Robin Hood, 54 mm $15
Playset figure, space alien or robot, 45 mm $8
Playset figure, Tonto, 60 mm $20
Playset figure, Yogi Bear, 60 mm $30
Prehistoric Times, #3389 . . . .$180
Prehistoric Times, #3398 . . . .$150
Rin Tin Tin, #3628, play set $300
Rock'em Sock'em Robots, in good box $125
Roy Rogers Double R Bar Ranch, #3989,
　　play set $300
Squad Car No. 1, windup, 11˝ . . . .$150-$250

Mattel

Baby Secret, doll, talker, 1965 . . . .$45
Barbie Queen of the Prom game, Mattel, 1960 . . . . . .$60
Barbie, Fashion Queen doll, 1963 . . . .$145
Barbie, Ponytail #1 doll, 1959 . . . .$4000
Bugs Bunny, hand puppet, talker, 1960s . . . .$30-$40
Chatty Baby, doll, early issue . . . .$85-$95
Chatty Cathy, doll, early issues . . . .$125-$150
Dr. Doolittle doll, 24˝, talker, 1969 . . . .$130
Hot Wheels, Beatnik Bandit, 1968-71 . . . .$10-$20
Hot Wheels, Custom Volkswagen, 1968-71 . . . . . .$10-$15
Hot Wheels, Deora, 1968-69 . . . .$40-$60
Hot Wheels, Mantis, 1970 . . . .$15-$20
Hot Wheels, Red Baron, 1970-79 . . . .$10-$20
Hot Wheels, TwinMill, 1969-71 . . . .$10-$25
Ken doll, flocked hair, 1961 . . . .$100

Little Kiddle, Bunson Burnie, with firetruck . . . .$30-$35
Little Kiddle, Calamity Jiddle, complete . . . .$60-$70
Little Kiddle, Peter Paniddle doll . . . .$25-$30
Matty Mattel Talking Boy, MIB $200
Skipper doll, straight leg, 1964 . . . .$50
Skooter doll, straight leg, 1965 . . . .$55
Woody Woodpecker, hand puppet, talker, 1960s . . .$50-$60

Milton Bradley
Bash! . . . .$10-$15
Beatles Flip Your Wig Game . . . .$75-$125
Beverly Hillbillies Set Back Game $20
Bullwinkle Hide & Seek Game, 1961 . . . .$30-$40
Candyland, 1949 . . . .$50
Captain Kangaroo, 1956 . . . .$65-$85
Captain Video Game, 1952 . . . .$75-$125
Dastardy & Muttley, 1969 . . . .$50
Howdy Doody Adventure Game, 1950s . . . .$50-$75
Howdy Doody's TV Game, 1950s $50
Huckleberry Hound Tiddly Winks, 1959 . . . .$25-$30
Lost in Space Game, 1965 . . . .$75
Snoopy & the Red Baron, 1970 . . . .$35-$40
Voyage to the Bottom of the Sea, frame tray
     puzzle, 1964 . . . .$100-$125

Misc. and Unknown Manufacturers
Block City, Plastic Block City Inc., 1960s . . . .$35-$45
Captain Video figure, alien or robot, 2″ plastic,
     Lido . . . .$15-$20
Davy Crockett charms, 1950s-60s . . . .$5-$8
Davy Crockett Roll Caps, Halco, 3000 shots . . . . .$20-$25
Davy Crockett wallet, vinyl, various designs . . . . .$15-$25
Dream Dolls, Dakin, miscellaneous . . . .$8-$12
Dream Pets, Dakin, miscellaneous . . . .$10-$20
Frisbie Pie tin . . . .$45-$50
Howdy Doody Quiz Show, 1950s, Multiple . . . . . .$50-$75
Irwin Hard Top Convertible, 9″, hard plastic . . . . . .$35-$40
Maverick wallet, vinyl . . . .$15-$20
Rat Fink, plastic charm . . . .$5-$15
Rat Fink ring . . . .$10-$15
Rat Fink Slot Car, Revell, 1966, MIB $250
Spiderman, 8″, Mego, 1972 . . . .$20
Super Winky Dink TV Game, kit #250, 1954 . . . . . .$50-$60
Winky Dink Magic TV Kit, Toykraft, in bag . . . . . .$75-$150
Winky Dink Magic Crayons, in box . . . .$10-$20
Zip the Monkey, Rushton, plush and vinyl . . . .$50-$75

Parker Brothers
Clue, 1949 . . . .$25-$40
Clue, 1960s . . . .$15-$20
Davy Crockett Frontierland Game, 1955 . . . .$40-$50
Disney Mouseketeer, 1964 . . . .$50-$60
Mary Poppins Carousel Game, 1964 . . . .$30

Peter Puppet
Davy Crockett Guitar, 1950s, 24″ long $175
Flub-A-Dub, marionette, 1950s $375
Howdy Doody, marionette, 1950s . . . .$150-$200
Peter Pan, marionette, 1950s $130

Remco
Hawaii Five-O Game, 1960s . . . .$75-$90
Melvin the Moon Man, 1960s . . . .$75-$85

Renwal
Doll house mantle clock . . . .$10-$15
Doll house radio phonograph . . . .$25-$30
Doll house sewing machine . . . .$35-$40
Doll house telephone . . . .$15-$20
Gasoline Truck, 4-1/4″ . . . .$20-$25
Speed King racer, 3-1/4″ . . . .$20-$25
Speed King racer, 4-3/4″ . . . .$20-$25
Speed King racer, 6-3/8″ . . . .$45-$50

Schaper
Cootie, game in box with single Cootie on top $25
Don't Spill the Beans, 1967 . . . .$15

Tee-Vee Toys
Howdy Doody figures, 4″, early to mid 1950s,
     each . . . .$15-$20
Howdy Doody figures, 4″, with painted features,
     each . . . .$20-$25

Tonka
Dump Truck, #180, 12″, 1949 . . . .$150-$200
Dump Truck, #6, 1960 . . . .$85-$90
Mini-Tonka Cement Mixer, 1964 . . . .$75
Wrecker, 1954 . . . .$200-$250

Transogram
Ben Casey MD Game, 1961 . . . .$20-$30
Dragnet Game, 1955 . . . .$50-$60
Eliot Ness and the Untouchables Game, 1961 . . . . . .$70
Flintstones Stone Age Game, 1961 . . . .$45
Green Ghost Game, 1965 . . . .$75-$90
Jetsons Out of this World Game, 1963 . . . .$125-$145
Johnny Quest Game, 1964 . . . .$500
Rin Tin Tin Game, 1950s $50
Rin-Tin-Tin Paint By Number . . . .$50-$75

Uneeda
Wishnik, hula Troll doll . . . .$30-$35
Wishnik, two-headed Troll . . . .$50-$55
Wishnik, graduation gown Troll . . . .$20-$25
Pee Wee, doll . . . .$5-$8
Pee Wee Doll Box, paper dolls, Whitman/Uneeda,
     1966 . . . .$10
Pee Wee Tote, Ideal/Uneeda . . . .$10-$12

Wham-O
Cheerios box, 1969, Superball and Frisbee offer $30
Frisbee, 1966 . . . .$15-$20
Mars Platter . . . .$50-$60
Mini Frisbee, 4″, 1967 . . . .$15-$25
Pluto Platter . . . .$225-$275

Whitman
Family Affair Game, 1967 . . . .$35
Fury, frame tray puzzle, 1950s . . . .$20-$25
Hot Wheels T.V. Show, frame tray puzzle, 1970 . . . .$10-$15
Jetsons, frame tray puzzle, 1962 . . . .$30-$35
Lassie, frame tray puzzle, 1957 . . . .$20-$25
Little Lulu, frame tray puzzle, 1959 . . . .$25
Rin-Tin-Tin, jigsaw, 1950s . . . .$20-$25
Ruff & Reddy, frame tray puzzle, 1950s . . . .$25-$30
Zorro, frame tray puzzle, 1950s-60s . . . .$20-$25

Acknowledgments

I wish to extend thanks to Martha Borchardt, for a great many reasons; Brian Klein, who will be disappointed at a few omissions in the Top 100 (Well, he won't be alone) - that water rocket is still sitting here waiting to be photographed; Robert Johnson of Comet Toys, for discussions and photos; Ken Boyer, for toys and talks; Merry Dudley and Sharon Korbeck, of *Toy Shop*; Elizabeth Stephan; Paul Kennedy, Andrea White, and Don Gulbrandsen for their roles in the early stages of this book, and Barbara Case, in the later; Robert Coppinger, for discussions; Dave Christenson; Becky and Jeff Stubbe; Charles and Kikue Rich; Tim and Mindy Borchardt; Mike and Les Plonsker; Marge Kluck and Sue Buza, for putting up with toy babbling when I should have been otherwise working, and Kay Felmer and Lin Beranek for good company; Chaz and Gerry Steltenpohl; Dave and Rosalie Borchardt; Tippi Blevins, for her Tinkertoy memories; Bill and Mai Larson; my long-suffering siblings Kenneth, Beth and Barbara, who unknowingly collaborated in my research years ago; Victor Malafronte, for some last-minute helps; and all those others of you who have helped in one way or another, knowingly and unknowingly. Any mistakes in this book I happily claim as original to me.

Additional Reading

The following list contains some of the many sources available that help shed light on the subject of Boomer toys. They range from excellent, well-researched histories, such as *Say Kids!*, *Toy Wars*, and *The Box*, to pictorial guides, such as *Toy Bop*, with its wonderful photographs but strangely incomprehensible text. I have not listed the many vintage catalogs I consulted, although you will find several books that reproduce catalog information below.

Davis, Stephen, *Say Kids! What Time Is It?*, 1987, Little, Brown & Co., Boston.

Frey, Tom, Douglas, Jim and Brodeur, Dick, *Toy Bop*, 1994, Fuzzy Dice Productions, Inc.

Fritz, Peter, editor, *The Big Toy Box at Sears*, 1997, Classic Toy Soldiers, Inc., Leawood, KS.

Hanlon, Bill, *Plastic Toys: Dimestore Dreams of the '40s & '50s*, 1993, Schiffer Publications, Atglen, PA.

Harmon, Jim, *Radio & TV Premiums*, 1997, Krause Publications, Iola, WI.

Heaton, Tom, *The Encyclopedia of Marx Action Figures*, 1999, Krause Publications, Iola, WI.

Hoffman, David, *Kid Stuff*, 1996, Chronicle Books, San Francisco.

Holland, Thomas W., ed., *Boys' Toys of the Fifties & Sixties*, *More Boys' Toys of the Fifties & Sixties*, and *Girls' Toys of the Fifties & Sixties*, 1998, The Windmill Group, Sherman Oaks, CA.

Huxford, Sharon and Bob, *Schroeder's Collectible Toys*, various years and editions, Collector Books, Paducah, KY.

Kaplan, Louis and Michaelson, Scott, *Gumby: The Authorized Biography of the World's Favorite Clayboy*, 1986, Harmony Books, NY; intro. by Art Clokey.

Kerr, Lisa, and Gilcher, Jim, *Ohio Art: The World of Toys*, Schiffer Publications, Atglen, PA.

Kisseloff, Jeff, *The Box: An Oral History of Television, 1920-1961*, 1995, Viking Penguin, NY.

Korbeck, Sharon, and Stephan, Elizabeth, *2000 Toys & Prices, 7th Edition*, 1999, Krause Publications, Iola, WI.

Liljeblad, Cynthia Boris, *TV Toys and the Shows That Inspired Them*, 1996, Krause Publications, Iola, WI.

McMahon, Jeff, "Where the Frisbee First Flew," in Freestyle Frisbee Page, www.frisbee.com, Tom Leitner, site wizard.

Melillo, Marcie, *The Ultimate Barbie Doll Book*, 1996, Krause Publications, Iola, WI.

Miller, G. Wayne, *Toy Wars: The Epic Struggle Between G.I. Joe, Barbie, and the Companies that Make Them*, 1998, Times/Random House, NY.

O'Connor, John E., editor, *American History/American Television*, 1983, Frederick Ungar Pub. Co., NY.

Santelmo, Vincent, *G.I. Joe Identification & Price Guide: 1964-1999*, 1999, Krause Publications, Iola, WI.
   - *The Complete Guide to G.I. Joe, 2nd Edition*, 1997, Krause Publications, Iola, WI.

Sommer, Robin Langley, *"I Had One of Those": Toys of Our Generation*, 1993, Crescent Books, NY.

Strauss, Michael Thomas, *Tomart's Price Guide to Hot Wheels*, 1993, Tomart Publications, Dayton, OH.

Stephan, Elizabeth, editor, *O'Brien's Collecting Toy Cars & Trucks, 3rd Edition*, 1999, Krause Publications, Iola, WI.
   - *O'Brien's Collecting Toys: Identification and Value Guide*, 1999, Krause Publications, Iola, WI.

Wells, Stuart W. III, *Science Fiction Collectibles Identification & Price Guide*, 1999, Krause Publications, Iola, WI.

Index